Heroines on Horseback

The Pony Book in Children's Fiction

Jane Badger

Girls Gone By Publishers

Published by

Girls Gone By Publishers
4 Rock Terrace
Coleford
Radstock
Somerset
BA3 5NF

First published by Girls Gone By 2013
Main text © Jane Badger 2013
My Favourite Pony Book (1–5) © authors as shown
Illustrations © see pages 196–7
Index © Laura Hicks 2013
Design and layout © Girls Gone By 2013

The moral right of Jane Badger to be identified as the author of this book has been asserted by her in accordance with the Copyright, Designs and Patents Act 1988.

All rights reserved.

Without limiting the rights under copyright reserved above, no part of this publication may be reproduced, stored in or introduced into a retrieval system, or transmitted, in any form or by any means (electronic, mechanical, photocopying, recording or otherwise), without the prior written permission of the above copyright owners and the above publisher of this book.

Neither Girls Gone By Publishers nor any of their authors or contributors have any responsibility for the continuing accuracy of URLs for external or third-party websites referred to in this book, nor do they guarantee that any content on such websites is, or will remain, accurate or appropriate.

Edited by Tig Thomas
Cover design by Ken Websdale
Lionel Edwards images on front cover by courtesy of Felix Rosenstiel's Widow & Son Ltd., London
Typeset in England by Little Pink Cloud Limited
Printed and bound by CPI Group (UK) Ltd, Croydon CR0 4YY

ISBN 978-1-84745-154-5

CONTENTS

	Introduction	7
1.	'I Remember the Day I was Born' ***How it all began***	10
2.	The Fantastic Riding School ***Primrose Cumming and Silver Snaffles***	27
3.	The Battery Thunders On ***The pony book in wartime***	31
4.	Skill, Courage and Determination ***The Pullein-Thompson sisters***	38
	My Favourite Pony Book (1) *Susanna Forrest:* The Black Beauty's Family *series by the Pullein-Thompson sisters*	59
5.	'I Don't Want to Grow up a Long-faced Horsy Woman' ***Monica Edwards***	60
	My Favourite Pony Book (2) *Linda Newbery:* Spirit of Punchbowl Farm *by Monica Edwards*	69
6.	The Beautiful Golden Dream ***Ruby Ferguson's Jill Books***	70
	My Favourite Pony Book (3) *Stacey Gregg:* A Stable for Jill *by Ruby Ferguson*	83
7.	Galloping On and On ***Pony book series fiction***	84
8.	Rather than Fame, Give me Horses ***Famous pony book writers***	96
9.	'Boot, Saddle, to Horse and Away!' ***The 1950s***	103
10.	An Unexpected Pleasure ***The 1960s***	117
11.	'And a Fast Horse Gave you Wings' ***Patricia Leitch and Monica Dickens***	129
	My Favourite Pony Book (4) *Sarah Singleton:* Dream of Fair Horses *by Patricia Leitch*	144
12.	And Feet that Iron Never Shod ***Wild horses***	146

13.	A Short Horse is Soon Curried	151
	Pony annuals and the short story	
14.	Gilding the Lily	161
	Pony book illustrators	
15.	What Happened Next	175
	The 1980s and onwards	
	My Favourite Pony Book (5)	181
	Janet Rising: Flying Changes *by Caroline Akrill*	
	Bibliography	182
	Acknowledgements	195
	Index of Authors	197

Dedication

Jonathan, Fred and Miranda
With love

INTRODUCTION

My first horse memory is of the piebald who bit me. Our garden in Bedfordshire backed onto a riding school's fields. I remember standing at the fence, holding up long grass for the horse next to the piebald, and him biting me, hard, on the arm. My mother, who came from a farming family, and had grown up with working horses, knew the piebald was trouble, and I was absolutely not supposed to hang over the end fence and feed him. I treated the piebald with considerably more wariness after that, but nothing stopped me haunting the end of the garden, endlessly watching the horses, and surreptitiously feeding the ones who I knew were gentle.

When we moved to Northamptonshire, there were no more horses at the end of the garden. Our old farmhouse had long since had its fields sold off and built on, and the stable yard too had been sold and turned into garages. I could see the old stable yard from our bedroom window, and if wishing could have done it the cars and buses would have gone and horses would have filled the stables again. There was just one double stable door still left, in the far corner, and it called me like a siren. Those stable doors promised horses. Once I did see in: a kindly man who worked in the Bus Yard, as it was called now, opened the doors for me. There was nothing there, only dark, the smell of damp and the ghosts of horses. I don't know what I had expected—perhaps a magical survival, a real, live horse—but I had expected something. I remember the man trying to cheer this strange child up, telling me about the horses he remembered here, and what it was like when the whole place breathed horse and was alive with them, and how much he missed them.

When I was seven, and my sister five, our parents bundled us into the car and up the hill outside the town. We pulled up at a wide gravel car park outside a red-brick house next to the church. I had no idea what we were doing there but I noticed the stables as we walked in—all empty. We walked on past a low, black, wooden building and through another open gate. At the end of a stretch of bare earth with an occasional plant left uneaten in it was a small paddock. We walked up to the fence, and there were ponies and children and a riding instructor. Would we, my mother said, like riding lessons? Because she had booked us some, and wanted to make sure we really did want them. Horse heaven had come. The instructor smiled. She would see us, she said, next week. And she did, the next week and for years afterwards.

We had now found real, live horses. Shortly after that, I found that horses lived in books, my other obsession, too. Whole new worlds opened up: girls utterly unlike me, who had ponies of their own or, if they didn't, managed to get them. I drank in their stories obsessively, and a whole new gaggle of children joined Badger, Mole, Winnie-the-Pooh and the Famous Five. My first pony book was Diana Pullein-Thompson's *Riding with the Lyntons*: the 1960s Armada version with the dung-brown cover and Mary Gernat's spiky, lively children surrounding a black pony.

By the time I was ten I had nearly a hundred pony books on my shelves. I was not short of new ones to read: pony paperbacks appeared in bookshops, newsagents, and even Boots, which sold books and toys in the 1970s. There were pony stories in magazines and annuals, pony stories in comics. Our local library had plenty: whole shelves of golden and black stallions, wild Australian brumbies and jolly gymkhana girls jostling for space. By the time I entered my teens and had a temporary break from equine literature via an ill-considered detour into the German author Herman Hesse, I thought I must have read most of what the English pony book market had to offer. I had moved on. My pony books were packed up long before I went to university.

I have often wondered what it must have been like for my mother, having a child who lived so much in her own head, and, when not there, in the world of the horse. My mother had never had a pony of her own. My sternly practical great-grandfather (with whom she lived) refused to have a pony on the farm that did not work for its living. Mum was allowed to ride the driving pony occasionally and ride the plough horses back to their stables, but that was it. As far as I know, she's never read a pony book. She kept my boxed-up books for years, and they were waiting for me when I wanted them: when I was in my mid-twenties and the horses in my brain had begun to wake up again.

I opened the taped-up cardboard boxes sitting on the floor of the landing in my tatty London house, which abutted a football ground, not a horse field. The books were creased, tattered, spines hanging off. There were Pullein-Thompsons and Jills, my few precious Monica Edwardses; Silver Brumbies and Black Stallions; even a full set of the Dragon partwork Mary O'Haras, never read, their separate nature making me shy away from them, suspicious of their unfamiliar format.

I still thought, looking at them, that I must have just about everything that ever had been published. Then, years later, back in Northamptonshire and with ponies at the end of a different garden, I found a couple more titles in a second-hand bookshop. I was intrigued. What else was out there? I started researching the pony book, but with little idea just how many more titles I would uncover. There were hundreds of British pony books: indifferent, bad and, occasionally, very good indeed.

This book is about what I found.

THE SCOPE OF THIS BOOK

When I was asked to write this book, I had grand ideas of covering the three hundred or so pony book authors I knew about. It very soon became obvious that lines had to be drawn somewhere if I wanted to do the genre justice. Rather than provide an encyclopaedia of every author there ever was (which is, anyway, already available on my website) I have looked in depth at how the most significant ones contributed to developing a genre that had its beginnings in the Victorian animal story.

Where to stop was reasonably straightforward: by the end of the 1970s, fewer pony books were being published and most of the major writers in the genre had written their best works. If there was a Golden Age of the British Pony Book, it ended in the 1970s. That is not to say the genre is dead: it has made a partial recovery. Numbers published in the twenty-first century rival those of the 1960s, but much of what is published now in Britain is generic series fiction, dominated by a few authors producing multiple titles. All is not lost, though: there are shining lights like Linda Newbery's *The Damage Done* (2001) and Meg Rosoff's *The Bride's Farewell* (2009). Girls will probably always like horses, and writers will still write for them.

There is a vigorous online community of people who read horse and pony books, and I've quoted from many of them. They, like me, absorbed, sponge-like, anything that had a horse in it. My definition of the pony book is necessarily wide. To concentrate just on the girl-and-gymkhana type would be to ignore large parts of readers' childhood experiences. I have therefore included authors like Vian Smith and Monica Edwards, and galloped briefly on the mountains where wild horses roam. Some of the best writing about horses occurs where there is not a single gymkhana in sight.

Jane Badger
2013

CHAPTER 1
'I REMEMBER THE DAY I WAS BORN'
How it all began

It's difficult, looking at the many titles which are still published now, to think of a time when the pony book did not exist; but the pony story was a relative latecomer to children's genre fiction. School stories and adventure stories for boys and girls were already well established by the 1930s, when the first genre pony books appeared. This is not surprising: the well-brought-up Victorian or Edwardian girl would never, ever have ridden anywhere without some form of chaperonage, making dashing adventure a little tricky. Direct care of the horse opened up to women when they began to take the place of grooms during and after the First World War, and the pony book emerged as women's position in society changed—as the equestrian world itself changed. Riding as a leisure activity filtered down the social hierarchy during the 1920s.

The pony book is not the same thing as the animal story: this had had a firm place in children's literature since the 1700s, but its focus was different. Nonetheless, it was out of these early stories that the pony book developed. Although human beings appeared in these stories, it was the animal that told its own story. The pony book has gone on carrying the banner raised in 1800 by Dick, the earliest narrator of a pony book I have been able to find:

> … and if my strictures tend to procure more uniform favour to my kind, or to soften one obdurate heart among the lords of creation, I shall not regret that I have written, nor shall my history be read without improvement.

Thus says the hero of *The Memoirs of Dick, the Little Poney (Supposed to be written by himself; ...)*. Dick is a grey Welsh pony whose life follows a trajectory that was to become familiar in story after story in the twentieth century. He has an idyllic foalhood. He is stolen by gipsies, and gelded by them (an early and virtually never repeated description in equine junior fiction). After recovering from the trauma, Dick is kindly treated by the gipsies, but is sold on to the spoiled offspring of a local squire. He is broken in, taken over by a farmer after he fails to jump a cow he is set at by the squire's son, and then acts as a helpmate to two children who are dying, we presume of tuberculosis. He is then taken on by another squire, finally ending up serving out a dignified retirement after becoming a true family pony who has taught a whole family of sons to ride.

And as Dick went quietly, at the end, into some peaceful field, so too did Anna Sewell's *Black Beauty* (1877) in the model for all didactic horse stories. This book has wrung tears from every generation that has read it, who wince at the idea of the bearing rein, and cry as the dead horse is wheeled past in the cart, sure it is Ginger. Anna Sewell (1820–78) was born in Great Yarmouth, Norfolk. After an injury to her ankle, she found great difficulty in walking, and relied on the horse to get about. She was horrified by the ill treatment she saw meted out to horses, and wrote *Black Beauty* to 'induce kindness, sympathy, and an understanding treatment of horses' (Mrs Bayly, *The Life and Letters of Mrs Sewell*, 1889). Sewell died five months after the book's publication. It had already been well reviewed and sold several thousands, but it only saw huge success after her death.

Black Beauty, like the earlier Dick, had a wonderful foalhood, only marred by the death of his brother Rob Roy in a hunting accident. Beauty's good start continues when he is sold as a carriage horse to the enlightened Squire Gordon, who treats his animals and staff well and never uses the bearing rein, that strap attached to the harness of a driving horse to keep its head up. (Although a loosely adjusted bearing rein can be useful in preventing a horse from evading control, Victorian fashion decreed such tight bearing reins that horses' heads were forced out of their natural carriage, and kept there for hours at a time.) While Black Beauty is at Birtwick Park, life goes well; but the horses are sold up when the Squire and his wife move abroad for her health. Beauty's next home is Earlshall Park, where he experiences the horrors of the bearing rein and the drunken Reuben Smith. After an accident in which Beauty's knees are so badly scarred that he is no longer considered fit for a grand stable, he is sold; and so his long slow deterioration starts, as he is sold from one owner to another. He experiences the full range of human stupidity and ill treatment, eventually collapsing through overwork. Unlike many horses, he is fortunate enough to be rescued, and eventually serves out a contented retirement, back with one of his early grooms.

Black Beauty's enormous popularity influenced the equine story for decades after it was published in 1877. The major exception to the trend, Rudyard Kipling's short story 'The Maltese Cat' (1898), is a moment in time, not a horse telling its story, though the polo ponies are the narrators. It is about winning, losing and perseverance. Taut, exciting and brilliantly characterised, it still stands as a highlight in equine literature, but not, alas, a model that was generally followed. Horse after horse, pony after pony, each told its own life story. Most of these stories follow a remarkably similar progression: a wise first owner, the standard by which all succeeding homes are judged; a decent enough second owner, followed by a downward spiral until, by a massive stroke of luck, the pony is rescued by its original owner, even though it's tottering, scrawny, down on its luck and virtually unrecognisable. From May Wynne's *Heather* (1912) to Cecilia Knowles's *Hippo, the Story of a Welsh Cob* (1960), ponies rose, sank and rose again.

Working within these limitations, there was little else to be done with the equine biography, though attempts were made to invigorate it. Ursula Moray Williams aimed at the younger market with her superior pony biographies *Kelpie, the Gipsies' Pony* (1934) and *Sandy-on-the Shore* (1936), and used her own and her twin sisters' experiences with ponies in *The Twins and their Ponies* (1936). Other writers set books abroad: Colonel C M Enriquez's pony, Khyberie, lived in India and then Burma (*Khyberie, the Story of a Pony on the Indian Frontier*, 1934), and Joan Penney's Melka in Africa (*Melka, the Story of an Arab Pony*, 1934). Different breeds were featured: Allen Seaby ran the gamut of native British pony breeds from Exmoor (*Exmoor Lass*, 1928) to Shetland (*Sheltie, the Story of a Shetland Pony*, 1939); and Richard Ball fictionalised a well-known horse (*Bronco, an Imaginary Biography of a Horse*, 1930).

The shining light in this procession of equine autobiography came some fifty years after the publication of *Black Beauty*. 'Golden Gorse' (Muriel Wace) wrote what is one of the classics of pony autobiography, *Moorland Mousie* (1929). It has a maturity and subtlety of viewpoint lacked by most equine autobiographies. Muriel Wace (1881–1968) was the youngest of five sisters whose mother died when she was eight; their father, Ashley Maude, then devoted himself to bringing the family up. Theirs was not a settled childhood: the family moved often, and the girls had fourteen governesses. They did, however, have ponies. A keen rider himself (and still riding the Quantock Hills at the age of 82), Maude bought the girls two unbroken Welsh ponies. He soon sold one, which was too wild, but he made a partial attempt to break the other in. However, he became bored by long-reining it, and at that point he passed the pony, still at the earliest stages of its education, over to his daughters and told them to ride it. The pony was more than up to their efforts, and would scrape them off with whatever was handy—an overhanging branch or the park railings.

In adult life Wace, with her doctor sister Mrs Young, for whom she kept house for a while, became a pioneer in riding astride. After her husband, the Revd Henry Wace, retired as bursar of Brasenose College, the couple moved to Crowcombe, near Taunton, where Wace's interest in the Exmoor pony, a small native British breed, began. Her first book, *The Young Rider's Picture Book* (1928), describes the process of schooling the two Exmoor ponies on which the heroes of *Moorland Mousie* were based. Her early experience with the wicked Welsh pony made an impact, and she frequently stressed the importance of a well-schooled pony: '… if a pony is well-broken he will be without tricks of any kind.'

The real Moorland Mousie

Moorland Mousie was Golden Gorse's first fictional work. Moorland Mousie is an Exmoor pony, born on Exmoor. He spends his earliest years on the moor with his mother, aunt and cousin, Twinkle, until the ponies are rounded up and Mousie and Twinkle are sold to a Colonel Coke and his daughter Patience. Patience is not experienced enough to control Mousie when he gallops off downhill. She is swept off the saddle by overhanging boughs, is concussed and subsequently is no longer allowed to ride. Mousie must be sold. The Cokes hope a more experienced child will buy him, but none does. Mousie remains in the field doing nothing, until the Colonel decides that he must be sold 'even if he goes to drag a cart'. Drag a cart is precisely what Mousie does, though his master, Gammon, is a good one. Sadly, though, Mousie moves on to other, less kindly, owners, which gives him the opportunity to spout advice. *Moorland Mousie* is just as much of a morality tale as *Black Beauty*. It shows the people who ride only because it is smart, and who care not one jot for their animals' welfare, and those who think only of what they want, not what the pony wants:

'It's quite clear your pony doesn't care for too much petting,' said Mr X … 'Some ponies are like that, and if you are wise children you will understand.'
   But they didn't want to understand. The truth is that they patted me to please themselves because I felt warm and silky and alive. I do not call that kindness. How can it be kindness to us if we do not enjoy it?

At last, Mousie is discovered, poor and broken down, by the Cokes, and returns to them.
Moorland Mousie follows what had become the traditional plot of the horse story, but what makes it stand out from its fellows is the portrait of Mousie. Golden Gorse does not just tell us what the pony thinks of himself: we see him as others see him. Mousie is very pleased with himself, but Old Jem, who breaks him in for Colonel Coke, shows us another side to him: he's nervous, and not ideal as a child's pony:

'I can't speak quite so well of the brown—not for the little lady, I mean—I wish she had had a little more experience, and then I should feel more confident. He hasn't a spark of vice, but he is a little nervous and high-strung, and no breaking will alter that … I'm not saying he won't come right,' he finished, 'but he wants watching.'

Mousie disagrees:

'Much Old Jem knows,' I thought; 'I wouldn't hurt a hair of her darling head.'

Golden Gorse continued Mousie's story with *Older Mousie* (1932), but with her last pony book, *The Young Horsebreakers* (1937), she explored the new ground broken by Joanna Cannan, and told the story from the riders' point of view. She was still just as keen to educate her readers, but the advice was no longer straight from the horse's mouth. In this book, Uncle Tom corrects and helps Janet and Felicity as they attempt to break in some young Exmoors. The ponies no longer speak for themselves.

Golden Gorse was not alone in exploring new ground for the pony biography. Primrose Cumming's first book, *Doney* (1934), while still being the biography of a pony, is a typical example of the way the focus was shifting towards the human characters. Primrose Cumming (1915–2004) was born on the Isle of Thanet, Kent, and educated by a governess who recognised her writing ability and encouraged her. As a teenager, Cumming was so keen on ponies herself that she would sneak out and ride farmers' horses in the fields. With the proceeds of *Doney*, which she wrote at the age of nineteen, she bought her first horse, Black Jack, and used what she earned from the book's successors to keep him. *Doney* tells the tale of an ordinary pony who has no particular point to make but lives a contented life with a family who treat him well. By the standards of the pony biography which preceded it, this should have made the book an uneventful plod, but it does not. Doney is unusual from the start in being a pony who has had a poor start in life but then finds a better existence. He is 'a middle-aged gentleman, rather stout and short of breath', not the attractive, lively youngster more typically the pony hero. Although Cumming wrote this book at such a young age, she still manages to populate her book with attractive characters, and some humour. Doney and Janet win the musical chairs only through Doney's fit of temper:

> The grey had about eighty yards to go, Doney fifteen at the most; but, in spite of the differences in distance, it was the grey and not Doney who got to the chair first. Doney, in a moment of blind anger and disappointment, blamed Janet and put all his remaining strength into a mighty buck. Janet flew over his head, luckily still clinging to the reins, and landed in a heap on the chair …

The interest in the book comes from Doney's reactions to the changes in his life. It is in the nature of things that ponies are outgrown, and Doney's brief downfall is caused when he is so upset by the thought of being supplanted in Janet's affections by the show jumper Topnotcher that he runs off, only to end up in the hands of the Burchers, who owned him before and abused him.

Cumming was an astute writer: she rarely trod the same ground twice, and her succeeding novels did not include another equine biography but struck out to cover farm stories, the first riding school stories (in the Silver Eagle series, which started in 1938), and fantasy, where her talent for characterisation could find more realistic expression.

Although realistic characterisation was undoubtedly an issue, the major limitation of the story-told-by-or-about-a-horse format was the plot. With the horse or pony being the focus of the story, there was little chance for the human element to have adventures, develop in personality or focus on competition. Authors started to explore different ways to write about horses and ponies. John Thorburn produced a story which took the equine autobiography theme and shook it by the scruff of its neck by allowing the horse to talk to its humans. The result was *Hildebrand* (1930), a manic cross between fairy story and equine biography.

Hildebrand is christened by his new owners, and one of his equine fairy godmothers unwisely gives him the ability to talk. Like Saki's Tobermory, Hildebrand turns out to have a gift for saying that which ought to be left unsaid. He insults the last fairy godmother to give him a gift, Sal Volatile the Night Mare, a 'terribly common' horse who drops her aitches. This does not go down well:

> 'Starts with "an aitch" does it?' she shouted. 'I'll give you haitches! I'll give you so many haitches that from now hon heverything you heat shall 'ave to start with a haitch, too. And I 'ope you're 'ungry you hinsolent beast …'

John Thorburn: Hildebrand

And so Hildebrand is condemned to eat only that which begins with an 'h'. The children are incidental in his story, there simply to provide a foil for Hildebrand's wickedness. He is absolutely the last horse one can imagine patiently teaching a small child to ride. He is far more likely to strand it on an island, or leave it agog as he shares a hen supper with his fox friends Hengist and Horsa.

Hildebrand galloped off on a cul-de-sac of his own; the obvious part of the storyline to develop was the human, and books told from the children's point of view, rather than the ponies', started to appear. When she was fifteen, Moyra Charlton wrote what is probably the earliest adventure involving children and ponies, *The Midnight Steeplechase* (1932). Moyra Charlton (1918–2000) was educated at home, apart from a period at school in Washington, where her father was British Military Attaché. Her first book, *Tally Ho* (1930), written when she was only eleven, is a standard equine autobiography. Her next book, *The Midnight Steeplechase*, is the story of six children: Dick Northcliffe and his brother Peter, Kenneth and Molly Stapletown, and Joan and Tony Montgomery. The action centres on

John Thorburn: Hildebrand

"HE HUNG ROUND THE INDOMITABLE NUTTY'S NECK"

Moyra Charlton: The Midnight Steeplechase

Burndon Castle, where most of them live. Dick is bored and decides that a midnight steeplechase would liven things up. The story includes what would become an obligatory feature of pony books, the gymkhana, but it happens near the beginning of the book, and is a plot device that really only serves to put one of the 'chase participants out of action and show a different and better side to Dick. The main focus is the children's determination to carry out the steeplechase, despite its looking a worse and worse idea. It goes horribly wrong, and the first part of the story closes with a long list of the expenses incurred by the children—it's something of a morality tale. Dick closes this part by saying: '… I am not ashamed of it. Of course I must admit it *was* mean of us to take advantage of Uncle Frank's going away and I feel that we never ought to have let him down. Still, we'll never do that again.'

After a gap of ten years, the children meet again, grown up. Dick is due to be sent back to India with the army, and fixes on the idea of having another midnight steeplechase. This goes rather better than the first, though it is touched with poignancy as Dick is going off on active service.

The Midnight Steeplechase was really pioneering stuff, more remarkable perhaps because of the youth of its author; the book is a surprisingly mature piece of work. When Charlton's books were published there was speculation in the press that she had been helped by her parents, but she stoutly maintained she had not; her first book was presented to them as a fait accompli. Perhaps Charlton wrote what she herself wanted to read: a book in which children featured as much as, if not more than, ponies. Her book was of its time and her class, with an indisputably wealthy county background. There is none of the longing for a pony that marked out the vast majority of later pony books. Money is not a problem for any of the children in this book; they could have any number of ponies. This book, however, marked an important development in the history of pony books: the realisation that children who rode ponies could, and did, tell more interesting tales than the ponies themselves. There is a certain neatness in a child producing one of the earliest examples of a genre intended for children.

Marjorie Mary Oliver, another author working in the early 1930s, also explored the theme of children and ponies; but her child heroes are not, as Moyra Charlton's are, children with untrammelled access to the country, animals and ponies. They are in need of what Oliver, and many of her successors, saw as the healing power of the countryside. The superiority of countryside versus town became a dominant theme of the pony book. Child after child moved out to the country, and their dreams came true because of it. Oliver's first three stories, written with Eva Ducat, are the loosely connected *The Ponies of Bunts* (1933), *Sea Ponies* (1935) and *Ponies and Caravans* (1941). All have what is more or less the same plot: children who are constrained in some way experience the liberating effects of the countryside through a woman who is determined to defy convention and live surrounded by a collection of children and animals (though mostly ponies), children and animals alike being managed with casual authority.

The perceived dangers of constraining children in an urban existence are hammered home. The pathetic little creatures met at the beginning of *The Ponies of Bunts*, Diana and John Ridley, are 'poor little townies—they do look peaky'. They are driven to Bunts, where they are to stay for the summer, in a trap pulled by the Dartmoor ponies Rice and Timmie. Their mother is convinced this ride will be too much for them, but they are glowing and delighted when they arrive at Bunts. The most pathetic of them all is Roger, in *Sea Ponies*. Sent to England and his aunt for his health, away from his parents and India, he is muffled up even in the heat of summer. Hideously fussy Aunt Matilda thinks pips in jam are dangerous and seizes every chance to forbid indulgence in the lethal substance, and in anything else that might be even remotely fun.

All the children cast off convention and their urban shackles, and flourish. They learn to ride, they relax, they gain independence. The miraculous wonders of the ponies and countryside are described rather breathlessly and with a certain lack of realism; everything is *so* handsome, *so* glossy and shines *so* beautifully. In keeping with this wide-eyed feel, there is a tendency for most of the children, particularly the townies yearning for the countryside, to be awash with innocent enthusiasm and not much else as they are let loose in this magical world.

That is not to say that Oliver cannot write more developed characters. Her observation of children probably reached its height in her early books with *Sea Ponies'* Roger. The repressed nature of Roger's existence is contrasted with the utter lack of care for what anyone may think that is expressed by Chris, one of the children who lives with Miss Rhoda and her collection of animals and eventually takes Roger on and sets him free. Waiting with some of the other children and ponies to meet a train, she stands casually on the back of her pony. She so inspires Roger with her insouciance that he throws his hated muffler and hat onto the station roof. Poor subdued Roger is convinced that Chris and her friends must despise him. As he trails along after Aunt Matilda, he turns and looks back at the children:

Chris was again standing like a circus rider on Tag, and as he turned she raised her hand and waved to him, and then Bunch and Geoffrey waved too. Roger dropped behind Aunt Matilda and waved back with all his might.

It's such a vivid picture: the child slouching along and suddenly exploding with enthusiasm. Unfortunately, Oliver's early books lack the narrative development which would make the most of her character observation. The books' conclusions lack any poignancy to point up the happy endings: all end in a glorious sunlit world where everything

Roger found he could make Tag go to right or left, just as he wished.

Marjorie Mary Oliver:
Sea Ponies

has worked out (and everyone lives in the country). Nevertheless, she was a pivotal figure in the development of the pony story, a writer for whom the pony was a means to a better life, emphasised by the use of photographs as illustrations: the wonders of the countryside were so evident they didn't need the possibly fanciful interpretation of an illustrator. Oliver really believed that freedom allied to the countryside could only do good.

Eleanor Helme, like Marjorie Mary Oliver, made the superiority of the countryside over the town the theme of her earliest pony books, *Jerry, the Story of an Exmoor Pony* (1930) and its sequel *The Joker and Jerry Again* (1932), both co-written with Nance Paul. Eleanor Helme (1887–1967) started her writing career as a golfing correspondent for the *Yorkshire Post* in 1910. She was an excellent golfer herself, and played for England. Writing on golf allowed her plenty of opportunity for observing the world in the sometimes long intervals between events worth reporting:

> … I enlivened a dull day's reporting by watching, and describing, a butcher bird in a thorn bush. He was much more engaging than watching the golf.

Helme went on to write several animal books for children, and a group of pony and farming stories, mostly based on Exmoor, where she came to live with her sister after the Second World War. Her first two books, featuring Robin Marston, his family and the Exmoor pony Jerry, are about children for whom having a pony is a rite of passage. The family is well off enough to buy the pony, and the only thing that stops their plan to ride is their inconvenient location in London. When Robin sees an Exmoor foal, he is given it, but the foal has to be kept by a local farmer until the family move down from London to Exmoor. Fortunately for the progress of the story, this move takes some years, by which time Jerry is old enough to be broken in and ridden about the moor. The books are gentle stories of countryside events; Helme's feelings about London's artificiality are made plain in her description of the pony class Robin and Jerry enter at Exford Show. One of the competitors is an overdressed London boy, with his beautiful black pony which has won at Olympia. It is made quite clear that the Londoner shows bad form; besides being dressed in clothes which are loud and exaggerated, he has 'artificial show-ring mannerisms' and has come down from London specifically to win at a small country show (a vice labelled in later pony books as pot-hunting). Not only that, he relies on a groom rather than looking after his pony himself, a character defect that was to resonate through many pony books to come:

> 'Now then, Jerry boy, we're just going to beat him. He's not going to come down from his old Olympia and think he can mop up everything just because it's a little country show. It's a jolly good show, and I'd like to see him out on the moor … And what d'you think, he's only just gone out—hasn't done anything for the pony himself, and there's the Olympia prize ticket stuck up on the post where the pony is!'

The Londoner is a good rider, but Robin and Jerry eventually vanquish him; the honest, hardworking countryside wins out over the affected, idle town. This nameless boy was among the first of the stock villains of the pony book: the over-moneyed rider who thinks more of success than of his pony.

Helme's *Mayfly* (1935) is a far better treatment of the theme of the move to the countryside. The Chatton family are wealthy enough to keep horses and ride in London (then, as now,

The Show

Eleanor Helme: Jerry, the Story of an Exmoor Pony

an enterprise that demands considerable resources), but the novel opens with Mrs Chatton and her son, Tony, learning that the family money has been lost. Their Knightsbridge flat, country house in Surrey, five horses and staff must go. Fortunately they have been left a house, Nutscombe; unfortunately the money to go with it has been left to animal charities. Unlike many succeeding pony novels in which poverty is overstated—it's a rare family that is so ground down it must dispense with its staff—Helme recognises that the state to which her fictional family has been reduced is still considerably in excess of what the majority of 1930s Britain could expect. Tony asks if they will be really poor, and his mother tells him that they won't. They are simply at the point of having to buy a good saddle locally rather than at Champion and Wilton. Changes must be made, however, and money must be earned. Tony comes up with the idea of running a riding school, and thus another stalwart theme of the pony book, earning a living through horses, is born.

This is a more sophisticated story than the Jerry ones. Although the countryside is seen as superior to town, *Mayfly*, rather more realistically than the Jerrys, closes with the two children, Tony and Diana, back in London. Diana is there because it is where she lives now that she is a professional musician, and Tony has an exhibition of his paintings there. However much one loathed London, it was undoubtedly useful.

This book foreshadowed much that was to become standard in the pony book: the love of the countryside and the concentration on the concerns of the horse above one's own. (There is no bathroom in Nutscombe, but who cares? Come and look at the horse trough and the beautiful stables.) The distinction between town (bad) and countryside (good) is subtly drawn: Cyril, whom Tony first meets at the Islington show, and who is very obviously a villain, caring not at all for his pony, lives on Exmoor. It is his upbringing and character that make him selfish, thoughtless and vindictive.

Helme's later stories, such as the Adam series (*Shanks's Pony*, written in 1946, *Suitable Owners*, 1948, and *White Winter*, 1949*)* were more descriptions of life as it was lived by a particular class on Exmoor than the girl-gets-pony book. They have a very vivid sense of place, and *White Winter* is a wonderful evocation of the sheer hard slog of living through the long and vicious winter of 1946–47 on Exmoor. Although the books are nominally about the Exmoor pony Adam, by far the most spirited character to emerge is Miss Popham, a 'resourceful old lady', capable and straightforward. *Mayfly* was the nearest Helme came to writing what became the classic pony book; but she was more interested in portraying character than children's dreams.

Charlton, Oliver and Helme all wrote stories which involved girls and boys equally. It was Enid Bagnold who made the first step into portraying those visceral longings girls have for ponies with *National Velvet* (1935), one of her two children's books. Enid Bagnold (1889–1981) was born into a wealthy family. After being educated in England and Switzerland, she plunged into bohemian life in Chelsea, studying art under Walter Sickert. During the First World War she was a nurse at the Royal Herbert Hospital in Woolwich, and wrote of her experiences there in her 1918 *Diary without Dates* (which was so critical of the hospital that she was dismissed). She continued with her war work as a volunteer driver in France. In 1920 she married Sir Roderick Jones, the head of Reuters. They bought North End House in

Rottingdean, Sussex, and it was here that *National Velvet* was written, in 1935. The couple also owned a racing stable, and it was their involvement with horses that inspired the book.

Velvet Brown, the heroine of *National Velvet*, drifts through the early chapters of the book existing in her dreams. Although the family has a pony, Ada, she is old, obstinate, and meant to be used for delivering meat, not as a riding pony. What Velvet longs for is something she can ride, in the romantic sense, sweeping along the Downs at a gallop in a great, glorious charge, not pottering about on errands. She cuts horses out of newspapers, makes them tiny bridles from cotton, and takes them out for rides, carefully rubbing them down when she brings them back. Bagnold gave a voice to the girl who passionately longs for horses:

> 'I tell myself stories about horses,' she went on, desperately fishing at her shy desires. 'Then I can dream about them. Now I dream about them every night. I want to be a famous rider, I should like to carry despatches, I should like to get a first at Olympia, I should like to ride in a great race, I should like to have so many horses that I could walk down between the two rows of loose boxes and ride what I chose. I would have them all under fifteen hands, I like chestnuts best, but bays are lovely too, but I don't like blacks.'

This is not a shy desire: it is a great galloping passion, given voice. It is not, as the academic and pony book specialist Alison Haymonds points out, a passion that is ready to be directed towards marriage and children. Velvet says 'I don't ever want children. Only horses.' Velvet does indeed get horses, in a splurge of excess. She wins the delinquent piebald The Pie in a raffle, and is left five horses by her father's customer Mr Cellini after a chance encounter with him when she delivers meat. None of these horses is ordinary: The Pie goes on to win the Grand National, and Mr Cellini's horses are the cream of the local equine community. Velvet is all fire and artistry on a horse:

> 'She'll sit on a horse like a shadow and breathe her soul into it. An' her hands ... She's got little hands like piano wires. I never seen such a creature on a horse.'

After Velvet wins the National, fevered public excitement is directed at her. The family is deluged with gifts, and Velvet and Mi, the slaughterhouse hand who has trained Velvet and The Pie, are mobbed when they try to catch a train at Victoria Station and have to be rescued by the police. None of this is what Velvet wants:

> Mrs Brown found an old trunk for the chocolate boxes and the flower ribbons and Mally's collection. It was April. The gymkhana summer was all before them.

Public excitement dies as soon as it starts, and the important stuff of living, the summer and gymkhanas, is left. *National Velvet* has some of what became the classic pony book themes: Velvet loves horses but does not have one; acquires one (actually several); overcomes adversity and wins a race; then settles into a calm procession of gymhana summers. Velvet, however, is ultimately unlikely to progress quietly through life: she is someone to whom 'things happen'. Her passionate intensity is not seen in most of her more sensible sisters: until Patricia Leitch's Jinny (1970s), pony book heroines lacked fiery passion, or at any rate the brilliance of Bagnold's depiction of it.

Captain J E Hance and Brenda E Spender used the introduction of children into the pony book to sugar the pill of instruction. Captain Hance's *Riders of Tomorrow* (1935), although nominally about a boy and a girl learning to ride, is more a manual of detailed instruction on the process of riding. Brenda E Spender's Tony series, which started in 1935 with *On'y Tony*, was less obviously didactic. It was aimed at the young reader still at the stage where ponies live 'in big square rooms with carpets of straw in a special house of their own'. *On'y Tony* is centred on the child hero of the series, Tony, and his learning to ride; like its contemporary *Riders of Tomorrow* it contains instruction but also has enough detail on Tony and his godmother, with whom he is staying, to lend the book charm.

Other writers started using ponies as one of the ingredients of adventures stories. They were a peripheral element in Kate Seredy's *The Good Master* (1935), set on a pre-First World War Hungarian farm, though it is more about family relationships than horses; Katharine Hull and Pamela Whitlock's *The Far-Distant Oxus* (1937) is a holiday adventure taking a group of children on a long journey. The book's opening leaves the reader in no doubt about just what is important to Bridget, Frances and Anthony:

> 'The ponies!' shouted Bridget, pulling back the stable door and gazing with adoring eyes at the long line of flickering tails.

The children rescue a foal, race their ponies and experience the joy of galloping over the moors: 'You heavenly pony. There is only you and me in the world …' The pony was now becoming a recognised element in adventure: not, in this book or its sequels, the be-all and end-all of holiday life, but a companion and an enabler.

Ponies are important to Bridget and her friends, and even at times that which allows them to shut out all the world but themselves, the pony, and speed, but they are not the focus of a grand passion. That great longing for a pony is what inspired much of the genre to follow. Girl after girl (and they almost always are girls) long and long for a pony, any pony. Like Velvet Brown, they cut out horses and ponies from newspapers; they stick them round their walls, and treasure model ponies. Velvet's successors, however, live a life unlike hers. *National Velvet* is as much the story of Mi, who drifts round racing stables until he ends up helping Velvet's father in the slaughterhouse, as of Velvet. The Velvets-to-come live lives where adults are a distant presence, if not entirely absent. It is their feelings and thoughts that matter, not those of the adults around them.

It was Joanna Cannan who set the pony book firmly into what became its traditional groove. In her *A Pony for Jean* (1936), Jean is the sun around which the story revolves. The rest of her family, parents, cousins and all, are more or less distant planets. Jean tells the story herself, so everything in the story is filtered through her. Although all pony-obsessed children can understand Velvet's wild longings, the possibility of taking part in the Grand

National as a teenager is vanishingly small. Being given a pony no-one else wants, learning to ride it and managing to compete in your first-ever show is rather more achievable. Cannan took the child-centred pony book and the gymkhana, told the story from the point of view of the heroine, and made it seem within reach of an ordinary child.

Joanna Cannan (1896–1961) had a childhood which encouraged story telling: she was thrown upon her sisters for company during her early childhood, as their nurse discouraged visits from other children. They entertained themselves by reading, writing plays and playing imaginative games, though their social circles widened once they attended Wychwood School. After leaving school, and a period in Paris, Cannan married Captain James Pullein-Thompson in 1918. He struggled to find employment once the war ended, and began writing to supplement his income. Cannan decided to breed Sealyham dogs and write, and see which was the more successful. Her first book, *The Misty Valley*, was published in 1922; her books sold, the Sealyhams retreated into the distance (replaced by cocker spaniels—less likely to

I GOT HOT AND BOTHERED

Joanna Cannan: A Pony for Jean

'I GROOMED CAVALIER AND MADE HIM LOVELY'

Joanna Cannan: A Pony for Jean

bite), and in 1935 she started writing *A Pony for Jean*. She had three ideal models on whom to draw: her daughters, Josephine, Christine and Diana, later to become stalwart producers of pony fiction, had ponies and ran wild, generally unfettered by school.

Cannan's heroine, Jean Leslie, lives with her parents in London, but as Jean's father has lost his money (after pepper went wrong) the family has to move to a small cottage in the country. As with *Mayfly*, the poverty is not catastrophic; Jean's mother does not have to go out to work, and they can afford to have someone in to cook, and to keep a pony. Jean's relative poverty is contrasted with the wealth of her cousins, who live near the new house and are a thoroughly superior lot. They have ponies of their own, and also a thin pony they call the Toastrack. Not caring much for him themselves, they give him to Jean. Jean's riding ability, as is made clear, is small. Unwilling to lose face before her 'despising' cousin Camilla, she attempts to jump Camilla's pony, Hesperus, and ends up with concussion. This first book sets Jean firmly at the hopeless end of the spectrum: no capable, moneyed child she.

A Pony for Jean was a completely different animal from what had gone before; told in the first person, it has immediacy and freshness. Jean, although not on the breadline, has a life which was rather more within reach of the average child than Moyra Charlton's castled children, and is an entirely believable character: she flounces, sulks and loses things, but has considerable charm. There are wonderful bits of observation, for example when Jean's aunt and cousins come to tea, and her aunt (Cousin Agnes) tells Jean about the Pony Club:

> 'I'll ask Miss Gosport to send you an entrance form,' said Cousin Agnes. 'It'll be great fun seeing you at the rallies.' She looked at the cousins and said, 'Won't it?' in the voice of a commanding officer.
>
> The cousins said 'Yes,' meekly, but I knew that it wasn't 'Yes,' that they were thinking.

Alas, Cannan's wry humour was not something that became a major feature of the average pony novel.

The pony book soon developed other standard themes. The rich had the best ponies, but were the worst riders. Children never moved from the country to the town, always the other way round. Winning a rosette in competition was the most important thing to a rider. Cannan was aware of these conventions as they developed, but she refused to follow them exactly. Although *We Met our Cousins* (1937) sees Tony and John, prissy little London children, shed their shoes and smart London clothes when they go to stay with their Highland cousins, the sequel, *London Pride* (1939), looks at what happens when Morag and Angus, the Highland cousins, pay a return visit to London. It is as if a whirlwind has hit the quiet London square in which Tony and John live. The four of them find and buy a badly treated pony, whom they name London Pride, and keep her in the square gardens (and even in the garden of the aunt and uncle's London house for a while, sneaking her in through the house) until they manage to wangle a countryside home for her. In her later *Gaze at the* Moon (1957), Cannan again played with the pony book conventions: this time her rural family are moving into town, and heroine Dinah is distraught. Nevertheless, she settles down and makes the best of her new surroundings.

In *They Bought Her a Pony* (1944), Angela Peabody is very rich but does not have a world-beating pony. She thinks she does. The riding-school owner who sold Flash to the Peabodys knew perfectly well that Mr Peabody was the sort who thinks the more expensive something is the better it must be: accordingly he sells Mr Peabody a very expensive bad pony. After Angela gets to know the bohemian Cochrane family, she eventually sees the error of her ways.

All Cannan's characters have their own particular attraction, but in Jean she created the original pony book heroine. Jean has the pony no-one else wants, wins prizes at the gymkhana, and in *More Ponies for Jean* (1943) she and her friend Judy fulfil the ultimate horsy girl's dream by opening their own riding school. Cannan had created the model on which the pony book was to base itself. Angela Bull in the *Oxford Dictionary of National Biography* says that in all the welter of rider-centred books that followed the Jean series, Cannan's books 'with their passion for animals and country life, and their stylish writing, remain pre-eminent'.

In the decades that followed, the formula was exploited and developed over and over again. Cannan's daughters, the Pullein-Thompson sisters, specialised in well-crafted stories combined with careful instruction. There were series: Jill, Jackie and Georgia riding their ponies in episodic adventures eagerly awaited by their fans. The pony book was used for promotion: the famous showjumper Pat Smythe's Three Jays series gave her young fans the chance to experience life at her home. Wild horses provided unfettered adventure, often in exotic locations. Stories were set in riding schools, in competition yards, and in paddock after paddock next to the young owner's home. In the flood of books which appeared from the 1940s to the 1970s, there were stories trite and stories derivative, but also stories that were genuinely exciting and well written. Joanna Cannan and her contemporaries had set the scene across which countless pony book heroines were to gallop.

CHAPTER 2
THE FANTASTIC RIDING SCHOOL
Primrose Cumming and Silver Snaffles

Writing at the dawn of the pony book, Primrose Cumming was lucky. Publishers were not obsessed with series, and were prepared to allow Cumming to experiment with writing pony books that, by the end of her career, included most variations of the genre. Her first three books shot off in completely different directions. *Doney* (1934) was an experiment with the horse-telling-its-story format, and *Spider Dog* (1936) an adventure more doggy than pony. With her third book, *Silver Snaffles* (1937), she made a leap into fantasy to produce the ultimate dream-come-true pony story. It has recently been reprinted and has been loved by generations.

Silver Snaffles's heroine, Jenny, has no pony but spends every spare minute talking to Tattles, who pulls Mr Pymmington's carrier cart. Tattles is past his best; he is elderly and his hard life has left its mark on him—'his backbone sagged with old age like a chair that has been too much sat in'. Jenny's father can't afford riding lessons for her; and if he could, the local riding school is run by Mr Kelley, who has a red face and shouts, and whose ponies are thin and tired-looking. Jenny pours all this out to Tattles:

'… I must ride, soon, Tattles, I must!'
  Jenny's last words rang out in the little stable. When they had died away the stable seemed very quiet for a while.
  'Through the Dark Corner, and the password is Silver Snaffles.'
  The words had come from Tattles. Jenny stared at him, her surprise making her sit bolt upright on the uncomfortable edge of the manger. Tattles had opened his eyes, but there was a far-away look about them as if he were dreaming. Jenny would have been frightened anywhere else, but you could not feel frightened in Tattles' stable with Tattles.

And so Jenny enters the Extraordinary Riding School where ponies teach the children. The only pupils allowed are those who have no pony—one of the major attractions of the book. It was for the unfortunate many, not the favoured few, that this world existed; the many, many pony-mad children who read pony books but would never have a horse of their own; and who would be lucky if they even had a riding lesson.

It is not a world that is sugar-sweet. Cumming's ponies do not exist in a dream world of unfeasible goodness, where every pony thinks only noble thoughts. Cock Robin, Tattles, Dragon and their comrades are distinctly tart at times; they have little time for human stupidity, as Jenny soon finds out. She learns exactly why she should start to think of things from the pony's point of view and not just her own:

> 'Now we're off!' she cried gaily, and dug her heels into his sides.
> 'Speak for yourself,' snorted Cock Robin.
> He neatly pitched her forward so that she slid over his head and fell on the grass, where she bounced several times like a rubber ball.
> 'Why did you do that?' gasped Jenny when she had finished bouncing.
> 'Why did you dig your heels into me?' asked Cock Robin indignantly.
> 'I thought that was the right way to tell you to start.'
> 'Well it isn't. An easing of the reins and a gentle squeeze with the legs is the way to tell me. A very gentle squeeze, please. You would be the first one to howl if I kicked you in the ribs.'
> 'I'm awfully sorry,' said Jenny, beginning to understand.
> 'I'll forgive you,' said Cock Robin nobly. 'Now try again.'

Anyone who has learned to ride must have wondered quite what the horse thinks of them; and every child must long for the ponies they love to talk to them. In *Silver Snaffles*, in simple and direct style, they do.

Cumming generally handles her alternative worlds neatly: while Tattles is working in the Extraordinary Riding School, he is still present in the real world. Jenny, unlike Tattles's owner, Mr Pymmington, can tell the pony is elsewhere:

> She went into the stable. Tattles was standing there, but he took no notice of her offerings. Even in the dim light she could see that his eyes had the far-away look which Mr Pymmington had noticed before. Then she knew that part of Tattles had gone through the Dark Corner, this time without her.
> She tiptoed to the manger and put the apple and carrot in it, ready for Tattles when he came back, then she went out again into the evening light.
> 'Tattles is day-dreaming again, I think,' she said.
> 'Very likely,' replied Mr Pymmington, 'but he's a good pony.'

There is a third world in *Silver Snaffles*, one beyond the lilac mist which surrounds the Riding School. There is an empty stable at the Riding School, which belongs to Pippin. She

A long red racing car swept by so closely that the wind of its passing blew up the ponies' manes

Primrose Cumming: **Silver Snaffles**

"*Oh, my dear, of course we have a pony*"

went through the lilac mist and has not come back. Jenny, another pupil, Peter, and two of the ponies go through the lilac mist to find her. There they find a world where ponies are almost unheard of, where 'raced streams of cars and motor-cycles, hooting on their horns, or back-firing with loud, banging noises like guns going off'. Pippin has been taken by Mrs Jostlepot, who is 'willing to pay anything in order to make a better show than our friends'. Jenny, Peter and the ponies manage to rescue Pippin, and, after a chase, succeed in getting back to the Riding School.

This second half of the book takes the focus away from learning to ride. It feels a slightly false step: the world of the Riding School has humour and balance, but the Jostlepots' world is a caricature land where the car is king and everyone thinks only of themselves. Once back from this world and with the Riding School, the book picks up its assured tone again. It ends with a hunt—though not one in which the fox dies:

> There was a stir among hounds as the fox suddenly reappeared at the mouth of his hole. He jumped on to the top of the bank and sat upon his haunches regarding them.
> 'Won't they kill him?' asked Jenny, who now wanted the fox to escape after giving them such a good run.
> 'Oh no,' said Tattles. 'We never kill here. I expect he is going to make a speech.'

Were ponies to teach one to ride, it is easy to believe that Cumming describes it exactly as it would happen. As with so many horse stories previously, she has points to make: ponies should be treated properly and their feelings considered; an obsession with the car is not healthy. This pill is well sugared, however, in those parts of the book set in the Extraordinary Riding School and the real world, though rather less so in the car-mad land beyond the lilac mist; but the enchantment of the speaking ponies, the appeal to the ponyless child, and the wryly observed characterisation of both ponies and people have created a book which will remain iconic.

CHAPTER 3
THE BATTERY THUNDERS ON
The pony book in wartime

The outbreak of the Second World War in 1939 certainly decreased the number of pony books published. There were other casualties too: Moyra Charlton's *Echoing Horn* (1939) had much of its print run destroyed, and the manuscript and illustrations of Michael Lyne's adult book *Hunting Here and There* were lost altogether. Whatever the privations of war, some authors understandably carried on as if war had not broken out: Marjorie Mary Oliver's *Ponies and Caravans*, published in 1941, is an idyllic holiday journey that takes its readers into a world where the most important thing was buying Dartmoor ponies. Josephine Pullein-Thompson's *Six Ponies* (1946) was written while Josephine was doing war work at the Reading Telephone Exchange. In an interview with her, I asked why *Six Ponies* made no mention of the war. It was a deliberate decision:

> I decided to leave the War out of the book. I was fifteen when it started, and after four years it began to look as though we would win and everything would change. No bombs, no blackouts, no rationing of food and clothes. Men would come home and organise

Horse in a Gas Mask, Riding *Magazine, April 1941*

things again. Pony Clubs would restart. There would be petrol for cars. So I tried to place *Six Ponies* in the future, but really it was set in the England of the 1930s.

War did, though, make its way into pony books, with varying results. Shirley Faulkner-Horne's characters were insulated from the worst effects; Primrose Cumming's were more directly involved. For Mary Treadgold's children, war ripped away all vestiges of a normal, comfortable life, and they were confronted with a world utterly changed.

Shirley Faulkner-Horne started writing early, publishing her first book in 1936, when she was fifteen. Her first fictional title, *Bred in the Bone* (1938), started a series of books placed firmly in the upper reaches of society, allying sound fact to characters whose existence is gilded. Faulkner-Horne does not ignore the war, but it does not have a major effect on her characters: in *Riding with the Kindles* (1941) Corona Kindle and her brother Ken cannot go home for the holidays from their respective boarding schools as London is being bombed. They concentrate instead on learning to ride better. Her next book, *Parachute Silk* (1944), is a straightforward spy-chasing adventure, the first title of the series featuring Ian and Veronica Paisley. Their dog Rufus finds a piece of parachute silk; Ian and Veronica are convinced this means that a German spy has landed, but no-one will believe them. It is quite possible that the author would have written more on these themes, had she been allowed to, but publishers were not always keen on the war being mentioned in children's books.

Faulkner-Horne's books are in some ways an odd mixture. She is good on description of the equine events—the polo lesson, the point-to-point—and her adventure stories are generally fast-paced. Her characters, however, are given to periods of moralising that detract from the pace of the story. Veronica, as she and her brother are off to investigate the innards of the mysterious saddle (*Mexican Saddle*, 1946), starts to discourse on the lack of perfection in the world, this being 'a warning that it is only a testing ground where we must prove ourselves worthy of a land of perfection. Here beauty is a slender promise and an encouragement.' Her brother soon stops her short, though it seems more likely that Veronica is intended to be 'deep' rather than irritating.

What is notable about many of Faulkner-Horne's characters is their utter self-confidence. They have never had to question their place in society: they are at the top. The critic John Birks's characterisation of pony book heroines as 'self-conscious little misses' would pass Faulkner-Horne characters by: they are generally blithely unselfconscious, completely comfortable in their settings, ready to 'take their place in forming the destiny of their country' (*Green Trail*, 1947). Jennifer Charrington, for example, in *White Poles* (1957), immediately addresses those she knows are her social inferiors by their surnames.

As time goes on there is some loosening of the social straitjacket, but only a very little. Philip in *Mexican Saddle* describes (with some lack of sympathy) how his grandmother has failed to adapt to the changes in society:

'She even expects the village school children to bow and curtsey to her. It's really rather pathetic; if she'd only come out and learn how things have changed she'd be a lot happier.'

Jennifer in *Look before You Leap* (1955) persuades her parents to let her work with horses and train to three-day-event. Once off the parental leash, she meets and falls for an amateur jockey. Jennifer is convinced her parents will not approve of someone whose only method of support appears to be racing, and she is right. But all is not lost: once it becomes clear that her beloved is from the top drawer, Jennifer's parents manage to overcome their opposition.

Primrose Cumming's characters experience something of the reality of war. *Silver Eagle Carries On* (1940) sees the Chantry family struggling to keep their riding school going in war conditions. They fight to keep their horses (horses were still requisitioned at the beginning of the war) and tackle petrol restrictions by teaching ponies to pull carts. *Owls Castle Farm* (1942), though it has minimal pony content, reflected Cumming's own war work. Brother and sister Brian and Sheelah are evacuated to their grandparents' house, near which is the neglected Owls Castle Farm. The farm's owner, Stephen Tabrett, is put under notice to improve the farm substantially within the next few months, or it will be taken over by the Government. Sheelah, and later Brian, set to, and after considerable hard work start to bring the farm round. The war is there as a constant presence; Sheelah lies in bed and listens to the aeroplanes droning overhead, returning from air raids. The foreign family lodging at the farm generate xenophobic reactions from the villagers. A German plane crashes and burns in the farm's spinney, leading to an invasion by souvenir hunters. The farmhouse is blacked out:

THE POTATO PLANTING

Primrose Cumming: Owls Castle Farm

It was one of the things by which she would most remember the war, Sheelah thought: this passing from a still fairly light world with blackbirds chattering up and down the hedges into night-time with curtains drawn and lamps lit as if it were quite dark beyond the windows.

The book is, at the end, hopeful. The farm is saved, and, as Brian and Sheelah survey the land, another formation of aeroplanes flies overhead, on its way home.

… they knew, too, that the future was worth fighting for … for the right to enjoy the good things of the earth.

Agriculture was important to Primrose Cumming: she saw it as the key to survival. Her characters meet the challenges of rationing and restrictions with gaiety and verve. Mary Treadgold's were placed right in the line of invasion.

Mary Treadgold (1910–2005) did not write conventional pony stories, but what she did with the pony book was important. She took the same starting points as many authors before and since—the golden beginnings of summer holidays, filled with ponies; visits to pony-mad cousins; the grand country house—but she did not leave her characters there. Her children have major issues to face, shattering events which are beyond their control. In *We Couldn't Leave Dinah*, leaving Dinah the pony fades into insignificance for Caroline beside coping with the reality of invasion in the Second World War. The children in *No Ponies* learn that war does not end tidily. Paul and Sandra, the heroes of the Heron books, have a cold and difficult world to deal with after the death of their parents.

After being educated at St Paul's Girls' School and Bedford College, London, Treadgold became Heinemann's first Children's Editor in 1938. Her work there coincided with the flood of pony stories inspired by Joanna Cannan's *A Pony for Jean* and its imitators. Among the books she received were 'a staggering number of manuscripts about ponies and Pony Clubs—a few, a very few, outstanding, the majority quite frightful'. Treadgold resigned from Heinemann in 1940 and, before she went to work with the BBC as a literary editor and producer, wrote her first book, *We Couldn't Leave Dinah* (1941), in an air-raid shelter: 'This was September 1940, and not being a knitter or caring for the sound of falling bombs, I occupied myself relatively painlessly in the air-raid shelter with trying to implement my own verdict: "I could do better myself!"'

We Couldn't Leave Dinah, which won the Carnegie Medal, has in its opening pages only the briefest hint of what is to come in the story. Caroline is busy living life as it has always been, daydreaming about the glories of competition:

Her eyes grew dreamy as she pictured herself in immaculate riding kit, leading a spirited, blue-rosetted Dinah round the ring with the judge stepping eagerly forward to shake hands. 'Never, Miss Templeton,' he would say, 'never have I seen a horse take that gate better …'

Caroline's golden dream is soon shattered by her six-year-old brother with the news that their Channel Island, Clerinel, is threatened with invasion by the Nazi forces. Caroline's first reaction to the news is to insist that they must take the ponies with them when they leave; then reality crashes in, but only briefly. Her father tells her straight away that the ponies must stay behind, but, wanting to give his daughter a little more of the golden world she has just emerged from, uses that classic tactic with children to soften the news: distraction. He reminds her about the next Pony Club event. It works:

> You couldn't really believe in awful things like Hitler when you were out in sun and wind and sea-spray and with people as absolutely marvellous as the Pony Club.

The Pony Club dream, however, fades utterly when Caroline and Mick are, in the confusion and panic of the evacuation, left behind. Treadgold shows conventional pony owning as the luxury it is. Both children quickly gain some perspective: despite the title, it is not the pony Dinah who is central to the story.

During the time the children spend hiding on the island, the ponies are used both to carry what they need when they hide in a cave before being able to escape and also as transport—to move around the island more quickly when they are attempting to find out the Nazis' true invasion plans. The ponies' position as part of life of the ruling class is emphasised by the German girl Nannerl, the young daughter of the German commander. Not only do her family take over the Templeton house, they also annex the ponies. But the ponies become the means through which the Templetons and Nannerl connect, the shared love of the horse being a common language, no matter who is the invader or the invaded. When Nannerl helps both Templetons escape, Caroline is able to take the extraordinary step of regarding Nannerl as more than just an enemy. She makes her an honorary member of the Pony Club:

> Nannerl was fumbling with the Pony Club badge. She held it out to Caroline. 'Zis is yours,' she said sadly. 'You most 'ave it to take to England.'
> Caroline looked at the little badge as it lay on the palm of Nannerl's broad, stumpy hand. Suddenly she had an inspiration. There was just one thing she could do for the small German girl who had rendered her so great a service.
> 'You keep it,' she said generously. 'You keep that, Nannerl. And I'll tell you what. There's a boy on this Island called Peter Beaumarchais. He used to be President of the Pony Club when we were all here. You find him and tell him Caroline Templeton made you a Junior Member of the Pony Club and gave you her badge. He—he'll remember me.'

Treadgold shows life in all its complicated muddle in her next book, *No Ponies* (1946). It does not take the story of the Templeton children on (that was done in the non-pony *The Polly Harris*, 1949) but looks at what happened to the ponies belonging to a British family whose home is in France but who had to leave to spend the war in Britain, leaving the ponies behind. The children who own the ponies do not actually appear: the book's heroes are their non-horsy cousins, Jane, Colin and Andy. After the war the three, with their aunt, are travelling through France by train to the house, where their cousins will later join them. Jane in particular loathes the very idea of ponies:

> 'It's just that I'm sick of being bad at things like games and—and riding. And it's all so lovely here, and next week it'll all be spoilt because I'll have to be trying not to mind being laughed at. And—and—it's not that I don't *want* to like riding either, because I'd *like* to like it, and I do *really* like Katherine and Anthony, oh—'

Like Jane, Treadgold does not deal in gymkhanas: these are kept at a distance. The rosette-winning, Pony-Club-going children of *No Ponies* are physically absent. They are simply there to act as a counterpoint to Jane's horror of the horse-obsessed.

Treadgold's novels ask questions: are people always what they seem? How does one cope with a horrible situation with no way out? Caroline and Mick Templeton see Monsieur Beaumarchais, father of their friend Peter, handing over their house to the German Army, and it is clear from what they overhear that he has been instrumental in the successful invasion. The true situation is infinitely more complicated than what they immediately imagine is true. In *No Ponies*, Jean, the cheerful French boy whom the children meet on the train, is really a Nazi youth leader being smuggled out of Germany to safety; and Pierre, denounced as a wartime collaborator, is anything but. However, Pierre does not end the book with his reputation restored: he knows he has to go on being loathed as a collaborator in order to carry on entrapping some of the remaining Nazis.

The occasional unlikeliness of Treadgold's plots (though this is true of any children's spy adventure) pales beside what Anne Carter, a contributor to *Twentieth-Century Children's Writers*, calls her 'shrewd eye for character and relationships'. Treadgold is particularly good at the interplay between brothers and sisters. The Templetons and Atherleys are entirely believable, and it is also apparent in her post-war novels. The relationship between Sandra and Adam, the brother and sister heroes of *The Heron Ride* (1962) and *Return to the Heron* (1963), is also beautifully observed. The children's diplomat parents have been killed, and the children have been shipped back to England, there to live with an uncle and his family, none of whom want them, or even particularly like them. Sandra has the worst of it, because she lives with the family full time; Adam is away at school, but recognises the shrivelling effect living in that loveless, noisy household has on her:

> Now he came to think of it, she had seemed to be smaller, and paler, and thinner than when they had been together at Easter. She had looked somehow—quenched. Staring down at the Long Meadow turf, Adam made a colossal effort with his imagination—she had looked like a girl who had been out in the snow and the winter cold for a long, long time …

Even after their charmed summer staying with Miss Vaughan, who understands and likes them, Sandra will have to go back to her grim Bayswater existence with relations who do not really want her. Nothing can be done about that; there is no easy way out, and Sandra simply learns enough to make it a little more bearable. Onkel Anton, the Hungarian refugee, who once worked at the Spanish Riding School in Vienna and teaches Sandra to ride, knows this.

> 'Nobody expects that you should like it,' answered Onkel Anton. 'Why should you? You have not much in common with your Uncle Arthur, I think. Why should one like to be with people with whom one does not share? Why should one think that one will fit there? And already look what you have done—you have begun to make your own way out—'

Return to the Heron breaks both Sandra and Adam out of their prison, but the book is not just about that: it is about loneliness, possession, and the love of beauty and what that beauty represents. At the end of the book, it is Adam, difficult and closed off from Sandra at the beginning of the novel after a terrible accident, who genuinely rejoices for her when she is to be bought a horse:

> To Sandra, Grant Maynard's voice seemed to carry right over the shadowed garden, right over Betsy's field. It seemed to carry right up to the sleeping Downs, where she would again ride Grey Horse. And, as she came down the terrace, speechless because of what she had heard, hardly yet believing, it was Adam's voice that said: 'Thank you. Oh, *thank* you.'

Treadgold, although inspired by the desire to write a better pony book than the examples which came across her desk, did not let herself be bound by the conventions the genre had already developed in its short life. She saw ponies in the round: as luxuries or childish dreams, but also as working animals, and as 'castles in Spain', a means of escape and comfort and a symbol of freedom. She saw too the love of ponies that brings people together across boundaries and politics. Her ponies are more than matched by their human owners. Treadgold is not a lazy writer: her characters are never stock stereotypes but are all intensely human. Perhaps her greatest success lies in the value she gives to her characters' feelings. They are never patronised for loving the horse, but neither are they treated as if loving the horse is some superior virtue. Mary Treadgold trod a brilliantly measured path, one trodden by few since.

CHAPTER 4
SKILL, COURAGE AND DETERMINATION
The Pullein-Thompson sisters

The Pullein-Thompson clan bestrode the pony book world; there were three of them, plus their mother, Joanna Cannan, and by the 1970s it was a rare pony-mad child who had not read at least one of their books. After Cannan wrote some of the earliest books in the genre, the daughters picked up the theme and ran with it. Brought up in bohemian surroundings in Oxfordshire, they lived the lives they wrote about. In their joint autobiography, *Fair Girls and Grey Horses* (1996), Josephine describes their childhood:

> But there was always a pony book flavour about The Grove: Cinderella, Ugly Duckling, Rags-to-Riches themes abounded. Beginning without skill, wearing the wrong clothes and riding untrained ponies, we failed for a time and then succeeded beyond all expectations. We bought ponies with bad names which became prizewinners, and in the role of the hard-up scruffy child, we managed to beat the richer, well-dressed children on their expensive ponies. We became convinced that skill, courage and determination could triumph over almost anything and we tried to pass this on in our books.

Josephine, the eldest of the sisters, was born in 1923, and twins Diana and Christine followed in 1925. The girls had relatively little to do with ponies until the family moved from Wimbledon to The Grove, in Oxfordshire. There their parents decided they should have a horse. Countess was not an immediate success: both parents were used to having grooms, and the practicalities of putting a bridle on the aged polo pony themselves caused some consternation. The children were unfazed, and the family horse soon became their province. They read the equestrian works of Henry Wynmalen out loud to each other, trying to improve, and they became good enough to work on other people's horses. Diana says:

> When Christine and I were eleven, we came, with Josephine, to an arrangement with [horse dealer] Mr Sworder out of mutual need. We needed ponies to ride: he needed riders to show off and school the ponies he bought to sell. If we could get more than the asking price for them we kept the change.

Mr Sworder sent the ponies to live at The Grove to be worked on. The girls went, briefly, to Wychwood School, where the staff did not appreciate Josephine's reading matter, asking that her beloved veterinary book 'be kept for holiday consumption, as it upset the other children'. In 1938, after a polio outbreak struck Oxford, where Wychwood was based, the Pullein-Thompsons were removed from the school. When they returned they were way behind their peers, and their parents used the girls' low marks as a reason for removing them permanently. They were then educated at home, so had every afternoon free to ride.

By 1939 and the outbreak of the Second World War, the girls had 'five or six' ponies, but, with the blockades of shipping, supplies of food for them became scarce and ever more expensive. In 1940 the Pullein-Thompson parents said they could no longer afford to feed so many ponies, and so, to raise money to keep them, the girls started 'to give riding lessons in earnest'. The school, based at their home, soon accumulated both more ponies and more pupils. The girls' reputation for sorting out troublesome ponies meant that 'anyone who wanted to sell a difficult pony rang the Pullein-Thompsons'. Some of these ponies became mainstays of the riding school, which soon acquired more clients as well as more ponies, 'lured by word of mouth or the typed postcards ... put in ... shops'. Many parents were working away from home all day, and so The Grove Riding School became a second home for their children: they would spend whole days there, and tasks like tack cleaning became social occasions. The girls flourished. Diana was at last *Diana*, not just one of the twins, and discovered that she liked being with a group of children. Josephine found teaching 'deeply fulfilling' and was fascinated by schooling; Christine was told she was the kindest instructor.

Running the school was hard, physical work. As well as teaching, mucking out, grooming, riding and cleaning tack, they had to contend with a world in which one did not nip into the car to get to one's pony. Some of the ponies were stabled two miles away, and six times a week the girls cycled or jogged to get them. Water came from wells, and had to be carried by yoke to troughs. They cut every spare area of grass for hay, and haynets had to be carried to the ponies every day in winter.

Although hard, the work was rewarding, and it prepared Josephine well for when she was old enough for war work. She left the riding school to work at a remount depot in Melton Mowbray, and then for a stint as a telephone engineer. The twins, then sixteen, were left in charge. After the war they opened a second riding school at Wolvercote, and by the 1950s were operating two stables with 42 horses. Diana's career with horses ended when she developed TB; she then went to London and worked with a literary agent. Christine went to America to work as a professional rider. All three carried on writing, continuing a habit that had started when they were small.

The girls achieved publication early. Their first article, written by all three, appeared in *Riding* magazine in January 1941. 'The Road to Ruin' was the next Pullein-Thompson effort to appear; again a joint work, this story appeared in the summer 1942 issue of *Riding,* and is a morality tale about the stupidity of sentimentality. Jester is a pretty grey pony who has gone to the bad. He has forgotten his early youth and his glittering early career, but remembers all too well his second home and owner, 'who by sentimentality had turned an almost perfect pony into a malicious and stubborn animal'. Tales told by the pony are legion; what marks this one out is that although it is a morality tale it starts off from the end result, rather than taking a chronological approach, which makes for a more interesting tale. The point could, however, have been brought home with a little more subtlety: it is hard for this sort of story not to slip into self-righteousness, and slip it does.

After this warm-up, the girls' next joint effort was a novel, *It Began with Picotee*. Although not published until 1946, it was finished by the spring of 1942, when Josephine was nineteen

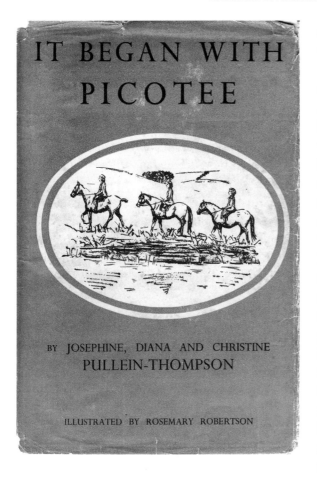

and the twins seventeen. The story, written during the ponies' rest days, 'emerged slowly as we argued over every word,' and 'giggled a lot'. *It Began with Picotee*, although written by all three, has a unified voice: it is very difficult to point to any particular bit as showing one sister's influence more than another. Olivia, Bridget and Griselda Douglas own Picotee, and are then lent another pony, Tony. Then they buy a chestnut foal they call Pengo, and then they agree to school Colonel Selcombe's half Shetland, and then they borrow Mrs Baxter's two ponies … And they end up with plenty of ponies. The ponies were based on those the Pullein-Thompsons themselves sold. Cocktail (of 'Cocktail Capitulates', their earlier short story for *Riding* magazine) reappears as Bronx the bucker. The plot, of girls riding ponies no-one else wants to ride so they can be sold on, is based on their own life. That the sisters were fully aware they were fictionalising life is clear. The Douglases plan to write a pony book to make money:

> 'It could be almost a true story, and none of the ponies need be stolen by gypsies or win at Olympia, as they do in most books.'
> 'It might be rather dull,' I said, 'if it was only about the things we do, especially if we put in all our quarrels and arguments.'

This is a little ironic, bearing in mind that all the Douglases ever, ever, ever do is ponies. And eat the occasional meal. And go into town occasionally to buy something horsy. The book is not without its faults: the action is episodic, and the characters are interchangeable and derivative. The narrator, Griselda, has more than a passing resemblance to Jean of *A Pony for Jean*, though without Jean's occasional focus on other things besides ponies. *It Began with Picotee* does, however, show the elements all three sisters developed in their books: the focus on the rider; that rider riding well; and realistic pony adventures. They took what they knew, and worked with it.

Diana Pullein-Thompson (b1925)

Diana was the first of the sisters to get within sniffing distance of being published. *Riding* magazine had a young riders' section, which ran monthly competitions. The November 1940 issue asked readers to write a critical appraisal of any article in *Riding*, and Diana, then aged fifteen, won the competition. *Riding* certainly got its critical review. *Riding* said: 'It is so much better to be fairly critical than just to say that all the articles in RIDING are lovely. Well, the prizewinner for the seniors produced a good and critical review, and well-written, too, and the lady's name is Diana Pullein-Thompson ...' *Riding* didn't follow their normal practice and publish her entry. Diana says:

> With all the arrogance of youth, I had chosen a piece by a well-established expert— was it Faudel-Phillips?—on jumping with the Weedon seat, which I tore slowly apart, unfavourably comparing the style he recommended with the Italian forward seat. For once *Riding* broke with tradition and did not publish the winning entry, for fear, I suppose of offending the expert.

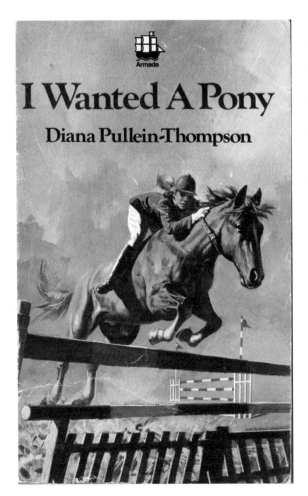

Diana's first solo pony book was *I Wanted a Pony* (1946). It is an astonishingly mature book for one started by a sixteen year old, and has retained its popularity for decades.

Despite its author's dislike of the book—she regards it as derivative, drawing its plot from her mother's *A Pony for Jean*, with its lone heroine beset by cousins—the book met with some critical acclaim. Mary Cadogan and Patricia Craig, not noted for their fondness for the pony story, talk of the author's 'unpretentious style', 'quality of detachment' and 'observant good sense'. Linda Yeatman, writing on the author in *Twentieth-Century Children's Writers*, calls it 'shrewd' and 'perceptive and amusing'.

The heroine, Augusta, is marooned at her cousins' house for the summer. Although she loves ponies, her riding efforts have been restricted to borrowing a friend's obstreperous half-Shetland, Dominoe. Augusta's cousins, successful riders all with glossy and successful ponies, despise her. Dominoe takes charge of Augusta during a bending race, and 'calmly but firmly' takes her out of the ring.

> Barbara, who is the eldest and fourteen, said, 'Oh! *really*, Augusta, you *did* look funny.' Stephen said that even the soppiest chap at his school could have stuck on Dominoe in the riding class, and that I wasn't holding my reins properly. Jill said that Dominoe was an awful pony and much too fat, and that I should have used a 'diagonal aid' when he started to play up.

After Augusta saves a farm from burning, she is sent a financial reward by the owner, enough to buy a pony. She cannot make her cousins listen to her tale of triumph, so she sallies forth to buy a pony on her own. Augusta bids on a pony at a local sale, and succeeds in buying it, and the fairy tale, we think, has been achieved. However, once Augusta tries to pay she finds that auctions are held in guineas not pounds, and that she does not have enough money to buy the pony (a guinea was 21 shillings, so Augusta needed fifteen pounds and fifteen shillings, not the fifteen pounds she thought she had bid). Augusta is horrified and ends up in tears outside the saleroom. However, she remembers her church hat, which is in her pocket, and goes off to sell it at a second-hand shop. The dealer is no pushover, and Augusta hands over more and more of her clothing until she remembers the silver buttons on her coat, sacrifices them, and the pony is hers. Although Augusta has a ride home of dreamlike bliss on the now safely bought Daybreak, all soon goes wrong again.

The critic Margery Fisher, although calling the Pullein-Thompsons 'the most successful exponents of the pony story', does not like *I Wanted a Pony* and saves especial venom for Daybreak's salvation:

> Few readers, whether they know about ponies or not, are likely to accept the situation in *I Wanted a Pony* … where Augusta discovers in a few minutes what everyone else (including the vet) has failed to deduce in months about the

Before catching Daybreak.

Diana Pullein-Thompson: I Wanted a Pony

grey pony—that its unpleasant habit of tossing its head is *not* due to a brain-tumour but to the fact that an unusually broad forehead makes all bridles uncomfortable. This contrivance to bring the pony within Augusta's limited means is unusually bad

It is Augusta's progression, without benefit of tuition, from a poor rider to an accomplished one that I find rather more difficult to believe. As with generations of other readers, though, I am willing to forgive this part of the story because of the author's creation of a completely plausible set of characters. Augusta's transformation into a talented rider might not be believable, but it is her cousins' reaction to it that the reader longs to see. While Jill remains self-righteous, Stephen and Barbara come through.

Coincidence and improbability are present in some of Diana's other novels. In *Janet Must Ride* (1953) her portrayal of a teenager working with horses has a plot which is not always helped by its improbability. Janet is a far more capable rider than any of her employer's children, and when the eldest girl, Miriam, is injured and unable to ride, Janet gets the ride (at Badminton), and does so well that she is taken on by an eventing stable. Once the equitation expert training Miriam is introduced, and Miriam's lack of keenness made plain, the plot immediately lacks tension: the only question is how long it will take for the inevitable to happen and Janet to take over. Then, as now, this situation was not impossible, but it was unlikely. Ruby Ferguson's Jill, and her succession of dead-end pony jobs in *Pony Jobs for Jill* (1960), was a much more realistic impression of what working with horses was like.

But Diana's ability to portray characters who convince pulls the reader past any weaknesses in plot. Her characters, unlike her elder sister Josephine's, are rarely part of a large family. As Linda Yeatman says, Diana has much 'sympathy with the loner'. Her books are almost always written in the first person, with some occasional variations of the technique: alternating first-person narrators in *A Pony to School* (1950) and four successive first-person narrators in *A Pony for Sale* (1951). Over the progression of the book, the narrator generally finds contentment. This is not necessarily within the group: although at the end of *I Wanted a Pony* Augusta's cousins are beginning to have a grudging respect for her, one suspects they will never be friends. Augusta does not mind; she has achieved what she wanted, a pony she can ride, and is happy to carry on living on her own terms.

Diana, in creating a succession of girls having trouble fitting in, was writing about what she knew. In *Fair Girls and Grey Horses* she described herself at school at Wychwood as 'an untidy girl struggling to be liked'. In an interview, she said:

> Very often I write about an isolated girl who wants friends, I suppose, don't I? *The Long Ride Home, Cassidy in Danger*, she's on her own. [There's a] family in *Pony Seekers*, but they don't have outside friends … I think it's because that's how it was for one, really … We were cut off, you see. We had no friends nearby … In the village, there were three single women, of course, who lived with mother. We always had a terror we might become like them. We didn't have any children friends in the village at all.

Diana's least successful book, *The Pennyfields* (1949), moves away from the first-person portrayal of a solitary girl with which she was most at home. The Pennyfields are one of those large families portrayed so often by Diana's sister Josephine. Chaotic and ebullient, they are short of money (in the traditional pony book sense only: the children go away to school and have a large house and a housekeeper, but they lack money for frills). They are trying to earn enough to buy a pony and a shotgun. The family's efforts are doomed never to work out quite as they should. After a very little while, there is a dreadful inevitability about much of it: an interesting event pops up, only to end in predictable disaster caused by one or other of this family whose members have little in the way of redeeming (or differentiating) features. The author was on surer ground dealing with the riding club children in *Three Ponies and Shannan* (1947), whom she was able to observe with the detachment that served her so well in *I Wanted a Pony*. In many pony books, having money is synonymous with being a villain. The rich girl has beautiful ponies she does not appreciate (and probably cannot ride), and they are looked after by a groom: never, ever, by her. In the final scenes of the book, she will be trounced in the local gymkhana by the poor-but-noble girl who has succeeded despite everything. Ruby Ferguson's Susan Pyke is probably the archetypal example. *Three Ponies and Shannan* is one of the few books to flout this convention. Only child Christina's father is a wealthy businessman, and the family move into Folly Court, and instantly smarten it up. Folly Court was owned by a local family who still live nearby. They were obviously reluctant movers, and are friends with Charlie Dewhurst, daughter of the local vicar. She has little money, a scruffy pony, and a massive chip on her shoulder. Christina, keen to make friends, invites Charlie to tea. It is a disaster.

> I could see that she was riding badly and making her pony refuse by pulling her in the mouth as she reached the wings, but I couldn't correct her, because of seeming conceited. At last I suggested that she might try dropping the reins on the take-off. Instantly she was furious and said that when she wanted teaching she would go to a riding school, not a pot hunter.

This attitude reflected what Diana saw in real life:

> I saw all around me how richer children were scorned, especially if they had grooms, so I deliberately decided to see life a little bit from their point of view. We had scores of pupils. And from my own experience there could be pleasant rich children and horrid poor ones, so yes, it was a deliberate decision [to write Christina as the heroine].

If Diana was making a moral point, it was that a pony demands things that are not reliant on financial and social background: tact, understanding and ability.

Pony books are often seen as depicting middle-class girls living an escapist dream with plenty of money, ponies and emotionally unengaged adventure: what Mary Cadogan and Patricia Craig call '[identifying] one kind of dumb thoroughbred with the behaviour and mannerisms of another'. The reality of owning an animal is, of course, different. Animals become ill; and, regardless of the social class of their owner, they die. As Alison Haymonds says: 'It was a love that brought with it a great deal of responsibility.' Diana was conscious of the responsibility of the need both to educate readers in how to look after another living being and to acquaint them with the reality of life with animals. In an interview with me, she said: 'Death is something you meet all too often when you are living and working with animals and, above all, I tried to be a realist.'

In *A Pony to School* (1950), Tilly and Piers own a grey mare, Seaspray. While Augusta and Christina, the heroines of the novel, are reschooling Clown, who rears, they take him out on hacks to visit Tilly and Piers in their house in the middle of the woods. The first visit is uneventful. The second is not, and with it comes a stark depiction of the reality of what happened to a pony in the 1950s if it caught tetanus.

> 'Do tell us what's the matter?' said Christina.
> 'Would you rather we went away?' I asked.
> 'Go into the stable and you'll see what's wrong. *Go* on. Don't stand here staring. You know the way, don't you?'
> 'All right,' I said.
> We took our ponies into the little paddock. 'It must be Seaspray,' I said.
> 'You go first. I'll hold Daybreak and Symphony,' offered Christina.
> I handed her my reins and walked to the loose-box; the top door was open; I looked over the bottom one and the sight which met my eyes is something I shall never forget; even now as I write I can recall it as though it was only yesterday that it happened. Seaspray was there standing in the far corner, but she was scarcely recognisable; her dear grey face was pinched and drawn; her eyes were sunken, her nostrils dilated and her mouth closed; her soft grey nose was poked out; her back was hollowed and her tail raised. She stood with heaving flanks, oustretched limbs and with such an expression of terror, as I had never seen on any animal's face before.

This is strong stuff. Although the bereft Tilly does get another pony—the reschooled Clown—the acquisition is overshadowed by Seaspray's death. To a child wanting a dream-come-true story, Diana's sometimes shocking realism can come as a jolt. In a further wrenching scene in *Riding with the Lyntons* (1956), the heroine is asked to take hay in to the two Dartmoor ponies, Jingle and Jangle. She does but, in a world of her own, can't remember whether she shut the gate or not. That night, the ponies get out. Jingle is hit by a car, and has to be put down.

> In a moment she would be dead. A corpse for hounds to devour. And it was all my fault. We walked in silence, and our ears were waiting for the shot which would mean Jingle's life was over. It came at last—a dull thud, not like the sharp crack of a pistol as I had imagined.

There are plenty of pony books which skim the surface of life and provide comforting puddings of reads: better to have some like Diana's, to add depth to a genre which often avoids the nastier side of life. Diana's books convince. Her children are more than simple, pony-loving souls. Her heroines are shy, awkward, lonely, but all are possessed of an inner determination and often a wry humour. They are faced with sometimes appalling reverses, but emerge at the other side. Diana never forgets that her characters are human beings first and foremost.

JOSEPHINE PULLEIN-THOMPSON (b1923)

Josephine's first solo work, *Six Ponies* (1946), was written on the roof of the Reading Telephone Exchange. The book is much more character-driven than *It Began with Picotee* (1946), the novel she wrote jointly with her sisters, and was the first of her popular Noel and Henry series, which together are possibly the best loved of her books. This five-book series, starting with *Six Ponies* and ending with *Pony Club Camp* (1957), illustrates the shift in attitudes to riding and schooling that took place in Britain in the 1930s and 1940s. British horsemanship in the 1920s and 1930s aimed mostly at becoming successful on the hunting field: dressage was despised and the backward seat while jumping was standard.

Six Ponies' inspiration was Charlotte M Yonge's *Six Cushions* (1869) which Josephine bought for her mother, who collected the author's work. Where Yonge describes six Victorian girls embroidering hassocks for a church, Josephine's book takes members of the West Barsetshire Pony Club and looks at what happens when six very different children take on the challenge of ponies who know nothing. 'It was,' Josephine says of *Six Cushions*, 'interesting because of its characters. I wanted a broad canvas for my first solo book, not a first person story, and this writer managed to tell you so much about six girls and their families by describing their trials and successes in making six cushions. It seemed to me the six people breaking in ponies would make a much more exciting story.'

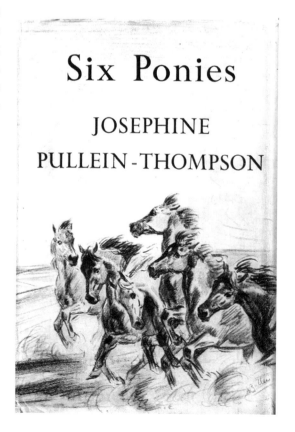

The plethora of twenty-first-century craft devotees would possibly not agree with her there, but *Six Ponies* has exerted a grip on the pony-mad ever since it was published. It developed the two strengths evident in the better books in Josephine's career: character, and what Clarissa Cridland calls 'solid instruction'. Far more than her sisters' books, Josephine's are technical and accurate. Jay Felton, a pony book fan who later became a riding instructor, says: 'I would read what the Major told them to do then go out and put it into practice—no riding schools where I lived. Many years later when I did my BHS exams I found how well she had taught me.'

Six Ponies opens with the Pony Club being set the task of breaking in six New Forest ponies, rescued from being sold for meat by a 'horsy' friend of Major Holbrooke's. The Major is about to take over the Pony Club, whose standard of riding is 'shocking'. The West Barsetshire Pony Club members are a varied group, a mixture of the arrogant, misguided and charming. Major Holbrooke is rapidly established as the fount of all equine knowledge, despite having met with instant opposition at the first Pony Club rally he held. Although he petrifies some of the Pony Club members—'already hot, tired and cross with the members for riding so badly, [he] exploded with wrath'—he is never less than fair, and is always willing to work to improve the members' horsemanship.

To a non-rider, there are sections of the books which must be completely incomprehensible, dealing as they do with dressage movements like shoulder-in and the turn on the forehand. In the hands of some of the less skilful authors who came after Josephine the desire to instruct could turn a book into a painful exercise in self-righteousness, but she avoids the unpleasantly didactic. Although we might not understand exactly how Noel, after intensive instruction in the art of equitation from Major Holbrooke, has turned from an inept rider carted out of the show ring into the most successful of the horse breakers, we can appreciate the fact that she has done it, and enjoy the process too. At the end of *Six Ponies*, the pigheaded have had their comeuppance, and those willing to listen their reward.

Josephine's characters are varied in their abilities and approaches to the horse: some are simply hopeless but willing to learn, others stubbornly determined to have their own way regardless of the effect on the pony. Noel Kettering, heroine of the Noel and Henry series, is the most notable of the hopeless but willing school. Characters like her are essential to the plot: without someone who is willing to change, there is no progression, no redemption and, for Josephine, no story. Josephine disagreed with Joanna Cannan's views on whether people could change their fundamental nature: 'Mama and I did not agree about people. Mama thought people were stuck with being horrid; I thought they could improve.'

Alison Haymonds, in the *International Companion Encyclopedia of Children's Literature*, talks about pony books' similarity to 'traditional fairy tales, with their stories of the transformation of gauche girls and neglected ponies and the recurring pattern of motifs and conventional events'. In Josephine's case, that transformation is always achieved through education. At the beginning of *Six Ponies* Noel has virtually no self-confidence (a characteristic she retains throughout the series, leading the Major, somewhat tartly, to liken her to Uriah Heep) but, most importantly, she can be taught. By the end of the series, she is teaching the younger Pony Club members.

The major male character in the series, Henry Thornton, Major Holbrooke's nephew, has a similarly erratic progress. Although Henry is riding one of the Major's horses with success at the end of *Pony Club Team* (1950), at the opening of the next book, *One Day Event* (1954), his dressage test on his horse Echo is a disaster:

As he rode the test, Noel's depression increased. Everything seemed to be wrong and she had so hoped he would do well. She didn't want to watch Echo's unbalanced strong trot; his unwilling transitions into the canter, his sorry attempts at turns on the forehand, his dawdling walk or his crooked halts.

In order to emphasise some characters' progression, a range of other equestrian points of view needs to be shown; Josephine has a varied cast to achieve this aim. The most long-standing equestrian villain is Evelyn Radcliffe, one of the large Radcliffe family who appear in the Noel and Henry series. To the unknowledgeable she does not appear a bad rider. Her ponies usually do what she wants them to do, but it is done by strength and force of character rather than finesse. It is Evelyn who personifies the traditional British point of view on the finer points of horsemanship:

'Look at the marks you can gain in the cross-country. A good hunter can more than make up any marks he may have lost in the dressage; he'd be more free-going than all these wretched over-collected animals ...' (*One Day Event*)

In addition to the moral imperative to improve one's riding, Josephine is, at least in her early writing career, firmly convinced of the corrupting power of money. Her next two books after *Six Ponies*, *I Had Two Ponies* (1947) and *Plenty of Ponies* (1949), are concerned with improving the characters of those ruined by too much money. Christabel, the heroine of *I Had Two Ponies*, is a spoiled and wealthy girl who ignores her ponies, so they are sold:

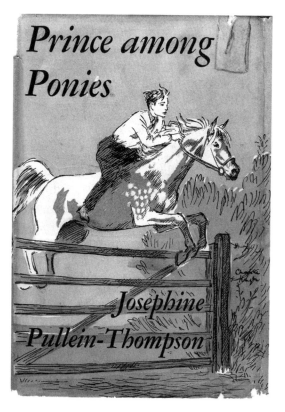

At first I felt cross and sniffed into my smart linen handkerchief, but after a few minutes I realised what a lot of unpleasantness it would save: Daddy wouldn't grumble because I didn't ride the ponies, my friends wouldn't be able to ask for rides and Small wouldn't be able to complain if I gave my friends rides. So I stopped sniffing and walked into the house and started to fiddle with the expensive radiogram ...

Christabel stays with the Westlake family when her parents go on a long business trip to India. The Westlakes are one of the large Bohemian families of which Josephine was so fond: examples of them appear in virtually all her early books. Christabel is underwhelmed by her first sight of the Westlakes: their car is 'battered and grimy', their children have 'queer names', and she has to wait for her lift from the station until the eldest boy has finished in the second-hand bookshop. The Westlakes are equally unimpressed with Christabel once they find out she did not make sure her ponies were sold to good homes, but sent them to a sale:

> 'So, just because you were too lazy to look after the wretched animals, you let them be sold in a beastly sale and never even bothered to find out who bought them,' said Lucy.
> This was really a bit too much. I felt my face go red with rage and I said, 'You ought to mind your own business and not be so jolly cheeky to your elders.'
> 'Kindness to animals is everybody's business,' said Lucy; while Simon murmured, 'Age is no criterion—'

Ironically, Christabel has come to visit the Westlakes determined to reform them, but she eventually sees the error of her ways. The book ends with Christabel thoroughly converted to the cause of pony: she has learned that one cannot judge by appearances, that the backward seat is bad, that looking after one's own pony is best. Despite the obvious coincidences needed to make the plot fulfil its themes of redemption and reward, it is still a sparky read. The dialogue is lively and realistic, and the family are thoroughly believable. The heroine is given added attraction by having her comment on her awfulness as she goes; she has an engaging honesty about her faults.

Plenty of Ponies, Josephine's next book, features the Esmonds, another large family, possibly once Bohemian but now ruined by cash. They were, the eldest declares, a reasonable bunch until their father came into money, but now their characters have suffered. Now they have ponies, a groom, and a large house. And has it made them happy? It has not.

> 'It's so difficult to think of unselfish acts to do nowadays,' said Lewis. 'At the cottage it was easy; if you felt virtuous you swept and dusted or peeled the potatoes … But now we're rich there's Maddo and Francine to do everything indoors, and Carter to do the garden and hardly allowing one to do anything for one's own horses; it's all very well for the parents to say that we're getting beastly and selfish, but it's much easier to be nice if you're poor.'

To which his sister points out that 'it's extremely difficult to be nice if you're really poor and don't have enough to eat and live in a slum', but the family resolve to improve their characters and turn themselves back into reasonable human beings. Almost all the book is taken up with their not doing this; they fail over and over again, which makes the book a sometimes unrelenting read. The moral point is hammered home, and the Esmonds, who actually seem a fairly reasonable bunch, have an over-lengthy struggle to overcome the moral disadvantage of Too Much Money.

In this book, as in Josephine's others, male and female characters have equal weight, and compete on equal terms. The male hero is not the most frequently found feature of a pony book, but Josephine and her sisters were proud of the fact their riding schools had as many male pupils as female, and their books reflect that. Pony Club member Richard Morrison's misogyny is dealt with tartly in *Six Ponies*: girls are seen as the equal of boys, and neither is better; they are different. Josephine breaks even more thoroughly with tradition by having boys as the principal characters in some of her books. *Show Jumping Secret* (1955) has a hero, Charles, who has to battle two things: his polio, which has left him with a lame leg, and the utter conviction of his horsy cousins that their way (legs forward, hands in lap) is best, and that his modern ways are strange. Charles eventually wins through, and he and his mare win a Foxhunter Championship—Charles progresses further than any of Josephine's other characters, in the competition sense at least.

Although Josephine was uncomfortable with situations of which she had little direct knowledge, she was on surer ground with emotions. Alison Haymonds says of the pony story: 'It ignores the world outside the stable yard, and most of the traditional conventions of storytelling—love and villainy, conflict and mystery.' While this is mostly true of Josephine's early works (after a gap of ten years during which she wrote mostly for adults, she returned to the pony fold with the mystery-based 1971 story *Race Horse Holiday*), the lack of romance at any rate was the fault of her publishers. Josephine included a lightly drawn romance between Noel and Henry in *Pony Club Camp* (1957), and it is clear from what the other characters say that they, as well as Noel and Henry, have the entirely normal preoccupations of teenagers.

> 'Susan … swears she prefers John Manners, and Judith's mad about the head boy at Frensham Park, but Carola and Polly think Henry's absolutely it.'
> 'What about Marion?' asked David.
> 'Oh, she has fits when she's all for Henry, but at the moment, she's fallen for Christopher, haven't you noticed?'
> 'Whew, has she really? I say, Christopher,' he yelled down the table.
> Nicolas stifled his words by putting a hand over his mouth and Gay said, 'Shush, do show some tact. Christopher's quite keen on her.'

Whatever Josephine, and indeed her readers, wanted, Collins, her publishers, were not keen on romance. Although *Pony Club Camp* generated the most fan mail of all Josephine's titles, 'with people begging "Please, please, can they get married",' Collins told Josephine that it must be the last of the series. They preferred what Josephine called 'Peter Pan characters'. She, however, saw her characters as real children and took pleasure in knowing them as they grew up.

This was certainly true of one of her most accomplished books, *All Change* (1961). It was her last pony novel of the 1960s, and her personal favourite. In it the Conway family are another numerous and well-delineated set. They live on a large estate of which their father is the agent; the owner has died, and the estate has been sold on to a London financier, Mr

Smithson. The book is a full-blown clash between the traditional way of doing things and more efficient, but possibly more heartless, modernisation. The children are desperate to stay in their home while determined not to antagonise its new owner.

All Change skilfully blends adventure, a believable family background and a tension between old and new which is satisfactorily resolved in a realistic compromise. It marked a break in Josephine's output of pony books while she concentrated on writing detective stories for adults. She returned to pony books in the 1970s, but moved away from the instructional novel that had been her forte with a series of pony adventure stories known as The Moors books, and a collaboration with her sisters with the historical Black Beauty's Family series. In the 1980s, as The Moors series was coming to an end, she started the much stronger Woodbury Pony Club series, which saw a return to the instructional format and the Pony Club.

In all, Josephine wrote 32 pony books in a writing career which stretched for over fifty years. Her books, and those of her sisters, were eagerly awaited by the pony fraternity: 'Books by the Pullein-Thompsons … are in the top class,' wrote Colonel C E G Hope, editor of *Pony* magazine. No-one reading the sisters' books could doubt that hard work and perseverance could bring success. As Alison Haymonds says:

> [girls'] life with ponies was a trial run for the sort of life post-war women had to learn to cope with, juggling relationships, responsibilities and family.

Josephine's best books are those in which the vigour of her characterisation sugars the pill of her instruction: the reader is never preached at, but absorbs the information while being thoroughly caught up with the characters and their adventures. She is equally at ease with adults as with child characters, and her stories, while not stuffed full of plot, are thoroughly believable portraits of children and their ponies.

CHRISTINE PULLEIN-THOMPSON (1925–2005)

Christine was the most prolific of the sisters by far, and to date is the British author with the most pony books to her name. Her bibliography numbers over a hundred titles, ranging from non-fiction to early readers, children's adventure stories and, of course, classic pony stories.

Her first solo novel was *We Rode to the Sea* (1948), very different from the first solo books her sisters produced. Josephine's *Six Ponies* and Diana's *I Wanted a Pony* were domestic riding adventures; Christine wrote about Scotland, adventure and escaped prisoners. *We Rode to the Sea* opens in a whirl of chaotic activity on a train from Glasgow to the Highlands as the Macgregor family journey to Fort Frederick to start their riding holiday. After mangling an unfortunate fellow passenger's knitting to a heartbreaking extent, the children set themselves problems from the start by leaving their map on the train. Nevertheless, they launch forth, mapless, into the Highlands, get lost, battle with their recalcitrant camping gear and then find that two German prisoners have escaped. The Macgregors decide they must catch them. Eventually, of course, they do.

This first foray by Christine into what she described as her 'Scottish obsession' is written with enthusiasm and verve, but this is not enough to overcome her characters' irritating foibles, of which they have plenty. Their own 'Scottish obsession' takes the form of endless digs at the English; ironically, bearing in mind that the family live in Glasgow, Lowland Scots are not favoured either. The family are prone to peculiarly Scottish exclamations and, having read the poetry of William Aytoun, spout it frequently and curse 'by the blighted hopes of Scotland':

> 'Oh, losh, don't say we've lost it,' exclaimed Christina. 'It would be too awful, after all we told Daddy about being practically grown up and quite capable of looking after ourselves.'
> 'I believe you're right …' said Alister. 'I did have it in the train. Now what, by the blighted hopes of Scotland, could I have done with it?'

The adventure itself is weak. Why the two escaped Germans are such a danger is never satisfactorily explained; they are simply faceless examples of convenient evil. Being dashing is confused with enthusiastic ineptitude: the Macgregor family are horribly prone to wishing, after their latest disaster, that they had thought ahead, and then promptly failing to do so in their next crisis.

Christine returned to the adventure formula in later novels, with more success. She worked in Virginia as a professional rider, and drew on the experience when she wrote *Phantom Horse* (1955). It is an interesting study of English children living in America and experiencing the differences between American and British horse life as they plot to catch a horse running wild in the mountains. *Ride by Night* (1960) is Christine's most successful adventure story. It has a very similar plot to *We Rode to the Sea*—as if the author, recognising the earlier book's weaknesses, wanted to try again once she had matured as a writer. Set in Scotland, it tells the story of children who decide to go on a trek. They are persuaded to take an adult with them, but he is soon out of action after the dressage horse he has borrowed is lamed. The children become lost, and come across two Rumanians (as it is spelled in the book) who have escaped from a nearby Russian ship and are seeking asylum. The children try to transport them to the nearest town. All the characters are better differentiated than those in the earlier novel, and the adventure is believable and flows more naturally from their actions. Sheila Delmore, who with her brother came up with the idea of the trek, initially despises a fellow trekker, Jennifer, who is 'sure to cry'. In fact, Jennifer proves herself stalwart, brave and with unexpected talents, including one it was probably fair not to expect: the ability to speak Rumanian. Sheila generously admits her mistake:

> I said: 'I think it's taught me not to judge people. We despised Jennifer and really her nose was broken which is probably enough to make anyone keep crying. And then she knew Rumanian and saved the day.'

As in *We Rode to the Sea*, the villains—the Russians—remain only a shadowy presence, as evildoers were to be in most of Christine's adventure stories. Her villains are wicked because of what they represent: oppressive Communist Russia in *Ride by Night*, teenage bikers in *The Open Gate* (1962), one of her Riding School series. This last-mentioned series does, however, give us one of her more convincing villains: Jim Morgan, the criminal who tries to sell off his horses for meat in *The Empty Field* (1961), emerges as a more realistically malign presence, a man who sits outside his shack doing nothing in the day, and surviving by sometimes vague but usually illegal means.

After *We Rode to the Sea*, Christine wisely left the territory of the adventure novel for a while; with her first series, the Chill Valley Hunt, she wrote about what she knew, and with much greater success. As did her sisters, she made full use of the riding school they ran as well as her experience as whipper-in to the Woodland Hunt. The Chill Valley Hunt trilogy, *We Hunted Hounds* (1949), *I Carried the Horn* (1951) and *Goodbye to Hounds* (1952), is a considerable literary step forward from her first book. The plot, which involves two families of teenagers starting their own hunt and battling to gain supporters, provided Christine with a firm narrative framework within which she worked to produce a series with vivid characters and credible action. The third book, *Goodbye to Hounds*, shows her style maturing: there are well-delineated tensions between the Dashwoods and the Days when the Days' farm, which is on a short lease, must be sold.

There is considerably more hunting in Christine's pre-1970 output than in her sisters' books, and indeed than in pony books generally. This makes some of her books unattractive now to a population either more squeamish or more principled, depending on your point of view, than its forebears. Her books reflect a time in which hunting was generally accepted. It is integral to many of her titles: in *The Impossible Horse* (1957), Jan, who has started a business schooling horses, has to convince the local equine community that the horse Benedictine is safe by hunting him successfully; David, the hero of *The First Rosette* (1956) and its sequels, helps out at the hunt kennels and has a hunt pony, Sinbad, on loan; and *A Day to Go Hunting* (1956) is about precisely that.

The Chill Valley Hunt series has not met with unqualified approval. It is not too harsh to say that the distinguished children's book critics Mary Cadogan and Patricia Craig loathe this trilogy (but fortunately appear not to have read *We Rode to the Sea,* an infinitely worse book). Cadogan and Craig are entirely right to find some aspects of the hunting novels unpleasant. *Goodbye to Hounds* sees the hunt riding over gardens and being selfishly unmoved by their trespass:

> We rode into the garden belonging to the largest of the two houses. We rode up some steps, across a rockery and through a tennis court. We heard shouts behind us, but we didn't care because we had seen a little wicket gate giving access to the wood, and because this was probably our last hunt with the Chill Valley Foxhounds and we wanted to enjoy ourselves more than anything else in the world.

Whatever one's views on hunting, this is not impressive. Christine was, however, an author who learned as she went, and later books go a little way towards acknowledging that there is another point of view. *A Day to Go Hunting* sees the frantic efforts of the hunt to keep hounds out of the deer park owned by a woman who disapproves of bloodsports. They fail; the Master goes to apologise, and after an hour's hard talking over tea manages, in one of the book's less credible moments, to talk the owner into supporting the hunt. It is highly unlikely that the hunting novels would be published today, but they provide an insight into the sport, and of how it began to change.

Christine's books reflected more than just changes within hunting. The Pullein-Thompsons were not unaware of changes in society. Josephine's *Patrick's Pony* (1956) dealt with a boy living at an orphanage; Christine's more credible *The First Rosette* of the same year had one of the earliest working-class heroes to appear in a pony book, David Smith. He is the youngest son of a family where money really is an issue: they genuinely struggle, and there is no money for riding lessons, let alone ponies. David manages to learn to ride through a combination of luck and graft: after he catches the pony of the Master's daughter when she falls off, he is invited to tea and offered the chance to borrow a pony. He works for the pony's keep at the kennels, and, for extras, does a paper round.

David's poverty and need to work to achieve his ambition of showjumping success is contrasted with the altogether easier life of the Master's daughter, Pat. She is expected to be a debutante, and sure enough the riding school she and David run together in *The Second Mount* (1957) is broken up once Pat moves to London. David is thrown back on his own devices in *Three to Ride* (1958), though by a massive stroke of luck it is Pat who rescues him after his disastrous experience working in a London riding school.

Although it was laudable to try to step outside the typically exclusive realms beloved of the pony book, Christine was a better writer when remaining within the world she knew best. Her working-class characters—who, after David, included Janice and Mick in *The Lost Pony* (1959) and the comprehensive school pupils from *Riders on the March* (1970)—are all prone to the same mercurial swoops from happiness to gloom. It is as though Christine's desire to sympathise with the difficulties of being poor leads her to over-write their emotions. Without any direct experience herself, she seems to assume there must be a heightened emotional response to life generated by being brought up in difficult circumstances. This is particularly noticeable in the Janice and Mick books (*The Lost Pony* and *For Want of a Saddle*), where Janice exists in a constant state of resentful envy, her rare moments of cheer being transformed by the slightest setback into a cry against the unfairness of life. Her brother Mick, while more positive in outlook, is prone to the same see-sawing of emotions. Janice and Mick lived with their parents in a one-room flat, but have been put into foster care now that the arrival of twins has meant hopeless overcrowding. Their foster home is in the country, and brother and sister are both desperate to ride. They find a stray pony who has returned to his now-deserted old home, and they decide to look after him and treat him as their own. Predictably, disaster ensues when the pony goes down with colic, but they manage to find a vet. The pony is stabled with the now grown-up David Smith, of *The First Rosette*, who puts the family in touch with

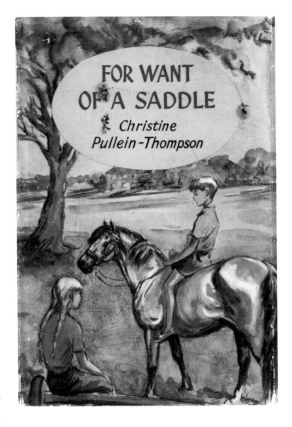

the possibility of a job and cottage. The family get the cottage, and the next book, *For Want of a Saddle* (1960), tells the story of what happens when the family move to the country. They have to work out how to survive through market gardening, and how to improve their riding on the landlord's pony when they have no saddle. This seemingly Elysian improvement in their circumstances still does not seem enough to cheer Janice up:

> Nothing was as she had expected it to be. She had expected a large rambling market garden, divided from a paddock by a wire fence, and in that paddock she had imagined a pony—the pony David Smith had said Mr Stone was anxious for them to ride. But the garden had been a garden for years, and had straight, neat, paths and fruit trees trained to climb walls, and there was no pony to be seen anywhere. It seemed to Janice that she was to be disappointed as she had been so often before. 'Nothing ever comes right for us,' she thought, staring at a cluster of snowdrops without seeing them. 'One might as well give up hoping …'

Perhaps it is personal taste that makes the constant swinging between despair and delight wearing: Margery Fisher finds the children 'engaging and probable'; the publisher Clarissa Cridland, however, finds them 'rather annoying'.

Christine's literary style does not help. Her constant use of the word 'suddenly' always seems to herald an emotional plunge of some sort:

He had meant to tell Pat about Tornado, to say, 'You should have seen her up and down the hills and over the bunkers,' but suddenly there didn't seem any point any more. (*The Second Mount*, 1957)

We had been fighting to save a man's life, or so it had seemed; and we had been fighting for our own survival. But now suddenly we were facing life as we had lived it for so long. Suddenly Tom Thumb's cracked heels mattered ... (*Ride by Night*, 1960)

Her characterisation is better when she is dealing with settings and events that are familiar to her; being freed from the need to construct an adventure allows her to concentrate on her characters rather than a whirl of events. Her most successful characters are her teenage girls. Jan in *The Impossible Horse*, determined to prove that the horse Benedictine is not dangerous, Olga in *The Horse Sale* (1960), shocked out of her passivity by the imminent sale of the borrowed horse she has schooled, and Debbie in *I Rode a Winner* (1973) are all realistic and sympathetic portraits.

I Rode a Winner is one of Christine's better books. Set in the world she knew best, that of the professional horse person, the book opens with Debbie Ravenswood having to move out of her family home because her parents have just split up. Her father is moving to Oxford and her mother to London; her brother has offered to have her while her parents sort themselves out. He is much older, running a dealing and livery stable with his wife, Tina, and Debbie barely knows him. She, understandably, feels completely unwanted, and Christine does a fine job of conveying her sense of dislocation and loneliness:

'Daddy and I will be keeping in touch,' continued Mummy. 'Daddy wants you for Easter and you're definitely coming to me for Christmas.'
　　I started to feel like a parcel, something wrapped up in brown paper waiting to be posted somewhere for Christmas. I was trying not to cry again.

Debbie feels hopelessly out of her depth when she reaches her brother's stables. Everyone working there seems alien. Tanned and capable, they even walk differently. She struggles to fit into the frantically busy atmosphere, and the groom Derek is blisteringly unsympathetic about the fact that she knows nothing of horses. She slowly starts to learn what to do, and then meets the mare Cleo, branded as a problem pony. Unlike the vast majority of pony books where the heroine longs to have a pony with which to have a special relationship, in this book the fact that Debbie does have that relationship flows naturally from her circumstances. Feeling lonely and with no-one to love, she looks to the mare for all the emotional support she is not getting from her family. Cleo is supposedly a girl's ride, but no-one has yet appeared who can ride her. Debbie realises that Cleo needs more freedom, and not to be stuck in a stable: she starts riding the mare, and succeeds so well that Cleo becomes a promising, and sought-after, jumper. But for Simon and Tina's stables to continue, Cleo must be sold: she is worth a lot now that Debbie has unlocked her potential. Debbie's battle is as much a battle with her circumstances as with her emotions:

> I tried to eat, but tears ran down my cheeks like a river and everything tasted salty. I wasn't just crying for Cleo now, I was crying because I had no home, because my parents were parted, because I couldn't decide what to do.

I Rode a Winner is not the easiest of Christine's books to read: its ending is not fairy-tale, but it is a convincing picture of a girl trying desperately hard to pick up the pieces of her life.

Romance is not a feature in that book—Debbie probably didn't have enough emotional capital left to cope with it—but Christine's characters are allowed a little, most notably so in *The Impossible Horse*, much of which is taken up by the stirrings of Jan's romance with the handsome Guy. This book originally appeared under a pseudonym, Christine Keir, possibly because it did tread those shores some publishers so feared in the 1950s. It was issued in paperback under the author's real name in the less inhibited 1970s. Christine did include romance in her 1960s Riding School series, in which Nick and Bromwyn have an on-off relationship, the fracturing of which provides much of the interest of the third book in the series *The Doping Affair* (1963; reissued in 1987 as *The Pony Dopers*).

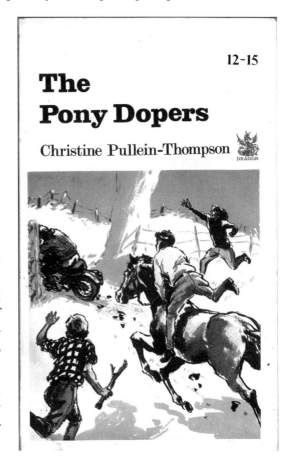

The sheer volume of Christine's books, allied to the number of different story types she tried, can sometimes obscure her real achievements in the pony book genre.

Strong narrative frameworks showed Christine at her best: both *The Horse Sale* and *A Day to Go Hunting* take a situation (a horse sale and a day's hunt respectively) and look at the way in which a widely differing set of characters react to it. *The Horse Sale* shows various teenagers and children coping with loved ponies being sold, and in some cases looking at, and changing, their own behaviour. It is a satisfying read: without being too overtly fairy-tale, it shows the struggle some of the characters have with themselves and their situations to achieve their dreams. *A Day to Go Hunting* has a similar premise: characters both adult and child find that their lives have changed after fog descends during the hunt and causes chaos. Many of them start the day in one situation and end, once the fog has literally and metaphorically lifted, in another. Angela has proved herself through coping with an accident to Jane and her horse; Jane's uneasy relationship with her employers has been resolved by her finding another job; the useless whipper-in, Captain Freemantle, has been sacked.

Christine's novels are usually engaging, but although all her stories successfully whirl the reader along, involving them in the plot, there is a definite difference in quality between them. Those with a background closer to her own tend to lack the awkwardness from which some of her attempts at social awareness suffer. As the 1970s progressed, Christine moved back, with the Phantom Horse and Black Pony Inn series, to children with whose backgrounds she was more in tune. During the later part of her writing career she wrote pony books for younger children and series which concentrated on animal rescue. In today's publishing climate, by no means as accepting of the pony book as it once was, it is unlikely that any British author will ever match her output. Even worldwide she has no equal. The Saddle Club series created in America by Bonnie Bryant is enormously long, but the books are written by several authors. By the end of her career, Christine had produced pony stories covering pretty well every aspect of the genre, from tales of a wild horse to holiday adventure, rescue stories and hunting.

To any reader of pony books in the 1960s and 1970s, the Pullein-Thompsons were a key part of their reading experience. This was due not only to the sheer number of books but also to their accessibility, and to the sisters' knack of producing books which stood re-reading. The pony-mad reader knew that with them she was getting good, solid instruction. If you wanted to understand why the backward seat was bad, they would tell you. If you wanted to understand how to ride sympathetically and well, they would tell you that too. If what you wanted was straightforward adventure, Christine provided plenty of it. The Pullein-Thompsons' characters stride memorably across the pony book. Noel and Henry, Augusta and Christina, David and Pat were the children you could meet at Pony Club, or who could successfully people your dreams if they were the nearest you were ever going to get to riding.

MY FAVOURITE PONY BOOK: THE BLACK BEAUTY'S FAMILY SERIES BY THE PULLEIN-THOMPSON SISTERS

You might pick up a pony book only because it has a horse on the cover, but by the time you set it down you will have learned far more. Years before I was taught history at school I absorbed it from the Pullein-Thompson sisters' nine-novella series of autobiographies of Black Beauty's extended family. While Anna Sewell informed a nineteenth-century audience of what was happening under their noses, the Pullein-Thompsons showed twentieth-century children how the world they lived in was made by horses as well as by humans.

These are autobiographies of the horse-drawn age, the period from the late eighteenth century to the end of the Second World War. Black Pioneer is raised on a plantation in the American South and, stolen by a runaway slave, finds himself a charger in the Civil War. Black Piper leaves an Ireland stunted by the potato famine and becomes a stagecoach horse. Black Blossom is condemned to a life of hard labour dragging overladen wagons through the underbelly of Victorian England.

The chief ingredients of the original *Black Beauty* are there: the horses pitched with little warning from one owner to the next, their circumstances changing through no fault of their own. They suffer hideous cruelties—tails amputated, the wire pushed into a mare's forehead to scar and form a white star—and the cumulative petty sins of bad owners such as musty hay, ill-fitting tack and bearing reins. Also vivid are the ordeals of the people around them: the Pullein-Thompsons describe the human cost of the coalmines, wars, workhouses and steel foundries. Children suffer as greatly as the pit ponies that Black Ebony meets. As the cynical brown mare Nutmeg tells Blossom: 'Oh it's a cruel world. The masters may be comfortable but the servants aren't.'

The small details have stayed with me: the white leather used to stitch Black Piper's torn shoulder; the young swell who pours brandy into his boots to warm his feet; the bundle of watercress thrown to Black Raven by Mother Massey. As in Anna Sewell's book, the reader agonises alongside the heroes and heroines, knowing what it must be like to have a stomach 'as empty as a bran sack' or stiff legs after being forced to stand for hours when you've fallen, and oh! all those broken knees! However, every horse in Beauty's clan is lucky. They all fetch up in good homes after a life of tribulations, and have full mangers and loving owners; and, mercifully, some of the humans even land on their feet too.

Susanna Forrest
Journalist and author of *If Wishes Were Horses*

CHAPTER 5
'I DON'T WANT TO GROW UP A LONG-FACED HORSY WOMAN'
Monica Edwards

The 1940s were a rich period for the development of the pony book. As well as the Pullein-Thompsons' novels, the less horse-centric but more complex books of Monica Edwards saw the light of day. Like Mary Treadgold, she is not a classic pony book author. Only a few of her books have ponies at their centre: *Wish for a Pony*, *No Mistaking Corker*, *The Midnight Horse*, *The White Riders*, *Rennie Goes Riding* and *Cargo of Horses*. With the exception of *Wish for a Pony*, her books do not follow the usual pony book format where the storyline focuses on a girl looking after the pony, schooling it, and going in for gymkhanas. Edwards had a broader view of the pony than that. For her, ponies were part of a full daily life. They get the children to school in the Punchbowl series, and are just one aspect of a life focused on many different animals: cows, hens, mice, and the wildlife of the Punch Bowl. Ponies may be integral to her plots—Cascade, for example, performs an heroic role in *Storm Ahead* (1953), and the ponies are used to help patrol the boundaries in *No Entry* (1954)—but the real interest of her stories is in her human characters and their lively and vivid interaction with the world around them, not in how a pony is schooled and how many prizes it wins.

Monica le Doux Newton, who wrote under her married name of Edwards, was born in 1912 in Belper, Derbyshire, the daughter of a vicar. She received what her biographer, Brian Parks, calls 'a fragmentary formal education'. From 1927 her father was vicar of Rye Harbour, in East Sussex, and Monica took full advantage of her surroundings, roaming the surrounding Romney Marsh and making friends with the fishermen and villagers who later became part of her Romney Marsh series. In 1933 she married Bill Edwards, and in 1947 they and their two children, Shelley and Shaun, moved to Pitlands Farm in Surrey, which Monica bought at an auction, and renamed it Punch Bowl Farm. The neglected house and farm, and many of the animals, including the ponies Tarquin, Bramble and Red Clover, were to provide the inspiration for the Punchbowl Farm series.

Cascade, many pony-lovers' dream pony and the equine hero of Edwards's first book, *Wish for a Pony* (1947), did not have a real-life equivalent. If the true pony book is defined as one which could not exist without the ponies in it, *Wish for a Pony* is probably one of the über-examples. It was written while Edwards's own children were young, and introduced the heroines of the Romney Marsh series, Rissa and Tamzin, as children utterly focused on just one thing:

> Both girls shared a single passion—ponies. And with both of them the main use to which brains and tact and energy were put was How and Where to get more riding.

The girls rescue a bolting pony belonging to a riding stable which has located nearby for the summer, and as a thank-you are allowed rides. A thoroughly satisfactory and pony-filled time follows, during which the girls compete in the obligatory gymkhana. Wishes come true, for Tamzin at least, when after a disaster at sea one of the injured sailors is brought to recuperate at her home. It so happens that Laurence, the sailor, knows a man whose daughter has been seriously injured in a fall from her pony, as a result of which he wants to get rid of the pony (though fortunately he does draw the line at having the pony shot, lest he upset his daughter). Tamzin finds this out, persuades her parents they can manage to keep a pony, and, after a few suspenseful days waiting to see if the owners agree, is told she can have it and all its equipment. Cascade is not just any pony either: he is half Arab, and a beautiful example of breedy bliss—'a really first-rate animal—an Anglo-Arab, or something—and quiet as a lamb'.

What rescues the book from being a spectacular sequence of coincidences is its exact depiction of its readers' dreams. Tamzin and Rissa are completely believable pony obsessives, and it is the simplest thing in the world for the reader longing for her own pony to identify with them.

> A young woman appeared round the corner of the stables. She wore breeches and carried a saddle and bridle on her arm. The girls smiled tentatively. She smiled back, called 'Lovely morning!' and went into the grey pony's box. Tamzin and Rissa listened with deep and silent interest to the sounds of preparation in the box; the ring of iron shoes as the pony moved over for his saddle, and the jingle of his bit as he settled it in his mouth.

Despite the sharpness of the writing, full of the minutely observed details that make the book spring to life, Edwards regarded it as full of faults. It was known in her family as *Wish for a P* because she explained its weaknesses so often and at such length. She wrote it as the presumably besotted mother of two small children, which possibly influenced the winsome portraits of Tamzin and her little brother Diccon that are contained in the first few pages of the original book. Diccon's baby language and Tamzin's wide-eyed enchantment with it were ruthlessly excised in the author's 1984 revision of the text for John Goodchild, and the book is the better for it.

"*They* are *lovely*," Rissa said.
Monica Edwards: Wish for a Pony

Edwards was keen not to be regarded as a pony book author. Horses and ponies were for her an important part of life, but not its sole focus. And so it was with her stories. Tamzin announces in *The Summer of the Great Secret* (1948) that she has no wish to become a horsy woman, and she doesn't. Neither of the two boys in the Romney Marsh foursome, Meryon and Roger, is a keen rider; that is left to Rissa and Tamzin. In fact, riding is one of the few things the all-rounder Meryon is not good at. In a scene in *The Midnight Horse* (1949), where it becomes plain that riding is not one of his talents, he plays the clown and knocks himself out trying to dive under a swimming horse; he has to be rescued by the girls. The Punchbowl Farm children all ride, but it is farming and wildlife that are the focus of the stories after *No Mistaking Corker* (1947).

As the Romney Marsh series progresses, the books become less horse-centric, though there are a few stories in which they are vital. *The Midnight Horse* is firmly horsy: the pony Banner is rescued from his neglectful tinker owners by Tamzin and Rissa, who come up with a scheme to raise money to buy him by collecting junk. While the four are camping out at Castle Farm with Cascade's previous owner, Lesley, Tamzin becomes obsessed with creating plasticine horses (which sparkling talent, alas, vanishes after this book), and the story centres on the true identity of the horse which gallops up and down the sands at night. In *The White Riders* (1950), Tamzin and her friends try to frighten off builders brought in to develop Cloudesley Castle by convincing them that the area is haunted by wild and ghostly riders. The most horsy of the later books is *Cargo of Horses* (1951), in which Tamzin learns that horses are being shipped off the coast illicitly to be used in the French horsemeat trade. She decides to rescue them and, with the help of Jim Decks and other sailors, the foursome transfer the horses to Jim's trawler, transport them to land and find them new owners.

Although ponies become a less important element in Tamzin's life as she gets older, the part an animal can play when human comfort will not do comes touchingly into play in the last of the Romney Marsh books, *A Wind is Blowing* (1969). Tamzin, overwhelmed by grief when Meryon rejects her after he is blinded trying to stop a bank robbery, seeks refuge with Cascade. It is a wonderful picture and completely unsentimental; Cascade's real interest, one suspects, is in his hay, but nevertheless his presence does what is required, and Tamzin is comforted:

> Crying bitterly and desolately for a long time it seemed as if grief and hopelessness began to go out of her with the tears, until there was only a clear calm like the sea after storm. She had been drifting in that storm, but now her boat was answering to the helm again, and there was a star to steer by.
>
> With a wisp of hay in his teeth Cascade turned to look at her as she leaned against him to re-read her letter.

The critic Margery Fisher says: 'Monica Edwards, since she is using real life, gives her young readers all of it.' And she does. As well as Meryon's traumatic efforts to make sense of life after he is blinded, the smaller but not often mentioned awkwardnesses of life appear. Pony books are generally a little light on the parasites that affect their subjects—but not so Edwards. In *The Midnight Horse*, Tamzin and Rissa have to deal with Banner's lice:

> … while Tamzin sprinkled sudden death on countless swarming lice Rissa gave him the first taste of oats that he had ever known.

The Punchbowl Farm books, too, are filled with the reality of farming: chickens are taken by the fox; a cow dies of yew poisoning; the pony Tarquin has to be put down after breaking his leg when Andrea gallops him over a field filled with rabbit holes.

The Punchbowl series begins with *No Mistaking Corker*, in which the Thornton family go on holiday in a horse-drawn caravan in another coincidence-ridden story, told in the first person by the younger Thornton daughter, Lindsey. After this rather uncertain start, the family find their feet once Edwards begins to use them in a real-life setting. The series which follows is far more than a simple renovation story: there is real conflict between Lindsey, who loves the wildness surrounding the farm, and her brother Dion, for whom farming is a vocation and who therefore wants the land to be as productive as possible:

> Five Y-shaped heads jerked up from eager grazing. Large frightened eyes started at her for a second, no more, and in swift lissom bounds the deer were gone.

"*It is in a valley*," Dion said, surprised

Monica Edwards: Black Hunting Whip

So they had found Dion's corn. It had been expected, but he would be furious, of course. How could he be expected to see how beautiful they were when his corn was being trampled down and eaten? (*Punchbowl Midnight*, 1951)

Dion had said that she was crazy, and that there was beauty everywhere in well-farmed lands and new buildings, but that she was too blind to see it. (*Spirit of Punchbowl Farm*, 1952)

The Punchbowl Farm series is, at first, much more domestic in scale than the Romney Marsh one. The books' initial interest comes from seeing the family struggle with the dilemmas of farming: breeding cows; coping with fences they can't afford to mend and the resultant escaping animals; harvest. As the series progresses, however, the plots become more dramatic. Punchbowl adventures usually involve a struggle against the elements rather than human villainy: the frantic scene in the mill in *Frenchman's Secret* (1956) when the family retreat further and further up to escape the rushing floodwaters is genuinely thrilling. The fires in *Fire in the Punchbowl* (1965) bring the characters up against the grim possibility of loss of life. Through all the drama, the ponies are a constant presence. Without them, key parts of the stories, such as lassoing deer or moving around swiftly during the fire, would be impossible.

Edwards's world is not one in which parents are conveniently banished. Mr and Mrs Thornton are a constant presence, while the Grey parents are intrinsic parts of the stories, providing a calm counterpoint to Tamzin's adventures. Without adult help, many of those would be much trickier: in *The White Riders* Mrs Merrow provides camping space, and

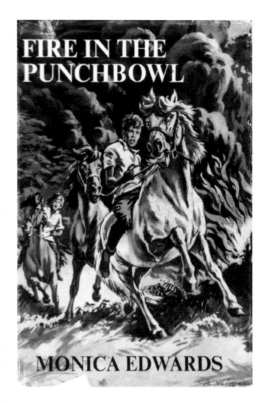

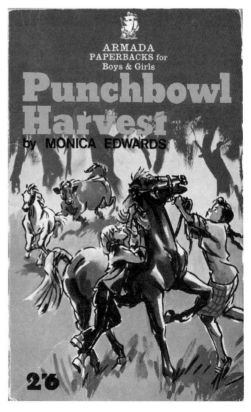

The filly swung round and glared, snorting, at the trap

Monica Edwards: The White Riders

her grown-up son Mike is himself an enthusiastic White Rider. In *Cargo of Horses*, once Tamzin knows about the fate of the horses shipped to France she immediately decides to do something about it. She and her friends will arrange for the horses' keep on the Marsh; Jim Decks, the local ferryman, is deputed to organise the actual rescue:

> Jim made a sudden despairing appeal, his netting-needle poked at Tamzin's face. 'Summer grazing!' he said. 'Winter hay! Horses will increase! *That* part's easy! You say all that, do you?' He waved the needle at her. 'You may well say it, but what I arsk you, gal, is *how're you going to get 'em?'*
>
> Tamzin drew her face back from the needle like a pony arching to the curb. 'Really Jim,' she said a little sadly, 'you a smuggler and a son and grandson of smugglers, owlers and White Riders, and a Marshman too, and you ask me that! I'm only thirteen and practically always at school, after all. I do think you might be more co-operative. I can think out the feeding and grazing part all right, but I should have thought you and the others could manage the rest.'

And Jim does.

Edwards's characters age naturally throughout the two series, which at points intertwine. She does not ignore the possibility of attraction, and in *No Going Back* (1960) Meryon and Tamzin's relationship moves beyond that of friendship. The nascent romance has an effect on the other characters. No longer are they a group of four friends; the balance has shifted, and Rissa finds this very difficult to deal with. After the relationship has been established, and accepted within the foursome, it is as if Edwards was unsure about where to take it. She still had plenty of adventures for her characters to undergo, but romance in those settings appears almost a side issue.

In one of her rare standalone stories, *Rennie Goes Riding* (1956), Edwards took the career novel and invested it with a psychological depth that was not always its lot. Rennie longs, as do so many girls, to work with horses, but there is very real doubt about whether she will succeed. Rennie does not find life easy. Having seen her mother killed in an accident, she is frequently ill, and stress makes her physically incapable: her hands or her legs stop working. Her family see her career choice as possibly foolish, but agree to let her try; her Aunt Lucy, who fears it will not work, is more than the conventional figure of opposition. She is prepared to use her savings in an attempt to help Rennie, even though she is afraid that her niece will not succeed.

Rennie *does* succeed in establishing a horsy career, but there are moments of very real doubt as to whether she will. Her health is problematic, and she leaves her settled job at a riding school to extricate herself from a situation where a fellow groom's boyfriend has become keener on Rennie than on the groom. The job she goes to is with the worst of horse dealers, whose horse-doping activities lead to a boy's death. Rennie realises just what she has become involved with, and leaves. She is still determined to work with horses, though she now understands something of the dark side of the horse world as well as the sheer physical slog and lack of monetary reward. Edwards was nothing if not realistic in her portrayal of life working with horses.

Another of Edwards's standalone titles, *Under the Rose* (1968), shows a different vision of the horse. Here it is a hidden one, part of the mysterious world of the shut-up country house, King's Somborne, that enchants the Black and Hunter children. The horse is a much wilder creature than most of Edwards's equines: he is a killer, and one of the children has a particularly terrifying experience before the horse relents in its pursuit. The Blakes' desire is not getting a pony but finding somewhere to live, now that their father has announced he wants the family house for himself and his new partner. The Hunter children have parents who live together, but their mother is so obsessed with doing good works that she rarely sees them. Theirs is a different world from the comfortable, stable families of the Punchbowl and Romney Marsh books, and the horse in it reflects that.

Edwards was ruthless in the pursuit of a good plot, and there are inconsistencies and oddities in both her major series. People and animals appear and disappear: the foal which Lindsey was supposed to be having as a reward for saving the polo ponies in *No Mistaking Corker* is referred to in *Black Hunting Whip* (1950) and the next book, *Punchbowl Midnight*, but after that is never mentioned again. The mill family of *Frenchman's Secret*, with whom the Punchbowl family share a truly terrifying flood experience, disappear completely in all subsequent books. This vanishing seems odd after they shared such a near-death experience, but their appearance might have made it harder for Edwards to focus on the relationships between the Romney Marsh and Punchbowl people, once the two series interlinked. If a plot would be improved by introducing something inconsistent with previous books, Edwards reorganised her internal world.

However, it is a tribute to Edwards's effectiveness as a writer that though the reader might well be aware of her occasional inconsistencies, the worlds of the Punchbowl and the Marsh are bewitching enough for them not to matter. Her books have a sparkling sense of place, and a wholly coherent world. Just as the Thorntons and the Romney Marsh folk live in her readers' minds, so do the ponies. They are as individual as her other characters: gentle Cascade, fiery Siani and the ever-patient Sula. Edwards's books are not simple holiday adventures. She did not patronise her readers, nor did she shy away from showing what can happen when life goes wrong. Her characters have concerns as relevant today as they were when she wrote the books, even if the stable families and close communities she wrote about have now been overtaken by the stresses of modern life. Her books are now another country, but still one intensely human.

My Favourite Pony Book: *Spirit of Punchbowl Farm* by Monica Edwards

Two authors who made me want to write were Monica Edwards and K M Peyton, both of whom transcend the pony book genre. I've loved and admired Peyton's work since reading *Flambards* in my twenties; here, though, I've chosen a novel by Monica Edwards, whose books meant so much to me as a child.

Wish for a Pony, a conventional tale of dream-fulfilment, began the Romney Marsh stories, while *No Mistaking Corker* established the characters for another and sometimes overlapping series, the Punchbowl Farm books. *Black Hunting Whip* took the Thornton family to the derelict Surrey farm, and nine more titles follow the joys, trials and dilemmas of the central character, Lindsey.

For settings, Monica Edwards used her childhood home at Rye Harbour (Westling in the stories) and Punch Bowl Farm, where she lived as an adult. She had a painterly eye, a feeling for weather, atmosphere and the natural world, and a deep affection for animals. Here is a routine moment, Lindsey putting out hay, made charming by close observation of pony behaviour: 'Clover's pretty head was shaking naughtily as she peered with bright, sharp eyes through her bushy forelock to find the very best heap of hay. Having found it, she drove Nanti and Sula away from it with flat little ears …'

A love of animals, wild places and traditional ways pitches Lindsey against her brother Dion, a dedicated farmer keen to modernise. In *Spirit* she fights for the yew tree that shelters the house, opposing Dion's determination to fell it after a cow dies of yew poisoning. For Lindsey, the tree embodies the spirit of the place. This is one of the few Monica Edwards novels to include supernatural elements: a haunting tune blurs the passing of time, and Lindsey glimpses a seventeenth-century disaster resulting from the destruction of an earlier yew.

The warmth of characterisation, both human and animal, sure evocation of place and reverence for the natural world give me an enduring affection for this author. As a bonus, this is one of three Monica Edwards titles illustrated with grace and sensitivity by Joan Wanklyn.

Linda Newbery
Prize-winning children's author

Ruby Ferguson:
Jill has Two Ponies

CHAPTER 6
THE BEAUTIFUL GOLDEN DREAM
Ruby Ferguson's Jill Books

Books based on a single character's experiences are particularly attractive to the reader: she can identify with that character and imagine she shares her world. When that world is the pony-centred arcadia described in Ruby Ferguson's Jill books, it has an enchantment all its own. These books took place in what the academic Nicholas Tucker describes as a 'mythical British countryside … an idealised setting'. Tucker further identifies some pony books as 'fantasies of perfect friendship with a loving, idealised companion'. With Ruby Ferguson's Jill, and the pony-obsessed girls who followed her—Gervaise's Georgia, Berrisford's Jackie and Leitch's Jinny—that was exactly what the reader got, over and over again. And the reader loved it: when the first Jill book, *Jill's Gymkhana*, appeared in 1949, it was an instant success. The series has been almost constantly in print since it first saw the light of day, and sixty years later is being reprinted yet again.

Jill has distinct similarities to the earlier Jean. Like Jean, she tells her own story. Like Jean, she doesn't have a great deal of money, gets a pony, and learns to ride him successfully. Jill has much of the freshness and vigour of Jean, but she is no mere copy. As the academic Liz Thiel points out, although both girls are eleven when their stories start, Jean is still a child, whereas Jill stands in front of the mirror wondering how she can look older. Jill's world is an idealised one, certainly, but the girl who strides within it is a real and fallible human being. She has a perpetual appeal, despite her author not being a rider and having to swot up on the equine world.

Ruby Constance Ashby (1899–1966) was born in Yorkshire to the Rev David Ashby, a Methodist minister, and his wife, Ann Spencer, of solid Yorkshire descent. On the dustjackets of her books, and in her (mostly fictional) 'autobiography', *Children at the Shop* (1967), Ruby claimed variously that she was descended from Danes and Highland Scots, that she came from a long line of Norfolk farmers, and that she had Highland ancestry and a childhood spent in Inverness. There is a whisper of truth in one of these: her paternal grandparents were born in Norfolk, but her grandfather spent most of his life in London as a successful Sydenham fishmonger. Ruby, as far as I can see, never lived in Inverness: the nearest the family got to Scotland was Newcastle, where they lived from 1906 to 1909. After this they moved to Woolwich, where David Ashby was a Methodist minister—not, as Ruby wrote in *Children at the Shop*, a chaplain attached to Woolwich Garrison. After Woolwich, the family returned to the north, with David Ashby next serving in Bradford. Ruby went to Bradford Girls' Grammar School, and then on to St Hilda's, Oxford in 1919.

After Ruby emerged from St Hilda's, she took a secretarial course and then worked as a private secretary to Alderman Mallison, of Cressbrook Hall, Derbyshire, and from 1937 to 1947 edited the women's page of *British Weekly*. She started writing as R C Ashby, under which name she published detective fiction and short stories, with her first stories being published by the *Manchester Evening News*. In 1927, Hodder & Stoughton published her first novel, *The Moorland Man*. Six detective stories followed. After Ruby married a widower, Samuel Ferguson, in 1934, her books appeared under her married name. Although Ruby and Samuel had no children of their own, Ruby had an excellent relationship with her stepsons, Bobbie and Alan, and with their children, her stepgrandchildren, for whom the Jill books were written.

The Jill books have a wonderfully distinctive voice: they are written in the first person, and that person is direct, funny and often acute. *Jill's Gymkhana* opens the series with eleven-year-old Jill Crewe adrift in a cottage outside the fictional town of Chatton, where she and her author mother have just moved. Jill's father has died while on a business trip abroad; her mother writes syrupy, but critically acclaimed, children's books. Jill is pony mad, but life is close to the financial edge for her mother and she cannot afford to buy Jill a pony. Then Mrs Crewe sells the serial rights to her book *The Little House of Smiles*, and there is enough money to buy Jill one, Black Boy. Jill has no idea how to ride or care for him, but she learns, thanks to being offered lessons by a pilot, Martin Lowe, who has been crippled in an air accident. Indeed, she learns well enough to win rosettes at Chatton Show. During the process she meets the girl who becomes her best friend, Ann Derry. The remaining eight books in the series deal with Jill's adventures: buying another pony, running a stable and riding club and, once she has left school, working with horses, albeit temporarily.

Jill's equine life is essentially small scale. Although there's the obligatory-in-a-pony-book rescue of a downtrodden pony, the stories are domestic; there are virtually no villains or daring rescues (and when there are, it generally

Ruby Ferguson: Jill's Gymkhana

isn't Jill who deals with them). Jill does not have the progression through the competitive levels which characters in other pony books (particularly the Pullein-Thompsons') do; her development as a rider plateaus. Having gained the heights of being able to win at Chatton Show, that is where she remains, occasionally riding in more advanced classes like the Grade C jumping when she is offered a ride.

The fascination in the stories comes from Jill herself and her life with her friends. Jill is capable and resourceful, obsessed with the horse, independent and the possessor of a wry sense of humour. In *Rosettes for Jill* (1957), she and two friends are taken to watch a major horse show. After the show finishes, she is left behind, unaware of everything, sitting in a 'beautiful golden dream'. It doesn't last long. 'Do you want to spend the night here by yourself?' said Melly's voice. 'Or have you sat on some gum?'

Jill is funny. The pony book was often earnest, occasionally dashing, but seldom funny. Some of the humour in the books is pure slapstick; when Jill tries to prop a letter up on the breakfast coffee pot, the pot goes flying:

Ruby Ferguson: Jill Enjoys her Ponies

> You wouldn't think a light little thing like a letter could knock over a coffee pot, but then you don't know the kind of things that happen to me unless you have read my previous books. The funny thing was, there was about ten times as much coffee all over the table as there had been in the pot. I sat thinking how this could be, while Mummy mopped frantically and tried to save the butter and marmalade from the flood ... (*Jill Enjoys her Ponies*, 1954)

And Jill has a dry sense of humour about her own affairs:

> Next I got out the wallet with my money and tied it in the thick cardigan that Mummy had made me put in for if it was cold, and put it at the bottom of a drawer with all my other things on top of it. I know that in books most people take care of money by putting it up the chimney or in the mattress where it is found about a hundred years later by somebody who buys the house or the mattress, but I wanted to have this myself, not my descendants. (*A Stable for Jill*, 1951)

Children generally like a moral framework to their literature. In the pony book, treating the pony properly and kindly is central: putting the pony first is best, and a great deal can be forgiven if a character does that. Jill's moral code is straightforward; the journalist Karen Dent says:

[in the Jill books] you try to play by the rules, you tell the truth, you don't go 'pot-hunting' at gymkhanas, and you always put your horse's welfare before your own. If you do that, you too can win the under-16 jumping at Chatton Show with your 'ordinary' ponies Black Boy and Rapide.

Jill's ponies always come first with her. She is not, however, quite so admirable in her relationships with her friends and family. The former—Ann Derry, Diana Bush and Val and Jack Hobday-Heath—and their relationships with Jill provide considerable spark to the books. These are realistic friends, who squabble and tease but enjoy each others' company, and make us enjoy it too. *Jill Enjoys her Ponies* opens with Ann and Diana trying to persuade her to come to Chatton Show with them. She can't ride as she's hurt her wrist swinging the hen bucket, so is refusing to go even to watch. '... I wish you'd both go away. I hate you,' she says. They do, but come and see her on the way back.

> 'Who was second in the under-fourteen jumping, anyway?'
> There was a slight pause.
> 'Me,' said Ann, going red under her dust.
> 'You dope!' I shouted, frightfully pleased. 'Why didn't you say so before? Where's your rosette?'
> 'I took it off George,' said Ann, opening her pocket enough for me to see the blue ribbon. 'I didn't want to look showing-off when you were having such a beastly disappointment.'

Jill is not the perfect sunny child of her mother's books: there's still a whiff of the sinner about her. In *Jill Enjoys her Ponies* a character called Dinah Dean appears. In any other pony book, Dinah would be its heroine. She's brave, resourceful, capable and put upon, and does acts of great heroism. She finds out that a local villain is buying up horses and ponies and selling them for meat, spirits three of the ponies away, and emerges triumphant with them, exposing Mr Towtle's villainy, at a local show. Jill, however, has an ambivalent attitude towards Dinah. She gives the girl her outgrown riding clothes but is horribly embarrassed when Dinah is seen out and about wearing them, proclaiming to one and all that Jill gave them to her. When Dinah turns up to thank Jill for them, Jill has a wonderfully confused reaction; her better self inspires her to take Dinah up and show her her room, but 'doing good' makes her feel 'hot and bothered' and she very pointedly tells Dinah to take herself off. Jill's battle between what she wants to do and what she ought to do carries on throughout the series.

If Jill were the only mesmeric character in the books, it would not be enough, but her enemies also have a charm all their own. Jill's cousin, Cecilia, in particular, provides a vigorous counterpoint to the horsy obsession and occasional self-righteousness that Jill and her friends express.

Jill has three nemeses: Cecilia, Cecilia's friend Clarissa Dandleby, and Susan Pyke. We first meet Susan in *Jill's Gymkhana*. She is everything Jill wants to be: she has a pony of her own, she is beautifully dressed, and she wins everything:

> I was wild with envy. It was like one of those radio quizzes where they ask you who, if not yourself, you wish to be, and at that moment I would have given anything to be Susan Pyke.

Ruby Ferguson: Rosettes for Jill

Susan very soon falls off the pedestal Jill has put her on: when she is out with her smart riding school class they pass Jill ineptly idling along the lane on Black Boy, wrongly dressed

Ruby Ferguson: Jill and the Perfect Pony

and with Black Boy very obviously in charge. Susan makes a remark about Jill which sets the whole ride off laughing, and Jill is mortified. However, Susan is rarely malicious after the first book, and once Jill realises she can ride better than her she shrugs off her comments.

Clarissa Dandleby is something of a caricature: she is obviously wealthy, with a groom to look after her ponies. Like Susan, Clarissa is not much of a rider, being more interested in being considered a 'hard woman to hounds' than in learning to ride her pony effectively.

Jill's cousin Cecilia provides a more interesting foil to her. They have nothing in common: Cecilia does not see the point of ponies; she likes school stories; she is neat and tidy; she enjoys pressing flowers and singing madrigals. When they first meet, Cecilia is fifteen and Jill eleven, and then as now there is a large gap between those ages. Jill and Cecilia first cross each other when Cecilia pays a visit in *Jill's Gymkhana*. Mrs Crewe buys Cecilia her requested breakfast of wheat flakes, but they are spurned:

> The next morning at breakfast Mummy put out the wheat flakes for which I had made my toilsome journey, but Cecilia only took one mouthful and then put her spoon down with a kind of patient-under-suffering look.
>
> 'Is there anything the matter with the wheat flakes?' asked Mummy.
>
> 'Oh no, Aunt Catherine,' said Cecilia. 'They're most awfully nice really, only they're just not a bit like the ones I have at home, so if you don't mind I'll just have a lightly boiled egg.'
>
> As you know, January is not what you'd call a lavish month for eggs, so Cecilia was pretty well appropriating our whole production.

Cecilia, like Dinah Dean, is one of those characters who in another book would be a heroine. She'd go down a storm in a school story with her contributions to the sale of work, and would, quite effortlessly, be head girl. Cecilia is beloved of grown-ups, and Catherine Crewe, Jill's moral arbiter as well as her mother, likes her. The pony-mad child would have shared Jill's opinion of Cecilia as an 'absolute blot'. She is incapable of seeing Jill without making a withering remark about her pony mania; she's still at it even when she's in her twenties and Jill has left school: '… Cecilia gave a delicate sniff and said, "Somebody's been around the stables."'

As the books progress, Jill does develop a grudging respect for Cecilia's abilities, though she carries on being at odds with her even when Cecilia learns to ride and turns up to the Greenlee Riding Club in *Jill's Riding Club* (1956). Ferguson keeps showing us Cecilia through others' eyes: she is a born organiser, incredibly efficient and a genius at extracting prizes. If she only liked horses she would be the ideal Pony Club District Commissioner. Whatever Jill thinks of Cecilia's craft efforts, other people like them: her table decorations and embroidery win prizes at the Whirtley Hall Fête in *Jill Enjoys her Ponies*, and she is photographed for the local paper. Aunt Primrose 'always knew Cecilia had it In Her to do Great Things'.

In the last book (chronologically), *Pony Jobs for Jill* (1960), Cecilia not only stocks with prizes the fête she, Ann and Jill are organising but also stuns the musical ride who have been giving Jill and Ann not a little trouble into awed and obedient silence:

So when the sixteen riders arrived that afternoon … instead of Us greeting them, there stood Cecilia in her pink jumper and skirt, and lipstick on, and believe me or believe me not, they all looked at her as if she was the crowned queen of Harringay … She bossed them like I've never in my life heard anybody bossed, and they took it! They rode in a silence that was uncanny, and even the kids at the back did it right … while they were clustering round Mrs York's tray of cakes she walked over to Ann and me, still twiddling her pearl beads, and said, 'There you are—positively easy'. We hadn't a word to say. Cecilia strolled into the house and left us to carry on.

It turns out the ride thought Cecilia was a famous showjumper, but nevertheless the point is made.

Ruby Ferguson: Pony Jobs for Jill

In much children's literature, and certainly in the pony book, the adult is absent. It is hard to have rollicking adventures if the heroes of the book are constantly being told to make sure they are careful. The adults in the Jill books, however, are an essential part of them. Parents, teachers and professional horsemen are all there, mostly portrayed positively. There are the equine role models: Mrs Darcy, owner of the riding school; Captain Cholly-Sawcutt, member of the British Showjumping Team and general good egg; and Martin Lowe, who teaches Jill to ride. Martin flourishes in *Jill's Gymkhana*, when he takes Jill from hopelessly inept beginner to reasonably accomplished rider. He fades from view in the series, alas, and the male point of view in the books is taken up by Captain Cholly-Sawcutt. He fails to teach his own bouncy and hamfisted children to ride, but Jill, helping at Mrs Darcy's stables, succeeds.

Jill's mother, Catherine, is central to the novels. Ferguson had a wry appreciation of the vicissitudes of mothers: a fair number of those appearing in the books are either convinced their little darlings are beyond criticism, like Susan Pyke's, or fussy helicopter ones, like the mother of the twins George and Georgina Fisher in *Jill has Two Ponies* (1952) who is sure both her children are brilliant, and that every minute of their riding lesson needs managing—by her:

> 'Oh no, darling, oh, you must be a good girl!' cried Mrs Fisher, dancing round in a flappish sort of way. 'Do it nicely, just for Mother.'
> 'I won't,' said Georgina, and began to slither off her pony, while Mrs Fisher grabbed her and tried to push her back. Wendy and I stood by helpless, looking at this awful exhibition and thinking what we would do to Georgina if we could have her alone and at our mercy for five minutes.

Catherine Crewe is the antithesis of all that motherly fussing. The relationship between Jill and her mother is one of the most attractive elements of the books: there's an obvious affection between the two, with Catherine combining an admirably hands-off attitude with a stern moral compass when needed. There are many occasions in the books when Jill does not behave as well as she ought. In *Rosettes for Jill*, two children of Catherine's school friend come to stay when their mother has to take her husband abroad to recuperate after an operation. Melly and Lindo Cortman are doggy people, not horsy; Lindo, to try to please Jill, paints her stable doors bright blue. Unfortunately she does not stop at the doors, and the windows, partitions and floor are painted too. The paint is not quick drying, and Black Boy ends up blue. Jill is furious and says she never wants to see the Cortmans again. She is unimpressed by her mother's initial efforts to put Lindo's point of view, but Catherine Crewe is not deflected from her ticking off:

> 'It's a funny thing,' said Mummy, 'but I seem to remember somebody else who did a lot of things that were meant to turn out well, and turned out very badly indeed for other people. But the people affected were rather decent and understanding about it. For instance, there was a certain Bring and Buy Sale where some things of mine got sold by mistake, things I valued. Perhaps I needn't say any more.'
> I felt very small and mere and wormlike. Looking back on my purple past I realised that practically everything I had ever done had caused somebody else a lot of trouble, and yet those other people had never said they loathed me and never wanted to see me again.
> 'Okay,' I said. 'I get it. Where is Lindo?'
> 'In the kitchen,' said Mummy. 'Crying.'

Catherine Crewe is firm but generally fair. Her eminent good sense when confronted with her daughter's failings, together with her wry sense of humour, does make me wonder about the fantasy goody-goody children in her fiction. Surely Catherine would have had more *sense*? It does seem very strange that Jill's mother is so grounded in reality, but her fictional children—Angelina the Fairy Child, Basil the Birdsong Boy and Barbie Brightside—are irredcemably *wet*. Jill describes them thus:

Ruby Ferguson: Jill has Two Ponies

It sounds awful to say it, but I never could get on with Mummy's books at all. They are all terribly up in the air and symbolic, about very whimsy children who are lured away by the Elves of Discontent to the Forest of Tears from whence they are rescued by Fairy Hopeful, and so on. (*Jill's Gymkhana*)

Ferguson was clearly having a dig at other children's authors here: Barbie Bright Side is perilously close to Eleanor H Porter's Pollyanna, and Enid Blyton and her Faraway Tree books, with their Fairy Hopeful-type figures, presumably did not meet with her approval either. Catherine Crewe is something of a paragon; perhaps Ferguson felt she needed a blind spot, and provided this in her complete inability to see the sentimental awfulness of what she wrote. Or, bearing in mind the eleven good papers which Jill reports as liking her mother's work, perhaps it is Jill who is wrong in her assessment of her mother's talents. Or perhaps Catherine Crewe has other similarities to Enid Blyton: an independent woman of considerable energy earning a very good living by peddling a picture of a world in which girls are good little home-makers, a vision she is ultimately keen for Jill to share.

Ferguson created an idealised world beloved by her readers, but problems came when she tried to introduce a real-world perspective. While readers were prepared to accept (and might even have welcomed) the total absence of romance in the series, they felt very differently when Jill was not allowed to take up the horsy career they hoped she would have. It is entirely normal in the series for women to work: Mrs Crewe supports Jill and herself through her writing, and the local stable is run by Mrs Darcy. It is never, ever doubted that Jill will work when she leaves school. In *Jill has Two Ponies,* Catherine Crewe says:

> 'When all is said and done, Jill is the one to decide. I should like her career to be entirely her own choice, and whatever it is I shall help her in every way.'

She has, alas, recanted these high ideals by the time the next book, *Jill Enjoys her Ponies*, appears. Jill gets the dream offer: a job after she finishes school in Captain Cholly-Sawcutt's stables. It is, as Mrs Darcy says, the sort of chance she really needs if she is to make horsemanship her career. But Jill says her mother wants her to take a secretarial course, and the implication is that however much Jill might want the dream job, her mother won't agree.

In *Pony Jobs for Jill* Mrs Crewe announces: 'A girl can't learn too young to run a home.' Jill and Ann would much rather run a stable. And so they do, for a while: having finished school, they take a succession of short-term horsy jobs, none of which leads to anything important. Catherine is not alone in her new views: Captain Cholly-Sawcutt appears to have thought again about his job offer. 'You're going to get yourselves seriously trained for some proper job, and you're going to keep up your riding for a hobby,' he tells Jill and Ann at the end of the book. And they do. In the very last paragraph of the book, Jill's set for a secretarial course, and feels she's 'secretary to the Prime Minister already'. She wanted to be an MP several books earlier.

The effect on Jill's readers was profound. To them, Jill was a role model who went out and forged her own way, but when she meekly accepted a limited and conventional view of what a girl should do their ideal world was shattered. Although some readers might, as the academic Liz Thiel says, go on to 'seek an explanation for Jill's heroic demise, to question the influences that have encouraged her to submit to conventionality and to consider the possibility of an alternative ending', those readers I have asked do not consider an alternative ending: they simply reject the one that is provided.

Jill's calm acceptance of the end of her dream came as an almost physical blow to me when I read it first as a child. Konstanze Allsopp, a pony book devotee, says: 'I will never forget the disappointment of reading that Jill book.' Fellow fans agree. Kate Hill says: 'So here is someone who, largely through her own determination, has progressed from knowing next to nothing to becoming a talented horsewoman, who is valued by Mrs Darcy and the champion Captain Cholly-Sawcutt, but who ends up doing a pedestrian office job. What a waste of all that experience and talent!'

Did Ferguson intend readers to question the ending she gave to Jill? Or was she reacting to the thousands of girls she felt she was inadvertently encouraging in ridiculous dreams?

Ruby Ferguson: Pony Jobs for Jill

She herself had done a secretarial course after Oxford. Maybe she too had had dreams, but they were dashed by the realities of finding work in post-war Britain. It is noticeable that Jill is still allowed to write: was writing Ferguson's escape? *Pony Jobs for Jill*, in which the moral voice of the sternly practical parent intrudes and rips apart the dreams we have all built up for ourselves and for Jill, is the least popular of the series. Ferguson made a romance of her own life: perhaps therein lies the key. Her best creations, and she knew it, were those in which reality was not allowed too free a rein.

In the last book in the series, *Jill's Pony Trek* (1962), Ferguson takes Jill back to her schooldays, when all she had to think about was enjoying the holidays with her ponies, and in the words of one of my forum users, Hazelhunter, 'sent Jill off into the twilight, always aboard Black Boy in her readers' memories!'. It is the Jill of the earliest books of the series whom her readers remember best: lively, pony-obsessed, and with a world of possibilities at her feet. And it is noticeable that the authors who wrote the pony book series that followed in Jill's footsteps kept their heroines firmly within the boundaries of their ideal, and pony-filled, worlds.

JILL—THE BLACK BOY QUESTION AND OTHER ALTERATIONS

When Jill fans get together, there is one topic that always exercises them. Was Jill's pony Black Boy black, or was he piebald, and was his name Black Boy or Danny Boy? The answer is 'both', and that it depends on what edition of the books you read.

In the original hardbacks, Black Boy was black. The first series of paperback reprints appeared in the 1960s; it was produced by Armada Books, the paperback arm of Collins, and generally included the original text and illustrations, though *A Stable for Jill* and *Jill has Two Ponies* had covers by Mary Gernat, and *Pony Jobs for Jill* had one by Peter Archer. It was in the late 1960s paperback reprints by Hodder, under their Knight imprint, that matters started to change. Knight commissioned a new illustrator, the New Zealander Bonar Dunlop, to provide covers and internal illustrations. He did six covers, including *Jill's Gymkhana*, and illustrated the first three titles; in all six, Black Boy has become piebald in both text and illustrations. In a further complication, Dunlop's cover for *Jill's Gymkhana* shows him as skewbald if we assume, as I think we can, that the picture is of him and Jill.

Two explanations suggest themselves here: first, that the publishers intended Black Boy to be renamed, although it is unlikely that the name would have caused problems of political correctness in 1968. Perhaps the winds of change were blowing over from America, post-Martin Luther King. The second scenario is that the illustrator failed to realise what colour the pony was supposed to be, and that, rather than ask him to redo the illustrations, the publishers decided to adapt the text to suit. As Hodder no longer has any records relating to the period, it has been impossible to pin down the true explanation.

Black Boy wasn't the only thing to change: titles did so too. Of the nine books in the series, three were reissued with different titles. *Jill's Gymkhana* appeared in America in 1950 as *A Horse of Her Own*: 'gymkhana' was not a term used in the USA, and Americans tended to ride horses, not ponies. Two books were given new titles in the UK: *Jill Enjoys her Ponies* became *Jill and the Runaway*, and *Pony Jobs for Jill* became *Challenges for Jill*. Both titles were thus made completely free of any double entendre.

Ruby Ferguson: Rosettes for Jill

MY FAVOURITE PONY BOOK: *A STABLE FOR JILL* **BY RUBY FERGUSON**

Classic pony fiction tends to tread a well-worn bridle path. The themes are universal. There's invariably a clash of both class and money, with our poor but worthy heroine versus the snooty rich girl who is heartless, spoilt and cruel. Then there are the ponies down on their luck that need rescuing, stables that are threatened with closure, runaway horses, frightful adults trying to ruin the fun and, at the end of it all, the glittering chance to ride to glory at the gymkhana.

I'm not claiming that Ruby Ferguson invented the genre—but I would argue that if she didn't do it first, then she certainly did it best. Her writing fairly leaps off the page with breezy wit and can-do attitude as she utterly ignores convention, frequently knocking down the 'fourth wall' and having her heroine, Jill, talk directly to us about her adventures. They aren't very big adventures, admittedly, not by modern standards anyway. These days young readers have been primed to expect life-changing events and high drama packed into every single page of a book. Well, they won't find them in a Jill book—those were slower and gentler times. Reading a Jill book is like taking a glorious country hack: remember it is the *journey* that matters.

A Stable for Jill is the second book in the series, in which our heroine finds herself promptly packed off at the end of the first chapter to stay with her dreadful cousin Cecilia for the holidays. Leaving behind her best friend, Ann Derry, and beloved pony, Black Boy, she is forced to spend her days pressing flowers with Cecilia, who is an 'absolute blot', under the auspices of her awful, unhorsy Aunt Primrose.

Jill despairs of having any fun at all until Chapter Three, when she meets Bar, Pat and Mike, the children of the local village vicar, who are horsy too. The vicar has demanded that they get rid of their pony, Ballerina, as she costs too much to keep, but with Jill's help they set up a riding stable in the back yard of the vicarage to pay the bills; soon more horses are on the scene and lots of jolly equine fun ensues. If all this seems a little far-fetched, I only have to remind myself that my own Pony Club Secrets heroine, Issie, once persuaded her mum to let her travel from New Zealand to Spain where she rode in a brutal no-holds-barred street race in order to win back her beloved colt Storm from the evil Miguel Vega. So let's just say a modicum of suspension of disbelief is vital to any pony book.

By any standards, old or modern, Ferguson's feisty, funny and unapologetically feminist Jill Crewe is a brilliant character. She is all the more remarkable when you consider that Ferguson wrote her between 1949 and 1962, at a time when Enid Blyton's saccharine, sappy Famous Five dominated the children's literary landscape. It's a widely held belief that Ferguson actively loathed Blyton, and that she wrote the character of Jill's mother, who is an author churning out books full of 'whimsical and sweet' children that Jill considers to be 'perfectly revolting', as a thinly veiled stab at her.

There is no whimsy whatsoever about Jill. She takes one look at a problem, rolls up her sleeves and gets stuck in. Jill, to use her own terminology, is a total brick. And she set the literary standard for all who came after her.

Stacey Gregg
Author of the Pony Club Secrets and Pony Club Rivals series

CHAPTER 7
GALLOPING ON AND ON
Pony book series fiction

After Jill, more heroines trotted and galloped their way through long series. The three longest, and the most republished, did nothing to move the pony book genre on; until Patricia Leitch's Jinny burst onto the scene in the 1970s, those of the 1950s and 1960s were the placid cobs of the pony book world: the ride was safe, but not particularly exciting. Their authors understood what to give the pony-mad child to keep her content, but did not seek to give her anything else. Mary Gervaise's Georgia Kane was happiest in the safe confines of her family, and Judith M Berrisford's Jackie lived in a world constrained by her need to conform. The showjumper Pat Smythe's Three Jays series was interesting for its insight into its author's world, but ultimately it offered nothing new. All of them provided safe and comfortable stories in which there was no danger of the characters challenging stereotypes. In this they were successful: all these series saw several reprints.

Mary Gervaise's Georgia series was born out of necessity: its author specialised in school stories, whose sales were starting to flag in the 1950s, and her publisher wanted a series that would sell. The author knew something about ponies, and decided to combine them with her school stories. 'Mary Gervaise' was one of the pseudonyms used by Joan Mary Wayne Brown (1906–98), who had a brief boarding-school education that came to an end after she got into deep trouble for bringing *The Adventures of Sherlock Holmes* to school. She was taken away and sent to another boarding school, but was unable to go to college after she developed anaemia. Instead she started to write, and produced 66 books as Mary Gervaise. The vast majority are school stories, which she wrote almost exclusively for a twenty-year period from her first title in 1928, *Tiger's First Term*. After that she wrote novels which would only count as pony books if the requirement for actual equine presence was fairly minimal. Gervaise does not relish the gymkhana, schooling or pony care; what interests her is character, both equine and human. As humans offer much more scope for character development, her books are necessarily biased towards them, and towards the idyllic family lives she relished.

Of the three series she wrote which feature ponies, the Belinda and Farthingale ones have the least pony content. Possibly because they have, as the children's-book specialist Sue Sims says, 'not really enough to satisfy the real pony enthusiast', they did not have a second printing, and faded from view long before the Georgia books, which were still in print in the late 1970s. The Georgia series is the most pony-orientated (and the one I shall therefore concentrate on), and was marketed as a pony series by Armada, who republished it in paperback.

The Georgia series opens (in *A Pony of your Own*, 1950) with a girl so beset by her own fears that her family have serious concerns for her (she is often referred to as Georgie throughout the series, but for consistency's sake I have called her Georgia). Georgia Kane is shy and awkward, terrified of many things but particularly of horses. There is good stuff in her, though. When a horse and rider have an accident outside her house, she manages to overcome her fear for long enough to sit on the horse's neck to stop it injuring itself further. Rather touchingly, when the horse is stabled in the family garage until it can be moved, Georgia feeds it apples with a toasting fork, being too terrified to feed it by hand.

In an effort by Georgia's family to help her overcome her fears she is then sent away to the Grange School, at which pupils ride. Although still terrified of horses when she arrives there, and bullied for it, she does manage to get over her terrors and thus sets the scene for a further nine books about her and her pony, Spot.

Gervaise's portrayal of Georgia and her family life is central to the series. The Kanes—Georgia's mother, her generally absent engineer father, younger twin brothers (known as Rough and Tough), elder brother, Peter, and beloved ginger cat, King Toby—provide a strong family setting in which a procession of

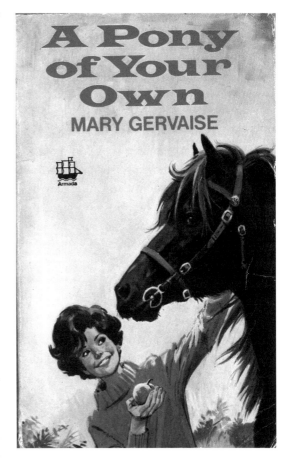

characters lacking something in their own family background can find succour. Georgia, awkward herself, is blessed with the ability to sympathise and put herself in others' shoes:

> 'A strange house is horrid, just at first,' said Georgie, very sorry for her. 'I know what you feel like—'
> 'You don't.' Patience spoke in a desperate little whisper, quite unlike her usually sedate tones. 'No one can possibly know. You see, I've never been inside a real home before, let alone stayed in one … It makes me feel—odd.' (*Ponies and Holidays*, 1950)

Georgia and her friend Susan Walker are bright and lively creations. Susan's impetuous nature adds spark and gentle humour to the narrative, contrasting neatly with her moments of thoughtfulness. After Georgia is injured in a fire, and a show of hands is needed in Assembly, Susan shows typical consideration:

> Twenty-nine hands shot into the air. The thirtieth, still bandaged, did not move, as its blushing owner was wondering what to do. But it was seized—quite gently—by Susan, and waved amongst the rest. (*A Pony of Your Own*)

Gervaise likes an outsider, and generates much of the tension of her stories through one or more. Once Georgia has fully entered the charmed world of the Grange, and made good and lasting friendships, it is her cousin Gerry who becomes the outsider. Formerly the confident one, she is unable to cope with the new, popular Georgia, and snipes at her constantly. There are other outsiders: in *Ponies and Holidays* a new pupil, Patience, is brought up by an elderly and old-fashioned guardian, until she finds that she is the long-lost daughter of the Daneforth family. In *Ponies and Mysteries* (1953) Patience's unhappy integration into her new family makes her still an outsider. By the end of the book she and her family are reconciled to their new situation, and Gervaise seems to lose all interest in her as a character. The next we hear of Patience, and her twin Pat, is that they have left school—and the series.

Although the Georgia series is nominally set in a school, Gervaise seems positively reluctant for her characters to experience any meaningful life within it. It is as though, having written so many school stories by that point, she is as desperate to get out as any girl condemned to learning Latin vocab on a particularly beautiful day. Out of a ten-book series, six are set during the holidays. Three are based at school, but the action and dialogue are set almost entirely in the girls' free time. *The Vanishing Pony* (1958) opens at school but swiftly moves to a nearby house. The ponies, too, are sometimes remarkable for their absence. With the exception of *A Pony of your Own* and *Pony from the Farm* (1954), they are not central to the stories. In most of them the ponies could be replaced with bicycles and they would progress just the same. In *Pony Island* (1957) the ponies are used to get the children to the island, but are redundant after that: they graze while the main drama, Margaret's rescue from the rising tide, takes place.

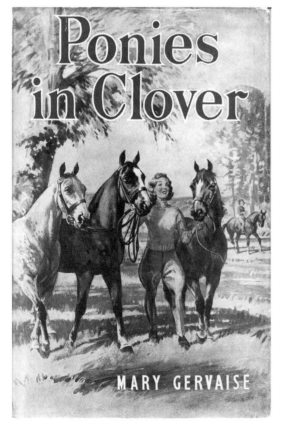

Nor does Gervaise enter fully into the world of the pony. In *A Pony of your Own* the whole school, plus ponies, is due to sail off to Lennet Fair and gymkhana, but Georgia doesn't go, as she thoughtfully stays behind to keep another girl, Teepoo, company. She is then ideally placed to save the headmistress's horse from a fire. There is a more fully described gymkhana in *Ponies and Holidays*, but its main purpose is to advance the plot and show the Kane family's reactions to the mysterious behaviour of the girl they think is their friend Patience, but who later turns out to be her previously unknown twin.

But what Gervaise does have a particular talent for, and what kept pony enthusiasts reading the books, is her portrayal of the ponies themselves. They are distinct and recognisable characters—something not every pony book manages. Georgia's chestnut Spot is a kindly soul, and Susan's first horse, Black Aggie, instantly endearing.

> ... Georgie felt a lump in her throat when she saw how pleased the little mare was to see Susan again. Black Aggie had never been to Dockleford before, but she did not seem to notice that she was on strange ground. She simply followed Susan, pushing against her so strongly that she almost knocked her down. (*Pony from the Farm*)

Ermyn's Widdershins, the pony who has been trained to do the opposite of what the rider expects, is unforgettable, and even the donkey Penelope emerges as a lovable character. The episode where Black Aggie dies is genuinely moving. Gervaise was best at creating characters and that is true of her ponies just as much as of her people.

It is Gervaise's strengths of observation and characterisation that make her books successful; her plotting tends to the obvious. When an author writes in the first few pages 'And after all,' she asked herself, 'what can possibly happen now?' the reader knows perfectly well the answer will be 'Quite a lot'. Arrangements for the Kane children to be looked after in the frequent emergencies which beset them have a regular habit of going wrong, and in the holiday stories they are often, conveniently, thrown on their own devices.

Gervaise's sympathy with the lonely, the awkward and the troubled, coupled with a sense of fun and the attraction of a strong (if idealised) family network, proved attractive enough to keep readers hooked.

Judith M Berrisford, a fellow 1950s author, did not focus on the family. Her heroes and heroines are generally firmly removed from parental influence pretty much on the first page, as the author whirls them off into incident and adventure. She wrote over thirty pony books, and was responsible for one of the longest British-written pony book series, clocking in at sixteen titles, as well as other, shorter pony book series, and many standalone pony books. It is remarkably difficult to find biographical information on her, for which there is good reason. *Contemporary Authors* gives her birth year as 1912, as Judith Mary Lewis, born in Staffordshire; the dustjacket of one of her gardening books, however, gives a birth date of 1921. Both, it appears, are right. I have not been able to find any record of a birth in 1912 under the name Judith M Berrisford, but there was a Clifford Lewis (a name under which the author also wrote) born in Staffordshire in 1912. Clifford Lewis married a Mary Berrisford, born in 1921, in 1945. Adrian Room's *Dictionary of Pseudonyms* has the solution to the mystery: it states that Judith M Berrisford is a joint name used by Clifford and Mary Lewis, the writers of animal books for children.

Berrisford's first book was *Taff the Sheepdog*, published in 1949. There were several short stories before this, including 'Pedro, the Terrible' for *Riding* in 1946, and an early series in *Pony* magazine, 'Silver Star', which appeared in 1950, as did the first pony book, *Timber, the Story of a Horse*. Unusually for a pony book, this has a male hero, but otherwise it is a standard story of pony and rider improvement. Berrisford's early books include, in 1951, the first of the Sue and Ballita series, *Sue's Circus Horse* (in which Sue buys the ex-circus horse Ballita), as well as other standalone pony books: *Red Rocket, Mystery Horse* (1952), *The Ponies Next Door* (1954) and *Pony Forest Adventure* (1957). These books established the Berrisford formula as 'fast-moving fun' (as a contemporary review put it), with plenty of adventures with willing ponies. Berrisford's stylistic quirks were well established by the time the Jackie series started: her writing fails to give her readers any room for their imaginations to work; she is prone to exaggeration to prove her point; her writing is generally pedestrian and unsubtle. Lest the reader have any doubt about what sort of series she was reading, the word 'pony' is used relentlessly—a forest isn't just a forest, it's a 'pony forest', and there are 'pony holidays', 'pony dreams', 'pony boys' and 'pony girls'.

In 1958 Berrisford launched the first of what was to be a sixteen-book series, *Jackie Won a Pony*. The heroine, Jackie Hope, acquires her pony, Misty, in the first book, and together with her cousin Babs goes on to have a series of holiday-based adventures in which the duo try to help out someone in need, fail (frequently), prove their worth, and help matters to a happy conclusion.

If the quintessential pony book is that in which a previously ponyless child gets a pony, *Jackie Won a Pony* loses no time in hooking the reader in. In the 1950s there were indeed competitions in which the first prize was a pony. *Pony* magazine ran several, perhaps the inspiration for the *Horseshoes* magazine competition in which Jackie wins hers. The title of the first chapter is 'Pony-Mad—And Ponyless', but in the very first sentence the heroine Jackie Hope's ponyless state comes to an end. There is no scene setting, no introduction of the character; straight away the plot gets going with the classic pony-mad person's daydream coming true:

Judith M Berrisford: Ten Ponies and Jackie

I'd won a pony! I simply couldn't believe it. Breathlessly I kept telling myself the staggering news as I hurried along the garden path, reading again the letter which the midday postman had just handed me.

There is no long-drawn-out process of choosing the pony either: within twenty pages or so, Misty is Jackie's. Berrisford was not interested in the conventional schooling-and-entering-a-gymkhana pony book model, or in the educational role of the pony book (when she tried this, in the Jane and Penny series, the results were depressingly turgid), or (as I shall argue) in showing strong and independent girls working out their own destinies. What she wanted was adventure, a relentless whirl of incident. As the reviewer of *Skipper and the Headland Four* in a 1958 *Pony* magazine says: 'There is never a dull moment in a Berrisford book.'

Each Jackie book progresses along a very similar path. The story establishes Jackie and Babs's absence from their parents and locates them at a pony-filled venue. It soon emerges that this place is in some sort of trouble. Jackie and Babs, enthusiastic and good-hearted girls, long to help. The plots, prone to coincidence, are not there to challenge the reader. Berrisford is the Enid Blyton of the pony book world.

The books follow the same basic format, and Berrisford even re-uses (virtually word for word at times) the plot of one of her earlier novels in a Jackie book. *Five Foals and Philippa* (1963) sees two girls staying at a pony stud that is under threat after an accident hospitalises the owner. *Jackie and the Pony Rivals* (1981) has a few minor changes to character names but is otherwise identical, and lifts, with only slight alterations, entire pages from the original.

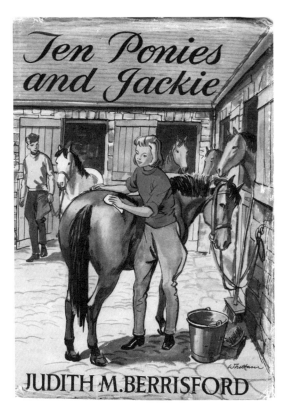

There is a constant rush of incident in the typical Berrisford book, often of a similar type. Berrisford is very fond of trial by water: wells, rushing rivers, bogs, the sea—particularly the sea. If Jackie and Babs are anywhere near water, something will go wrong. In *Jackie's Pony Camp Summer* (1968), Jackie and Misty are swept off a causeway from an island to the shore and have to be rescued. In *Jackie on Pony Island* (1977), Jackie and Babs are late leaving the island, and have to be rescued from deep water on the causeway.

These accidents and disasters nearly all happen because of Jackie and Babs's rash enthusiasm: they rush in where angels fear to tread. This need to have a continuous stream of incidents fuelled by the girls' ineptitude paralyses character development: if they genuinely learned from their mistakes (and they do,

Judith M Berrisford: Jackie and the Pony Trekkers

especially Jackie, frequently take themselves to task over their dimness) then there would be nothing to drive the plot. And so the girls are condemned to remain forever puppyish. The girls stay at around the age of fourteen for virtually the whole sixteen-book series, having summer holiday after summer holiday. These are not books to be read if you are keen on following timelines.

It is not surprising, bearing in mind the trail of disaster that attends them, that Jackie and Babs succeed in infuriating at least one older character per book. In virtually all the books up until the end of the 1970s, there is an older male character who holds a very low opinion of the girls. John Collins, the older brother of Jackie's penfriend Molly, runs the trekking centre the girls go to help at in *Jackie and the Pony Trekkers* (1963). He is alarmingly sexist in his attitudes—'Pony trekking's too big a venture to be run by a bunch of girls,' he says.

Dave, the older brother of the family Jackie and Babs help with the beach-riding scheme in *Jackie on Pony Island*, finds the girls a major irritation. After he has to save Jackie and Babs from their plunge into the sea off the causeway, he is livid, and condemns them as 'the silliest pony-girls I've had the misfortune to meet'. The most dramatic dislike occurs in *Jackie and the Pony Boys* (1970). Derek and Giles want absolutely nothing to do with Jackie, Babs and the latter's friend Pam at all. Jackie muses on their dislike:

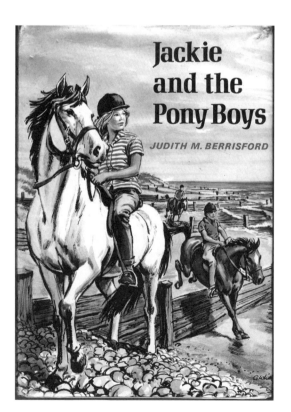

> We felt left out. The boys had made it only too clear that they didn't want us, and Derek had been downright unpleasant.
>
> Boys versus girls. Was that how it was going to be? Or were the boys going to ignore us during the rest of the pony-holiday?
>
> Must girls always feel inferior to boys, I mused? It wasn't fair—not to pony-girls, such as us. There were more pony-girls than pony-boys. Everyone knew that, *and* lots of champion girl-riders and showjumpers.

Judith M Berrisford: Jackie and the Pony Trekkers

Jackie and Babs are always hurt by their rejection, but they nobly work on, trying to do their best. In many ways they are admirable characters: they carry on in the face of considerable disapproval, time after time; they love their ponies, and treat them well; they treat others well; they always want to help. And yet ultimately it would be more satisfying if they were able to break out and construct their own world and succeed in it, rather than having to win over the disapproving male. It is telling that the girls always want the older male's approval. When they succeed at last, it is on the terms dictated by those older boys. They do not forge their own path but strive constantly to gain male approval. Jackie and Babs are not, ultimately, the good role models which Alison Haymonds finds in so many pony books.

Despite the occasional glimpses of something better, the Jackie series is essentially unsatisfying. Although goodness is always ultimately rewarded, the reward happens in a framework which is paternalistic and belittling, in a series of plots which have very little to differentiate them. They are the ultimate in comfort reading: minor reworkings of the same comfortable and limited world.

Judith M Berrisford: Jackie and the Pony Trekkers

The showjumper Pat Smythe's boy and girl characters were a more balanced lot: she was a woman who had succeeded in a man's world, and her girl heroines Jane and Jacqueline stand no nonsense at all from the other member of their trio, Jimmy. The Three Jays series was notable for being the first pony book series to sell on the back of its author's celebrity. Cassell, the publishers, pulled off a master stroke when they combined the twin popularity of the pony book, and the immensely famous showjumper. Showjumping is now a minority sport seldom seen on terrestrial television, but from 1947, when the Royal International Horse Show at White City was televised, until the 1970s, when the Horse of the Year Show was peak time viewing for the entire week it was on, showjumpers were household names.

Pat Smythe was a phenomenon. The first Olympic Games at which female equestrians were allowed to compete took place in Stockholm in 1956; she won a bronze medal. In the same year she won the *Grand Prix Militaire* at the International Show in Lucerne in 1956. Another woman rider came second, but the cup was presented to the French officer who came third, and it was his name that was engraved on it.

An immensely organised woman, Smythe managed to combine her successful showjumping career with writing over twenty books. Colonel Sir Harry Llewellyn, a friend and fellow Olympic medallist, said: 'No one filled her time more profitably than Pat.' Smythe had had little choice but to work hard. Unlike many other international riders of the time, she had no family or other money behind her. She and her mother ran their rented house, Miserden (which later appeared in her Three Jays series), as a boarding house for agricultural students and for children whose parents wanted them to have a country holiday; this, with a little horse-dealing, funded her riding. After the tragic death of her mother in a car accident, and the blindingly unsympathetic attitude of her bank manager, who rang on the afternoon of her mother's death to say that he was sorry about the accident, but please could she repay her overdraft of £1500 as soon as possible because she had no securities to cover the sum, Smythe had to run the show on her own. She cleared the overdraft by selling one of her horses, and hired a housekeeper to look after the guests. After the successful publication of her autobiography, *Jump for Joy* (1954), she moved her bank account.

Pat Smythe: Jacqueline Rides for a Fall

Two more non-fiction titles followed

(*Pat Smythe's Book of Horses*, 1955, and *One Jump Ahead*, 1956) before the first of her children's pony series, featuring the Three Jays, appeared. Published in 1957, *Jacqueline Rides for a Fall* sold well, reaching four editions by December of that year. The book was marketed with enthusiasm: a Three Jays club was launched with it, with a club newsletter every three months which included a letter from Pat. The club ran competitions, the first of which had a pony as a prize. Others offered visits to Miserden: a fourteen-year-old Lynn Redgrave was an early winner, and her prize was to go to a training demonstration there.

The concept of the series was a clever one; the stories are told by Smythe, and the reader feels part of her life, experiencing Pat's routine with her horses alongside the fictional Three Jays: Jimmy and Jane, 'second cousins' of Pat, and Jacqueline Field, who comes to stay as a guest. The traditional pony adventure is there too, but the real attraction of these books is the glimpses into the author's life. Smythe was writing mostly about what she knew, and the books are peppered with real-life incidents and anecdotes that occur again in her autobiographical works, such as her £5 grand piano bought from a chicken market, and the sign Colonel Llewellyn pinned on the horse Prince Hal's door, warning of his vampire tendencies.

Jacqueline Rides for a Fall is the story of how the two Jays become three. Jacqueline is the horribly spoiled daughter of a wealthy industrialist. When she arrives at Miserden to stay during the holidays, she soon shows herself to be appallingly conceited and wilful. She alienates the household with her rudeness, and, after having been strictly forbidden to do so, rides Pat's horse, Brigadoon, and gives herself concussion. Fortunately Smythe is determined to bring out the good qualities she sees in Jacqueline, and eventually she, Jane and Jimmy do manage this, though Jacky (as she becomes) remains prone to wilfulness throughout the books.

Besides giving an insight into how life was lived at Miserden, the books are also used to educate. The Three Jays ask questions Pat's youthful fans would want answered. It would be difficult for readers not to come away from the books knowing considerably more about showjumping than when they started.

> 'I wonder if you can tell me something, Pat, I've never really understood,' Jane said. 'I know Hal's a wonderful horse, and so's Tosca … It's easy to see now just why they're so good … But what I don't understand is how you came to pick them in the first place when they were younger … What's the answer?'
>
> 'Well, Janey,' I replied, 'that's quite a question and I could never give you anything like the full answer. And there's quite a lot of luck attached to it too you know … First, the horse should enjoy jumping and also have the athletic ability to be able to jump …'
> (*Jacqueline Rides for a Fall*)

And so she continues, for a good page or so. Smythe is clear and modest in what she wants to convey, but the long passages of information detract from the flow of the story. The dialogue is often sparky, but can degenerate into backchat and little else. The characters are lively, if not broadly drawn. To a pony-loving child, there is one element of the books that

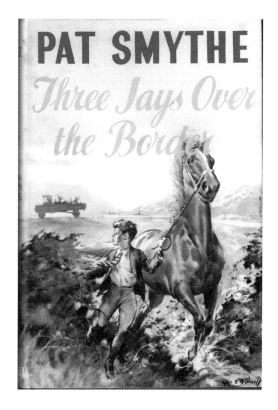

must seem peculiar: Jacky's pony, Pickles, is named, but although Jane and Jimmy both have ponies they ride while at Miserden, the animals are never named but just referred to as 'the pony'.

The series continued for seven books. Then, after a seven-year break, Smythe wrote the three-book Adventure series, in which she herself again features. This was straightforward pony adventure, using little of the involving domestic detail seen in the Three Jays books, and the new series was not as successful as the earlier one. With Smythe's retirement from showjumping, and consequent absence from the public eye, her books' popularity waned. The parts of the books where she is writing about her own horses are the best. Smythe is a better writer than her children's books would suggest, and her non-fiction work is remembered

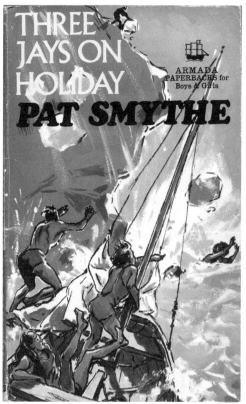

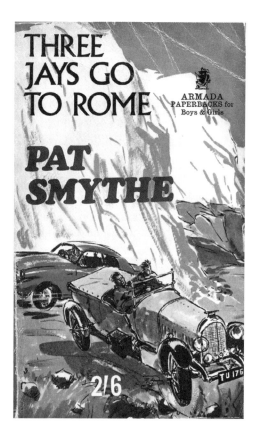

fondly: she writes well about her horses in books like *Tosca and Lucia* (1958) and *Florian's Farmyard* (1962), and her confiding style made her early books, at least, very popular. As a review of her work in *Riding* says, 'She treats the reader as her friend and seems to take him into her confidence.' But the books needed Smythe's celebrity to make them really come alive; without that, and the reader's desire to take part in her world, the books are not strong enough for the reader to make an imaginative leap into the series.

All three of these series show the pony book formula being used to give the reader undemanding fare of no lasting literary merit. None of them added anything of consequence to the genre; indeed Judith M Berrisford did the reverse, giving pony book fans heroines who no longer forged their own paths but judged success by whether they met male views of how they should behave. Pat Smythe's stories at least have girl and boy characters who are equally lively and resourceful, while Mary Gervaise shows how powerful a strong family can be.

CHAPTER 8
RATHER THAN FAME, GIVE ME HORSES
Famous pony book writers

In the 1950s the United Kingdom was slowly emerging from the privations of the Second World War. Rationing at last came to an end, there was little unemployment, and life seemed good. The pony book, with its portrayal of an arcadian Britain, chimed perfectly with the interests of a population beginning to have more leisure time and looking to a better world. In the late 1940s and 1950s it seemed that if someone with a horsy background could lift a pen they could get a pony book published. Foremost among them was Pat Smythe, author of the Three Jays series, who has already been discussed. Other stalwarts of the equestrian world attempted pony books (and also adult fiction, the racing detective novel being a particular favourite of the retired racing fraternity); the results were uneven. As Alison Haymonds says, 'Good riders do not necessarily make good writers.'

If Glenda Spooner (1897–?) had an opinion (and she had many), she aired it. She had considerable energy and drive. Born in India, she rode any horse she could find once the family moved to Scotland. Before settling to horses, she acted, worked in advertising, and flew. She was advertising manager and director of *Popular Flying*, and met her husband, Captain Hugh 'Tony' Spooner, at an International Air Race in Egypt. When he was killed in an air crash after only ten months of marriage, Spooner moved back to England and settled in Sussex, where she started a dealing business specialising in children's ponies. By the end of the Second World War she had become a recognised authority on ponies. Her Thoroughbred pony, Ardencaple, sired the Champion and Reserve Pony of the Year two years in succession. In 1953 Spooner started Ponies of Britain (now known as Ponies Association UK), whose aim was to support the welfare and survival of British pony breeds. She was involved with the International League for the Protection of Horses and the Brooke Hospital for Animals in Cairo.

Spooner wrote several books on showing, her speciality, as well as fiction titles for both adult and child markets. I cannot imagine any publisher being brave enough to insist that she follow a particular line or plot, and her fiction is, to say the least, varied in approach. *Royal Crusader* (1948) is an equine autobiography, *Minority's Colt* (1952) a post-war romance tied up with racing, and *The Perfect Pest* (1951) the story of a young child from whom less tolerant parents (I include myself here) would have sought refuge in strong drink. The *Silk Purse* (1953), Spooner's last work of fiction, was based in the world of showing, for which of course she had ample material. It is an uneven book: she has a tendency towards punning names for her characters—the Cheetems, for example—unnecessarily so, as her writing is good enough for readers to work out the characters' essential natures for themselves. Most of the book is a look at the showing world from the jaundiced but still affectionate point of view of the teenage heroine, Gillian, but it takes a frankly bizarre detour into fantasy halfway through.

The Silk Purse does not show the innocent sunny world of children's pony-showing classes seen in so many pony books. The thoroughly nasty dodges of the showing world are all displayed. Ponies who do not carry their tails properly have wintergreen applied under them; ponies over height are shod 'with ballet slippers'; and the judges' shenanigans are legion. The showing world is full of sharks waiting to gobble the unwary, and Gillian's mother *is* unwary. Her one aim in life is to see her daughter winning showing classes, and in doing so beating the Cheetem family who win all the time, everywhere. Gillian's mother has bought a pony she has been told will be a winner, but Tommy will never, ever win a showing class. Gillian, however, likes him as he is. She is eventually persuaded by her mother to trade Tommy in for a £1000 proven show pony, Perle, and it is at this point that the book takes off into strange territory—oddly so for a book so grounded in reality. Gillian, we think, wakes up, and spirits Tommy off on an early morning ride so he will not be there when the dread horsebox arrives to take him away. She goes to a blacksmith, who transforms Tommy by magic into a staggeringly beautiful chestnut pony called The Silk Purse. This fantasy lasts for a chapter or so before the book returns to the normal world of showing: it has all been a dream. In reality, Tommy is traded in for Perle, who alas, turns out to be another pup; only her original rider can make her go well in the show ring.

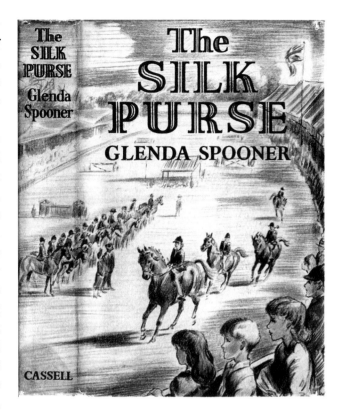

Once back in the familiar territory of the showing world, the book picks up. There is more to Gillian's mother than her showing obsession. When Gillian suggests that the mare's original rider might be free, and could ride her to success, Mrs Avery springs into action and goes to ring the girl's father.

> … at that moment Mother returned. She sat down without a word and picked up her knife and fork. For a moment I thought Mr. Trotton had turned her down flat.
> Father asked, 'Well, what did Trotton have to say?'
> 'I never asked him,' she said. 'I got as far as the telephone box and realized I'd rather never show again than have everybody saying Gillian couldn't ride that blessed pony.'
> Seldom have I been so astonished.

> I said, 'I'm very much obliged, I'm sure,' which sounded all wrong, but I meant it well.
>
> Mother seemed to know this for she suddenly leant across and kissed me, much to the waiter's embarrassment. I let her for I am beginning to see that Mother's urge to win is all mixed up with me. Whoever would have thought it?

When on ground with which she is familiar, Spooner's acute observation and often acerbic style make her, at her best, very readable indeed. Gillian and her parents bounce off the page, and the author's strongly held opinions lend an energy and a passion to *The Silk Purse*. That passion leads her into a fantastic cul-de-sac mid-story, but it does enable her to bound out again and finish the book on a convincing note.

Probably the most consistently good of this section of authors is Pamela Macgregor-Morris, but as she was an equestrian journalist this is perhaps not surprising. She was born in London in 1925, but when she was five her family bought a weekend house near Goodwood. Pamela acquired a pony and was 'hooked on the horse' for life. In 1946 the family moved to Dartmoor, where she wrote her first books as well as starting to write for *Horse and Hound*. She carried on her journalistic career by becoming an assistant to *The Times*'s equestrian and polo correspondent John Board, whom she succeeded in 1956. She bred hunters before running a stud of riding ponies with her husband. Besides her pony books, she wrote many general equine titles.

Macgregor-Morris's eight pony books were written over a twenty-year span, and covered most of the genre: the horse telling the tale of its life; a character earning a living through horses; the classic holiday story. Her earliest books, *Topper* (1947) and *High Honours* (1948), were both equine biographies, and were followed in 1950 by *Exmoor Ben*, the story of an Exmoor pony. Her better books were written when she entered directly into the world of her heroes and heroines, which she did most successfully with *Lucky Purchase* (1949). It is that rarest of creatures in the pony book universe, the story of a child who does not like horses. Jane is the daughter of a horsy family, and that is the trouble:

> ... at meal times, the three of them would sit and discuss horses for hours, while Jane would stare either out of the window or at her plate, wishing that she could be excused so that she could get away from the everlasting topic. It should have been enough, she thought to herself, that Dick was interested in horses—if only her family were satisfied with that, instead of trying to force her to be as well!

Poor Jane has been dragged along in the wake of her family, with no attention paid to what she wants. How, after all, could she not love the horse? After another woeful performance at a show, Jane's parents finally realise there is no point pushing her. They resolve not to mention the horse, and Jane goes off to stay with her unhorsy Aunt Frances at the seaside. There she is blissfully free of horse—until she meets the old and scruffy beach pony Kitty. There is something about Kitty that tugs at Jane's heartstrings. Her parents, equine snobs, are not keen on the idea of such a scruffy animal joining their stable, but they relent.

In a further move away from the traditional pony book, there is a tear-wrenching scene where the elderly Kitty, after a few months of good living with Jane, dies. Macgregor-Morris handles the death with a sure and economical touch:

'It's Kitty, Madam,' the distressed groom burst out, twisting his cap in his hands. 'I've just been out to her paddock, and she's lying by the stream.' He stopped, not knowing how to go on.

'Is she dead?' asked Mr Arbuthnot.

Harry nodded. 'She must have died in her sleep, I think, sir.'

For a moment there was silence.

'However are we going to tell Jane?' said Mrs Arbuthnot helplessly.

But there was no need. There was a sound from the doorway and the four people turned to see Jane standing there. She had come down the stairs silently in tennis shoes, and it was obvious that she had heard the conversation, or enough of it to know what had happened. She gave a stifled cry and, turning, ran across the hall and up the stairs again; a door slammed, and there was an awful quiet in the room.

This sureness of observation and character is also utilised in *The Amateur Horsedealers* (1951), which again plays with convention. The true heroine of this book is a grandmother. It is usually the children who make the most of parents being away, but this family's grandmother is thrilled to be off the leash too. The family have hit hard times, though this is pony book poor, where the family still manage to maintain a large house with staff, and a few horses. After the father of the family leaves his regiment because of cuts, he decides to go into horse-dealing to fund the family. The children are delighted, but their grandmother is appalled—at least until the parents go horse-hunting, when her true colours are revealed and she goes with the children to an auction to make sure they do not buy a dud. The grandmother is a wonderful creation, and once she enters the fray she sweeps the book along in a whirl of determined eccentricity.

Macgregor-Morris's last pony book, *Clear Round* (1962), showed that Collins, who had baulked at Josephine Pullein-Thompson's 1957 *Pony Club Camp* because it had the merest hint of romance, now realised which way the world was moving. Fiona is a horse-mad London girl from a resolutely un-horsy family, sent to do her BHSI at the sort of finishing school designed to win over parents who are anti-horse: French, flower-arranging and cookery are also taught. Here she meets Gavin, the owners' son, and, more importantly, Lucifer, their difficult young horse. Relationships blossom with both horse and man, and all ends in a thoroughly satisfying manner.

Macgregor-Morris, like Glenda Spooner, set her books against the background of what Margery Fisher called 'the big house'. In *Clear Round* the owners of the big house started up the finishing school in order to keep it going: proof that Macgregor-Morris, at least, was prepared to adapt to changing circumstances. Her moneyed children are vibrant characters, and their situations, particularly in *Lucky Purchase*, genuinely moving. And the rich child has a story to tell too.

Dorian Williams (1914–85) was the voice of showjumping on television. He commentated in the glory days of horses on television, when every evening programme of the Horse of the Year Show and the Royal International Horse Show was televised. Educated at Harrow, he had a full life: in addition to commentating, he was involved with the British Horse Society as a member of its council and as Chairman, and was instrumental in setting up the National Equestrian Centre at Stoneleigh. He was also Master of the Whaddon Chase Hunt. He used his family home, Pendley, for a Shakespeare festival, and set up a centre of adult education there.

As well as all this, he found time to write, and besides many non-fiction titles, and the Wendy series, produced two fictional works for adults, *Pancho* (1967) and *Kingdom for a Horse* (1967). The Wendy books explore what life was like for a working-class girl working with horses. The heroine is soon whisked away from her ordinary background (Williams, with what now jars as a spectacular bit of sexism, describes Wendy's mother as 'just a busy housewife looking after six children'.) In the first book of the series, *Wendy Wins a Pony* (1961), Wendy does indeed win a pony in an art competition, but the pony himself, Smiley, plays remarkably little part in the story. He is simply a device to get Wendy away from her family and into work. After Wendy has nowhere to keep her pony her guardian angel, Miss Rogerson of the local riding school, advertises on her behalf for somewhere to take her on as a girl groom with attendant pony. Wendy finds work with the Tivertons and their new residential riding school, and that is where the three-book series is based.

The series is an interesting one on several levels: it is a reasonably realistic portrait of what life as a girl groom would be like, with unrelentingly long hours, exhaustion and little time off. What can go wrong when working away from home is made a little more explicit. All is not plain sailing between Wendy and her employers. In *Wendy Wins her Spurs* (1962) she leaves, and gets a job with the Whittle family. It is difficult to see Mr Whittle as anything other than an older man who wants to get Wendy into bed, although this is never openly stated. He is constantly trying to get her alone, is obviously resentful when her friend visits and shares her room, and at one point comes into her room after she's gone to bed. Nothing happens, but it is difficult not to wonder where Williams was going with that particular plot line. In the end, Mr Whittle tries to dope a racehorse and is arrested—saving Wendy, the reader is convinced, from a much worse fate.

Was Williams trying to warn young

girls working with horses of what could go wrong? Perhaps he did not feel able to write directly about the threat from a male employer. (Susan Chitty's 1966 *My Life and Horses* has her heroine being chased round the feedbins by one of her employers, but this is treated as a joke.)

The series as a whole is still a readable one. Wendy is a young and rather naive girl living away from home for the first time, and her life with horses seems realistic. She has no major triumphs in the show ring: her horse wins at the White City show, but only when he is ridden by someone else. Any girl reading the series would come away with no illusions about the sheer slog involved in a career with horses, and perhaps an idea of some of the downfalls.

Marion Coakes (1947–) became well known as a showjumper with her pony Stroller, who, despite being considerably smaller than most showjumping horses, was phenomenally successful. Together they won a silver medal in the 1968 Mexico Olympics in the individual event. The pair were immensely popular during Stroller's career, and Coakes, with input from other contributors, produced three editions of *Marion Coakes' Book of Horses,* as well as a biography of Stroller.

Sue-Elaine Draws a Horse (1971) was Coakes's only excursion into fiction. It was written with Gillian Hirst, better known as the author Gillian Baxter, who had already produced a number of well-received pony books of her own when she collaborated with Marion Coakes on this one. In an interview, Gillian Baxter commented on how much she enjoyed the experience. 'Doing the research for the book with Marion was great fun: she was a lovely person. I went to visit her to find out how she thought of things, and the sort of words she used.' I asked if they had written the book together. 'No, I did that!' And who had the idea for the book? 'I did!'

Sue-Elaine Draws a Horse uses the same literary device of setting a story amid the background of your own stables that Pat Smythe had earlier used with considerable success. It is set at Coakes's stables, complete with the famous Stroller. Sue-Elaine is a fictional teenager who helps Marion with her horses. When they are at a show, Sue-Elaine sees, and falls in love with, Sea-Blond, a badly behaved palomino horse, and after helping to rescue him when he tries to kick his way out of his box she is allowed to have him on loan. The book reads awkwardly at first: Pat Smythe had an immediacy and freshness to her writing about her own horses which this book lacks, possibly because it was Gillian Hirst writing about them rather than Coakes herself. The story is, however, superior to Pat Smythe's books: the use of a professional author ensured that. Once past the scene-setting of the early chapters, the book takes off and is a well-observed picture of a girl's obsession with a horse, and of the appalling behaviour of some people in the showjumping world.

Public figures have always sold books: they have a ready-made fan base to buy them, and the writing ability of the public figure is not necessarily such an issue as it is for the non-famous. But it is a rare star autobiography that does not linger, unsold, in charity shops some months after it has been on the bestseller lists; books by public figures must be marketed strongly, and their appeal maximised, while the public figure still has a pull, and the lessons learned last century are being applied in this one: sales of Katie Price's Perfect Ponies series were initially strong, but have waned as her popularity has declined.

Pat Smythe's books' popularity has faded now, their plots and characterisation not being strong enough for them to stand on their own among a throng of better-written books. Ironically, Marion Coakes's *Sue-Elaine Draws a Horse* has faded from view because the book did not carry its real author's name. Had it had 'Gillian Baxter' emblazoned on it, it would have carried on appealing to her fans; she is still read today, whereas Marion Coakes's star has faded, as all sports stars' must. Dorian Williams and Glenda Spooner produced readable but more uneven work. Real literary talent will out: Pamela Macgregor-Morris's books are still appreciated because writing was her job; and she was good enough to succeed at whatever she turned her hand to.

CHAPTER 9
'BOOT, SADDLE, TO HORSE AND AWAY!'
The 1950s

More pony books were published in this decade than any other in the twentieth century. Pony book authors writing in the 1950s were fortunate. The children's author Geoffrey Trease says: 'In those days you could have sold *Richard III* if you had given it the right wrapper and called it A Pony for Richard.' Even Antonia Forest, one of the finest twentieth-century children's writers, contemplated writing a pony story when her publishers told her it would sell (she wrote about falconry instead, though ponies do play a minor role in her books). Publishers imported American series: Walter Farley's Black Stallion, Rutherford Montgomery's Golden Stallion, Marguerite Henry's historical horse stories and, the best of them all, Mary O'Hara's Flicka. And, as well as series born both here and abroad, endless home-grown holiday adventures with ponies were produced.

The critic Marcus Crouch argues that cosy holiday adventure was what was required in the post-war era—'the security of the family and the luxury of adventure without real danger'. The sheer amount of pony holiday adventure that was produced suggests Crouch is right. The post-war spirit was not the only thing that inspired these stories: Arthur Ransome's holiday stories played their part, producing a 'flood of family stories and holiday chronicles during and immediately after the war' (Crouch). Whether these imitations, which included legions of pony stories, were any good is doubtful. The pony adventure was certainly seized on with enthusiasm by authors—including some, one suspects, whose hearts lay elsewhere.

M E Atkinson (1899–1974) was a prolific children's writer, most active between the 1930s and 1950s and best known for her Lockett and Fricka series; the latter is an adventure series with some pony content. The standalone *Horseshoes and Handlebars* (1958) is more overtly pony-orientated.

Atkinson is an author with whom I struggle. I read with bafflement review after review in *Pony* magazine praising her books: *The Barnstormers* (1953) is 'a four-star story', *Hunter's Moon* (1952) 'a lively and delightful tale'. She is mentioned in the same breath as Monica Edwards: 'Books … by the Pullein-Thompsons, Monica Edwards, M E Atkinson, Primrose Cumming, are right in the top class … Later critics are not so welcoming, describing her as 'not particularly good' (Thwaite) and 'indifferent' (Haymonds). Perhaps Marcus Crouch has the explanation when he suggests that many of the holiday stories after the war appeared much better than they were, and that 'in retrospect one sees the thinness of the invention and the shallow observation which the writers' high spirits at first obscured'.

There are many other authors who have not stood the test of time well. Hilda Boden (the pseudonym of Hilda Morris Bodenham, 1901–?) started writing pony books in the 1940s. Her first was *Pony Trek* (1947), a conventional story in which Jennifer and John and their mother buy Welsh ponies, and ride them home from Wales. Boden's books include most of the major tropes of the pony book: a neglected pony is rescued in *One More Pony* (1952);

sinister adults threaten ponies in *Joanna Rides the Hills* (1961) and *Joanna's Special Pony* (1960); a pony is the means for healing in *Little Grey Pony* (1960). She does not enter wholeheartedly into the world of the pony: her books are generally free of competition and gymkhanas (though Colin, the hero of the 1958 *Pony Boy*, does win at the Summer Show); what interests her more is the struggles of her characters. Colin works to buy tack for his pony, and learns to ride from a library book.

Boden's books promise much more than they deliver. They often have unusual beginnings but end with a slide into predictable, feel-good conventionality. *Pony Girl* (1959) starts promisingly, with a reversal of the well-worn pony book opening device of a move to the country. Molly Mallory and her family live on a small and unprofitable farm in Ireland, separated from Molly's father, who has found work in London. The family sell up and move to London to be together, thereby scuppering Molly's plans to work as a lad at a racing stable. Their cramped existence in London seems initially unlikely to turn up a horse, but very soon Molly notices the tiny paddock behind their house and finds that a theatrical entrepreneur has left a pony there which is starving. Despite her own poverty, Molly manages to start rehabilitating the pony, but what could have been an interesting twist on the conventional plot soon rushes headlong into dream territory when Molly and her family end up finding a country billet with a family which they met in Ireland. Although Boden's children are generally resourceful and independent, their ultimate success can sometimes depend disappointingly on coincidence and the actions of fairy godmother figures. *Pony Girl* ends in utter conventionality:

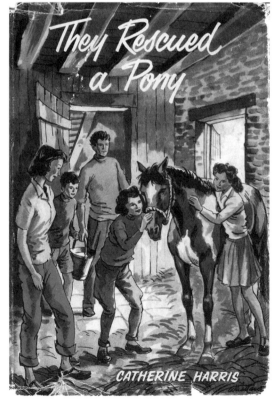

> 'We're lucky,' said Mother, cuddling both Paddy and Molly as they went into the shabby London house. 'Think. That dear little lodge—and a bathroom, in time—and green trees and fresh air to breathe …'

Other writers dealt with the adventure theme a little more successfully, if occasionally with alarming results. Catherine Harris's works improved as she went on. She began early, her first book, *We Started a Riding Club* (1954), being written in her teens. After this uneventful story of a family who (unsurprisingly) start a riding club, aided by their irascible MFH grandfather, Harris launched out on a four-book series about the Marsham family, described on the jacket of *They Rescued a Pony* as 'lively and impetuous'.

The books are mostly about the five older children: Flyn, Donna, Cressida and the twins, Jay and Janson. (There are six Marshams altogether: the youngest, Timothy, just escapes the winsome cuteness which often characterises baby brothers and sisters.) The characters frequently remind each other that they are Marshams, and must therefore be dashing. The twins in particular are endlessly wearing; they are rude, thoughtless, careless and obsessed with being flamboyant and adventurous.

This caused Harris problems as the series progressed. The first story, *They Rescued a Pony* (1956), in which the Marshams rescue an ill-treated circus pony, and the second, *The Ponies of Cuckoo Mill Farm* (1958), where the combined Marsham and Forrest families rescue cows from a flood as well as contending with the differences between the families, are more successful than the third, *Riding for Ransom* (1960), which fails in both characterisation and plot. Two boys are kidnapped in succession: young Timothy, when he is mistaken for the son of a wealthy American family staying with the Marshams, and then the real American boy, Simon. The Marshams then veer between the occasional grey-faced expression of worry and carrying on as if they have completely forgotten Timothy. Mrs Marsham's decision to allow Simon's father to choose whether or not to go to the police, because it was his boy the kidnappers meant to snatch and not hers, is staggering:

> 'I still think it's wrong, horribly wrong,' said Mrs Marsham, 'but it is up to Ensign to do what he thinks fit and we must abide by his decision, because the whole affair is centred around the Baddeleys and not the Marshams. It's only because of that stupid mistake over Timothy's identity that we're involved at all.'

When later, having found out that the other children have disappeared to rescue Timothy and Simon, she says:

> 'Aren't we lucky to have such original children? Oh Roger, wouldn't it be marvellous if this mission they've set out on were a success and they rescued Timothy and Simon and we never had to see another policeman?'

my disbelief clawed itself back from suspension and goggled.

The fourth book, *To Horse and Away* (1962), sees Harris pulling back from the absurdities of the kidnap plot, and placing her characters in situations where their adventures spring naturally from their characters, rather than being a wild crashing through unrealistic adventure. The four middle Marsham children are on a trek back to their home from Wales. The twins' stranding in a cliffside cave, with the tide reaching ever higher, is entirely convincing, as are their shaky attempts to comfort each other and their bravery when it looks as if they will be swept off the cliff. Harris's characterisation of the family, hitherto rather broad brush (Cressida, the poetic one, is given to coming to a full stop in the middle of the street as she composes verse), is much more subtle in this last story of the series.

Harris moved away from the Marshams in her final book—possibly feeling, with maturity, that an insistence on dash and headlong adventure were best avoided. *The Heronsbrook*

Gymkhana (1964) is much more domestic in scale, but it is her tour de force. It takes a single event, a gymkhana, and a set of characters ranging from the young to the about-to-be-married and the adult organisers, all of whose fears and hopes are explored within a convincing setting. It is an assured book. The ending is perhaps just a little too pat, with all problems solved and resolutions to behave differently made, but the process of getting there is thoroughly enjoyable, and Harris's acute observation of her characters' thoughts and behaviour makes it worthwhile reading.

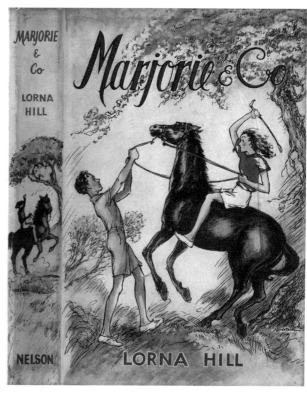

It is not parental attitudes that are alarming in Lorna Hill's pony books: it is the attitude of her hero, Guy. For the author he is clearly a dream of rugged bliss, but he divides reader reaction pretty sharply. Lorna Hill (1902–91) is not a classic pony book author: she is far better known for her two ballet series, Sadler's Wells and Dancing Peel, where the obsessive nature needed to succeed at ballet is vividly portrayed but is allied to the sort of take-me-I'm-yours romance that gave Mills & Boon a bad name. Her strongest series is The Vicarage Children, with a heroine both sympathetic and self-effacing, set against a sensitive description of the difficulties of life in a poor parish. Hill wrote from experience: her husband was a clergyman in just such a poor parish.

Hill wrote two series, Patience and Marjorie, which are classed as pony books. They were written for her daughter, Vicki, before she went to the Sadler's Wells Ballet School. The books are holiday adventures centred on the characters of the children who ride the ponies rather than on the equines themselves—in the Marjorie series, Guy and Marjorie herself are infinitely more memorable than any pony they might have ridden. However he was regarded when the books came out, Guy, with his penchant for physical punishment and stern and unbending ways, seems rather strong meat today:

'You mustn't beat Peter. Why, he was nearly drowned—'
   'That was my fault,' Peter broke in. 'I deserved a licking. And it's no use kicking up a fuss, Pan, because it's over and done with, and we're all square again, aren't we, Guy?'
   Guy nodded gravely. (*Border Peel*, 1950)

Josephine Pullein-Thompson's male characters meet their female equivalents on level ground; Guy is more likely to sling the recalcitrant female over his shoulder. At least these two series avoid what Angela Bull calls the 'syrupy romance' of the ballet books, although Guy is a character chafing at the pony book bit to escape into his rightful home, the romance novel.

The Patience books form a shorter series but a much more endearing one, at least for the first two books. Patience is a character with considerable charm, less brutal than Guy and less downright difficult than Marjorie. Patience's elder brother, David, the hero of the first two books, is patient and kind; he teaches the difficult Judy the right way to ride and behave without bullying. It was Guy, however, whom Lorna Hill's daughter and her friends wanted, and, after a testing-the-water appearance in *It Was all through Patience* (1952), it was Guy they got. David is marginalised in *So Guy Came Too* (1954), and in *The Five Shilling Holiday* (1955) he is removed from the action altogether after an accident.

There was not a great deal of competition on the ballet book front; there was considerably more, and better, in the pony book field, and Lorna Hill's books do not measure up. Their strong sense of place and the occasional shaft of decent characterisation are not enough to make them stayers in the race for pony book glory.

Kathleen Mackenzie (1907–?90) also went in for family adventure rather than conventional tales of gymkhanas and wanting a pony. Families, friends and their relationships were what really interested her. Her first book, *The Four Pentires and Jimmy*, was the start of a series featuring the Pentire family, Sarah, Frances, Vivien and Jane, who live on a farm. Characters are added as the series progresses, until in *Vicky and the Pentires* the author is handling a large cast. The author had plenty of inspiration in her own background for such multitudes of characters. She was born in the Argentine, but returned to England when she was three. Her father was one of ten, her mother one of twenty, and she herself was one of eight. She started writing when young, and was also interested in the stage, for which she wrote and produced plays.

The Pentire series features ponies as a means to an end: they are there to generate adventure, or enable it, but they are not the centre of it. *The Four Pentires and Jimmy* (1947) opens with the children taking part in a gymkhana where they have competition in the shape of the Rendle children, who are on beautiful ponies belonging to the local riding school. To the unwary it seems as if the conventional pony-and-gymkhana adventure is what will result, but instead the ponies are whisked away—quite literally: they are stolen. It takes the Pentires a little while to realise this is what has happened (they are similarly slow on the uptake in *Vicky and the Pentires*, where the ponies are being borrowed overnight for nefarious deeds). The plot then centres on the minutiae of their camping trip and their attempts to track the ponies down. The ponies themselves are absent until the end, when it is discovered they were stolen by that familiar personification of evil in the pony book, the gipsy.

The series continues with adventure being a key factor: helping a runaway (*We Four and Sandy*, 1947); catching spies in *The Badgers of Quinion* (1950); catching a criminal gang rustling dogs in *Vicky and the Pentires* (1951). Even in the more obviously horsy *Red Conker* (1952), in which Frances rides a chestnut horse found by the family, the horse is in

All three stared across the moon-silvered mud.

Kathleen Mackenzie: Vicky and the Pentires

danger of being stolen. The Pentires are a vivid lot, their ponies unfortunately almost entirely forgettable.

One wonders how much Mackenzie's heart was in writing pony stories. Even with her more overtly horsy books, like *Jumping Jan* (1955), it is the characters who stick in the mind, not the ponies or anything that happens with them. The family with whom sixteen-year-old Janice Maddever starts her working life are splendidly vile. Jan is nominally there to look after the horses, but it is the family, and Jan's effect on them, that the reader remembers. The family is dominated by Mrs Jervis, a minor actress of great beauty, who has made a very good marriage. She is devoted to emotional scenes, as are three of her four children. Mr Jervis stays aloof from the drama, to the detriment of his children's characters, and the elder daughter, Ellie, has her own ambitions, far removed from those her mother has for her.

Jan, though interesting enough, is another example of a type Mackenzie used over and over again: the lonely child, whose parents are dead or otherwise absent, contending with a problem. Jan has left her parents to start her first job; Tamsin and John's are away in Peru (*Pony and Trap*, 1962); Nigel (*Nigel Rides Away*, 1960) and Nancy (*Nancy and the Carrs*, 1958) are both orphans, and the relations with whom they are living are unsympathetic; Pippa's father has died (*Chalk and Cheese*, 1957). The children struggle on, bravely, and overcome all odds. Although Mackenzie is sympathetic to her characters' trials and tribulations, when read as a set the books are rather indigestible; the succession of brave, noble and capable children does sometimes make the reader long for one who, quite simply, fails.

Not all authors leapt into pony adventure with uncritical enthusiasm. A young one, Sheila Chapman (born 1942), grew up in Somerset. Her mother bought Post Office Savings Stamps until she had saved up enough money to buy Sheila and her sister their first pony, Queenie. This equine had a neat appreciation of who was in charge: when Sheila's mother was there she was a 'model pony', but when the girls were on their own she became 'a character-building challenge'.

Chapman wrote her four pony books when she was aged between twelve and fifteen. They are all relatively dark in tone; there are broken and unsympathetic families, and ponies die too. Carmen, the heroine of *A Pony and his Partner* (1959), has come to live with her cousins after her parents' death. Poor Yoland, in *Pony from Fire* (1960), has a blisteringly unsympathetic family. In a fire at the family home, her pony is killed and she is badly injured. She forgets the accident completely, but is so petrified with a fear she can't understand (and as the family refuse to mention it, ever, it is highly unlikely that she ever will) that she can no longer go near horses. Lynn, the heroine of *Ride to Freedom* (1961), lives with a grim foster mother who bullies her and threatens to sell her pony.

All Chapman's heroines find resolution of a sort: Lynn runs off with her pony, riding away to find her real family. Carmen finds a new home with her pony, Oberon (although in the 1960 sequel, *The Mystery Pony*, he dies). Yoland is sent to stay with more sympathetic relations, manages to conquer her fear, and wins through with Firecat. Chapman's books are not comfort reads, though they do all have positive endings. All her heroines have journeys to go through before they can find happiness, and the means by which they reach it are sometimes unrelenting.

In this sea of competent but ultimately unrewarding pony adventure, there was the occasional author who shone. Veronica Westlake, with her acutely observed families, Patience McElwee, with her biting observation on horse-world snobbery, and Gillian Baxter, with a series of superior books which took equestrianism seriously, all provided books well worth reading.

Veronica Westlake's characters exist in a more realistic post-war world than many of their pony book fellows. Born in Devon, Westlake (dates unknown) spent her childhood with her Irish cousins, horses and dogs. She worked as a freelance writer, but this was not her only job by any means: Routledge and Kegan Paul, who published one of her books, listed her other occupations as 'film extra, a private secretary, fashion model, school-teacher, riding-school instructress …'. These jobs gave her ample opportunity to observe children and their ways, and this is shown in the astutely observed characters of her four pony books: *The Ten-Pound Pony* (1953), *The Unwilling Adventurers* (1954), *The Intruders* (1955) and *The Mug's Game* (1956).

The Ten-Pound Pony is about three siblings, Jessica (the narrator), Ann and Martin. Their father has died in the war, and the family now struggle to survive in a cramped London flat, their mother supporting them with what part-time secretarial work she can find. When the family move to the New Forest so that she can take up a slightly better paid job, there is still very little money.

The family squabble and scrap in a thoroughly realistic way. There is a particularly neat scene where Jessica has the wrong shirt on, and has to give it back:

> 'But what am *I* going to wear?' I screeched, dancing round the room in a fury, clad only in my shorts, throwing open all the drawers and cupboards and burrowing into the tidy piles for the spare shirt I knew wouldn't be there.

Westlake is strong on the interplay between siblings. The plotting when a larger and heavier brother has done his sisters down is well observed:

Ann and I looked at each other. A frontal attack on Martin was never any good—he was much too strong for us. But he would be repaid—perhaps at some distant date when he was least expecting it.

The Ten-Pound Pony is, at first sight, a classic pony book fairy tale. After considerable strife and hard work, Jessica, Ann and Martin acquire a pony. At the very end they have a family reunion, a large house and stables too. But these children work very hard to get their pony. Westlake is keen on reality; even when the children find the ill-treated pony, Gipsy, which they want to buy, their mother provides a stern counterpoint to their romantic desire to have that pony. 'Even if you had the money,' she says, 'you couldn't buy a pony or horse in that sentimental fashion.' When they do achieve the miracle and buy the pony, there is a touching description of its arrival: usually in a pony book this is simply a case for rejoicing, but not for Westlake. The reality of owning another living being produces in the children almost a sense of awe:

Owning inanimate objects like books and bicycles was one thing—owning something that ate and breathed and depended on us for happiness and the continuance of life itself was quite different, and we felt almost afraid as we smoothed her rough coat and tried to finger the mud off it …

The ending is not a complete fairy tale: throughout the book the children are surprised by glimpses of their mother as a person in her own right, and when she and her estranged father are reunited they have mixed feelings about it. There is a particularly telling scene where, even after the family have been reconciled, Jessica remarks tartly on the effects of her grandfather's temper:

It appeared to worry him that Martin was too old now to 'get in anywhere decent'—I suppose meaning the Public School where he himself used to go. I heard him regretting that Martin's name hadn't been put down for it when he was born, and I couldn't help thinking privately to myself that if his wonderful school had taught him to control his own temper there would have been a chance of Martin going to it.

We finish *The Ten-Pound Pony* expecting more storms to come.

Life as a Westlake child is not necessarily easy; the author turned her clear eye on the pony obsessive (and her unsavoury siblings) in *The Unwilling Adventurers*. The Strickland family's mother has died, and they run rings around their father. When he is suddenly left a fortune, the family rejoice. They can have everything their little hearts desire—until, that is, their father hears them planning their future, is appalled, and resolves to do something about it. This he does in a manner that prefigures the infant Richard Branson being turned out at the age of five to find his own way home: having told his children what he thinks of their selfishness and different obsessions, he sends them off with £1 each, stout walking shoes and several pairs of thick socks and tells them to take a boat upriver for 25 miles, at which point they will learn the next challenge they have to undertake.

The children are, one by one, disabused of their over-inflated belief in themselves. The dénouement comes for Julie when she applies for a job looking after horses; puffed up with conceit, she rides with horrible enthusiasm and no sympathy for the poor horse. She begins to suspect that all is not well, and when she overhears her efforts being discussed by the staff her illusions leave her:

My whole misconception of myself had fallen like a house of cards about me, and my pride was flayed and quivering.

Westlake's adults are shown with a realism rare in the genre. Margaret Huggins of *The Mug's Game* is shipped off to stay as a paying guest with the Stacey family. Mrs Stacey is 'the businessman of the family' who 'earns pots of money', though rather sadly she hates it but has to do it to support the family. Mr Stacey stays at home, running a chicken farm, which he also hates but is 'the only thing he is any good at'. He paints too, very unsuccessfully. At the end of the book the Stacey parents are still in the same rather unenviable state they were in at the beginning; doing what they hate for the sake of their family.

Westlake wrote, with a detached and wry affection, of a middle-class world not without its challenges. She is one of the few pony book authors to inject humour into her books and, like her contemporary Patience McElwee, is well worth seeking out.

Patience McElwee (1910–63) was a fine writer best known as an author of books for adults; her three pony books, although nominally aimed at children, are really a far more successful read for the adult reader who enjoys a biting appreciation of the snobberies and silliness that infest the world of the pony. Her plots are straightforward—in all of them problems are overcome and a happier place reached—but it is in the observation of character and situation that the books are most successful. Perhaps it was McElwee's distance from the horsy world that helped. She was not herself a rider; her daughter Harriet Hall says: 'My father and I both hunted most weeks and my mother would come to the meets, but she was terrified of horses and never willingly had direct contact with one. She did, however, know a lot about the racing world and could talk horse brilliantly.' It was Harriet's experience of the Pony

Club that McElwee drew on, particularly for *Match Pair*, where the ruthless depiction of Pony Club parents stings: a portrait that could perhaps only be written by someone watching that world but not part of it.

The children in McElwee's books generally have considerably more sense than the adults: Jane Howell, the teenage narrator of *Match Pair* (1956), looks on the grown-ups surrounding her with an unsparing eye. Jane and her twin brother, Adam, have been shipped over from America, where they lived with their diplomat father, their stepmother and Mademoiselle, who 'looked after our stepmother's clothes and nervous system'. They are to live in England with their Uncle William (who is what McElwee's daughter called 'her standard hero, bad-tempered and taciturn': versions of him appear in her ten adult novels). Jane, on going to Pony Club camp, is a stern critic, as three quotations will demonstrate:

> A few more children had arrived, but mostly it seemed a gathering of men who had been waiting for just this opportunity to get away from their wives, judging by the way they threw their weight about in quite unnecessary directions …

> Miss Jardine thanked me nicely for having disentangled the pony, and Mrs Allibone said: 'Oh, Jane doesn't mind making herself useful, do you, dear?' as if she would have liked to say Jane is one to push herself forward on every possible occasion.

> I managed to buy my way into a faint sort of popularity by providing sweets for other people to eat under the bedclothes at night.

The poor Merry children of *The Merrythoughts* (1960) have a similarly bleak experience of human nature. The child who invites them to tea is only interested in them because their parents are on television. Any individuality is ruthlessly crushed out of the Merrys by Miss Baxter, their parents' secretary. In a scene which probably has a chilling resonance now for the children of some celebrities, the cold realities of the children's existence are spelled out:

> They were sometimes taken into the country on Sundays, but Miss Baxter saw to it that it was always to somewhere where they could be reached by the clicking cameras of reporters, and they were warned they might not stray away from their parents' side because viewers liked to think of them as the Perfect Family.

In all McElwee's children's books, her young characters have to contend with the selfish manoeuvrings of the adult world. Mrs Aston Pringle, the impeccably drawn grandmother of *Dark Horse* (1958), is concerned with keeping up appearances, marrying off her eldest granddaughter to someone 'suitable' and scoring points off her 'friends'. Her grandchildren long for a more scruffy and bohemian existence, like the one lived by Shamus and Tim O'Brien who are blissfully unconcerned with the finer things of life.

Each book contrasts the adult posturing with the more bohemian and free existence of those on better terms with the rhythms of the countryside. It is the sterling influence of the countryside and of the adults who appreciate it that saves the Howells, Merrythoughts and Hardcastles—the only pony book trope that McElwee used wholeheartedly. Perhaps her publishers, Hodder & Stoughton, hoped that in her books they had a second Jill (whom they also published). They did not. Jill exists in an Arcadian Britain, albeit one peopled with humour. McElwee's Britain is one where adults do not necessarily have children's best interests at heart, but for all that her children manage to come to terms with their situations.

The best of the 1950s authors might have started their careers in holiday adventure, but they realised its limitations. Real life happens outside the holidays. Gillian Baxter (birth date unknown) is another author who started young: she was fifteen when she wrote her first book. Her heroines often mirror the ages she was herself when writing, but she has a gift of observation and enough objectivity about her characters to create believable plots. Her books reflect the dream realised; they are about girls working with horses, and competing at a high level, and even the book she wrote with the showjumper Marion Coakes, *Sue-Elaine Draws a Horse*, is about a girl working with horses. Later in life she switched to writing books aimed at the younger reader, with *Special Delivery* and the Magic and Moonshine series. Baxter did not restrict herself to one particular horsy field, ranging over more disciplines than most authors: the Bracken Stable series is about showjumping and eventing, *The Team from Low Moor* centres on the Prince Philip Cup, and *The Stables at Hampton* is possibly the first novel concerned exclusively with dressage

Baxter's first book, *Horses and Heather* (1956), was a conventional but sound start in which her characters explore managing the adult world, as the author was no doubt doing herself. Christine and Colin Scott and their cousin, Alison, have been invited to stay at a small riding school. When they arrive they find that the owner has been taken to hospital, leaving the school with no-one to run into it. The Scotts step into the breach. (It is a risky business being a riding school owner in pony fiction. With an awful suddenness, an illness can strike that leaves you hospital-bound without having arranged cover for the horses. Patricia Leitch's 1967 *Afraid to Ride* and Justine Furminger's 1981 *Bobbie Takes the Reins* use the same plot.)

After her trot around the fantasies of pony-mad children wondering what the world would be like if they organised it, Baxter found her feet and delivered a succession of well-crafted and intelligent novels. Her books have a directness and freshness borne of experience. In an interview with me, she said: 'I wrote about the ages I knew, and stayed with [the characters] as they grew up. I think it's important to go with your characters.' She avoided the conventional pony book trope of getting a pony and having gymkhana success; the one major concession she makes to it is that her heroines are generally exceptionally talented riders.

Margery Fisher says of *Tan and Tarmac* (1958) that it has 'a refreshingly professional attitude to riding'. Nearly all Baxter's horse books are about people making a success of a horsy career, though not without a struggle. Even her books for younger children see her characters involved in the world of work. The children in *Special Delivery* (1967) help the hospitalised greengrocer by doing his deliveries with a donkey cart, and the Shetland ponies in the Magic and Moonshine series, begun in 1969, are working animals doing theatre performances. Baxter knew just how hard working with horses was. When she was seventeen she started as a working pupil with Robert Hall at the Fulmer School of Equitation; it was demanding work. Hall had two yards: 'One of my first jobs was to wash all the tails of the riding school horses: they hadn't been touched for weeks, only a quick brush. His other yard had his Lipizzaners and dressage horses and it was absolutely perfect. I had to groom the dressage horses, and when I did I had to knock out the curry comb on the floor outside so he could check how much grease I was getting out!'

The Bracken Stables trilogy (*Jump to the Stars*, 1957, *The Difficult Summer*, 1959, and *The Perfect Horse*, 1963) sees a girl ending her school career and launching herself into the world of work. Orphan Roberta (Bobby) is living with her aunt, uncle and cousin Ellen. Her aunt, Helen Camberwell, is a beautiful and selfish socialite whose family trail in her wake. The small but exclusive school to which the Camberwells send Bobby and Ellen allows riding, but only with a conventional and dull stable. Bobby discovers the Bracken Hill stables, where riding well, rather than trailing around the countryside on unfit horses, is what is important. The stable is run by Guy Mathews, who also buys and sells horses. This connection with trade damns him in the eyes of the headmistress, but Bobby manages to persuade her uncle and aunt to let her ride at Bracken Hill. After a distressing interlude when Helen Camberwell buys and mistreats Shelta, a horse Bobby has showjumped with considerable success, Bobby manages to buy Shelta herself, and settles down to work at Bracken Hill. Life is not easy. In a more sophisticated development of the children-running-the-riding-school plot, *The Difficult Summer* opens with a disastrous fire. Guy is hospitalised, and several horses are killed; the stables are partially ruined, and Bobby and a fellow groom, Heath, have to try to keep them going. The task is difficult and realistic, with the stable having to struggle back from the financial brink.

The nastier side of life is a feature of Gillian Baxter's other stories: Tamara, the dressage rider of *The Stables at Hampton* (1961), has to contend with a face badly disfigured in a fire. Laurence Croft, the show jumper who trains the unsmart Low Moor Pony Club team to compete in the Prince Philip Cup, had been blinded in a car accident he caused, in which his wife and young child were killed. Lindy Smith in *Horses in the Glen* (1962) has a brutal and dishonest stepfather, who assaults her so badly when he steals her prize money from her that she is left unconscious.

However, all is not gloomy. There are romantic relationships in many of Baxter's books—generally very lightly done, with an understanding being reached, and the possibility of a glorious future. After a three-book courtship, Bobby and Guy's future together is understood. *Ribbons and Rings* (1960) sees the reluctant debutante Leslie Marsh help Shaun O'Rorke make a success of riding a wealthy owner's showjumpers, despite the determined opposition of her parents. The most detailed exploration of a relationship comes with *Horses in the Glen*. Frandia Kendrick, the daughter of a Scottish landowner, is at first seduced away from what she sees as the unexciting life with a trekking centre which her boyfriend Stephen Hartley wants to lead to the whirl of competing and smart hunts led by her friends.

In contrast to Baxter's moneyed heroines are those who approach the horse world from the opposite end of the income scale. Lindy Smith, the gipsies' daughter of *Horses in the Glen*, has to some extent taken on the behavioural models of her parents when she decides to keep the filly she finds wandering on the moors, though she knows she must belong to someone. Furiously ambitious but poor, Edie, whose only hope of succeeding with horses is to work with them, causes an accident in the pursuit of her ambition in *The Team from Low Moor* (1965). The friction between characters from different backgrounds gives Baxter scope to explore her observational talents: Stephen Hartley is described in *Horses in the Glen* as a 'gentle failure', and his girlfriend Frandia (Fran) is utterly unaware of her condescension in her dealings with Lindy:

> To Fran, Lindy was her own private good work campaign, and hardly a real person at all.

Baxter's books are well worth seeking out. She writes a good teenager, and she has a fresh and realistic approach to the world of working with horses, whose vicissitudes she understood well. She gave the girl who worked with horses, but who would probably never have one of her own, a voice. In this she was unlike many pony book authors active at the same time.

There was a great deal churned out in the 1950s which ultimately failed to satisfy. Authors need to be able to sell their books in order to survive; the climate of the 1950s, with the push from publishers to produce pony books, was not kind to some. M E Atkinson might have written better books had she not felt the urge to shove adventure down her readers' throats. The good books in this period relied on character to drive the plots. Veronica Westlake, Patience McElwee and Gillian Baxter wrote about heroes and heroines who do not have everything dropped into their laps: they have to work for what they achieve.

CHAPTER TEN
AN UNEXPECTED PLEASURE
The 1960s

The 1960s was another productive decade for pony books, at least as far as the number published went. Although the Pullein-Thompson sisters went in other directions throughout most of the 1960s, many other authors active in the 1950s kept on writing: Mary Gervaise and Judith M Berrisford added to their series fiction; Gillian Baxter and Monica Edwards both continued writing. Publishers began to produce books in cheap editions to meet demand, Monica Edwards's *Wish for a Pony* appearing in both the Children's Press and Collins Seagull imprints. Lutterworth produced the Crown Pony Library, which made hardback books available to a wider public. Sadly, their titles were mostly written by second-rank authors like Elinore Havers and Catherine Carey, producing more of the competent but uninspired pony adventure so popular in the previous decade. Peter Grey wrote the formulaic twelve-book Kit Hunter—Show Jumper series for World Books in the late 1950s and early 1960s, taking pony adventure international as it followed a champion showjumper on her dramatic adventures all over the world.

The introduction of the cheap paperback made the pony book available to a much wider public. Puffin Books' editor Kaye Webb was not keen on the pony book as a whole, but she recognised the plums of the genre, and Puffin picked up titles like Mary Treadgold's *We Couldn't Leave Dinah* and Monica Edwards's *The White Riders.* The real explosion in availability came when Collins developed their Armada imprint, Hodder & Stoughton their Knight Books and Granada their Dragon Books. All sold popular children's titles from authors like Enid Blyton and Malcolm Saville, and raided their back catalogues (and other publishers' too) for pony books to feed the still-insatiable demand. The titles they reprinted were often abridged to fit into set book lengths. Dragon took the bizarre decision to reprint the American author Mary O'Hara's lengthy books in several volumes: *My Friend Flicka* appeared in two parts, and *Thunderhead* and *The Green Grass of Wyoming* both in three. However, without these new editions many readers would not have known about the works of writers like Monica Edwards and Primrose Cumming, whose classic *Silver Snaffles* was published in an abridged version by Knight.

Although many books in the 1960s carried on what had been seen before, there were a few authors in this decade who took the pony book and did something new with it. C Northcote Parkinson wrote his lunatic *Ponies Plot*, and Vian Smith produced a series of fine equestrian novels set in his beloved Dartmoor. At the end of the 1960s, K M Peyton took the pony story to a new level with her Flambards series and *Fly-by-Night* (1968).

C Northcote Parkinson (1909–93) was one of the small band of men who wrote pony stories: of the three hundred or so British pony book authors I know about, around ten per cent are men. Northcote Parkinson was a naval historian and the codifier of Parkinson's Law, and re-wrote his definition of Parkinson's Law ('Work expands so as to fill the time available for its completion.') to fit in with his pony book: 'Muck spreads so as to cover the stable floor available.' Northcote Parkinson ended his academic career as Raffles Professor of History at the University of Malaysia in Singapore. Besides a fictional naval series and numerous naval histories, he wrote one children's book, *Ponies Plot* (1965), in which the ponies narrate the story. His children's two ponies, Fairy and Spice, inspired the book. Fairy he memorably described as 'a Welsh Pony so musically talented that she might have had a career in Grand Opera'; Spice apparently ate a copy of the book. Parkinson wrote:

> In the ordinary run of pony books the story centres on a small girl who dreams of ponies, wants a pony, secures a pony for nothing (saving it from ill-treatment in a gypsy encampment), rides it with growing confidence and ends with First Prize in the Hunter Trials. Among ponies, however, the same story would be told with the pony as hero. Ill-treated and underfed, Blackie dreams about children, wants a child for himself, plans to attract Brenda's attention, defeats the scheme of a rival pony, saves the girl from drowning, wins over the reluctant parents and finally (guess what?) wins First Prize in the Hunter Trials.

Northcote Parkinson's ponies are more in the line of Thorburn's *Hildebrand*, hen-eater and confounder of his master, than Primrose Cumming's helpful riding school ones in *Silver Snaffles*: these are quirky ponies with an individual outlook on life who tell a story that has considerable inventive energy.

Vian Smith wrote with real sympathy for both humans and horses. Smith (1919–69) was an actor and journalist, born in Totnes. He spent many of his holidays with his grandparents on their farm in Dartmoor, which became the setting for most of his books. During the war he served as a sapper, and his first book, *Song of the Unsung* (1945), was based on his experiences. Smith's world is not the peaceful, optimistic one of the 1950s. His books ask questions which will be uncomfortable to those who want an unchallenging, secure world. *Martin Rides the Moor* (1964) sees Martin, newly deaf, dealing with the attitudes of those around him to his changed condition as well as with his own difficulties. The hero of *The Horses of Petrock* (1965) is a gang member trying to break free from his old friends and his past. In the 1960s the social order was changing, the unthinking acceptance of the social hierarchy faltering. *Come Down the Mountain* (1967) sees Brenda Carter defy her village to rescue a horse. She is awkward, overweight, an outsider mocked by most of the others on the school bus. The old, half-starved horse she sees every morning from the bus window belongs to the Bassett family. Day after day, as Brenda watches the horse, winter creeps closer and the horse deteriorates. The villageers know perfectly well just what state the forgotten horse is in, but they do nothing. The Bassetts own the village. If a fuss is made there will be trouble. Better not to think about it:

> The car stopped. George Carter leaned to open a door. His expression was pale and taut. It told her to get in and say nothing. He would do the talking as soon as he'd backed and shown the car the way home.

C Northcote Parkinson: Ponies Plot

'Behaving like a fool'

Brenda opened her mouth, but her father's glance was savage.

'I don't want to hear how bad he is. Do you think I can't imagine? But there're some things you can't alter.'

The village's reaction is entirely understandable. Brenda defies the Bassetts, helped by her father and her few friends, and, in the end, by the village. But the gulf between the horse's owner, Stephen Bassett, and the villagers remains just as wide. They have spent their own money and time rescuing a horse which will never make them a profit. 'Why? That's what baffles me. Why did they do it?' says Stephen Bassett. This is not a question generally asked in the pony book. Though there are plenty of other Stephen Bassetts in horse literature, their position is usually left unchallenged. In this book, we are left with the distinct sense that there might be considerably more coming to Stephen Bassett than he imagines.

The pony as a possible item on the menu is unthinkable in a pony book, but Smith in *Moon in the River* (1969) explored what made the whole pony book genre possible: the domestication of the horse. It is set on prehistoric Dartmoor, where the main preoccupation is survival. Horses are food. The book is a fascinating exploration of how the horse first came to be regarded as more than meat. Someone, somewhere, once made the decision to ride and not eat. The book tells the story of Kurt, Onah and their father, who escape the massacre of their tribe. Living on their own, they find life even more perilous than normal, particularly as winter is approaching. The logical, the sensible thing to do would be to kill the wounded mare they capture, but Kurt comes to see in her more than just food.

There is an intensity to this book: it is about survival at the most basic level, about fear and death. Smith's picture of the wild, wounded mare is a triumph:

The mare screamed for the stallion to save her. As darkness droned down and the first stars showed like pin-pricks, she fought rope and stake in a furious crescendo, her neck and chest curdled with sweat, her sides smouldering. She tried to rear, to drag out the stake.

Even in this world, there is still room for magic. Onah has never, ever touched a live horse:

Her fingers moved to the mane, to the line where the strong, coarse hairs grew upright from the neck. The warmth was magic. It comforted her fingers. She looked across, wanting to tell Kurt how wonderful it was.

But it is not all wonderful, after all. The book ends in the death of the mare, but with the recognition that the Rubicon has been crossed. Smith's books challenge the reader. He looked at the horse and real life: he writes an excellent horse and, more importantly, fine characters.

So did K M Peyton, probably the best author of pony books. She started writing in the 1960s, is still writing today, and has contributed many fine books to the genre, although some, like *Blind Beauty* (1999), are well outside the scope of this book. Her characters live with the reader long after the book is finished: they are far more than just vehicles for equine adventures. Her books are about obsession and desire, particularly the passionate longings of teenagers, whether for horses or each other. She has a keen appreciation of the difficulties that come when one is not blessed with money, or even when suffering from that lack of it that is pony book poor. She writes about the horse world in its entirety, the mix of people who love horses: the rich and comfortable, those earning their living through horses, and those for whom horse-keeping is a constant struggle. Peyton does not judge her characters, and she writes with a real sympathy for adolescent minds both male and female.

A horse obsessive from an early age, Peyton started writing young. Her first book was finished when she was nine, though it was never published; nor were its seven successors. Her first published book, *Sabre, the Horse from the Sea*, came out in 1948, when she was nineteen. It appeared under her maiden name, Kathleen Herald, as did her next two books, *The Mandrake* (1949) and *Crab the Roan* (1953). All were pony books, although her riding experience as a child was minimal. She says:

> I devoured technical horse books from the senior library—Henry Wynmalen, Sam Marsh, Geoffrey Brooks, Faudel-Philips, R S Summerhays, etc, so I knew a lot of theory but not much else, never laying a hand on a real horse, apart from three riding lessons a year on Wimbledon Common, saved up for from my pocket money, all I could afford—five shillings an hour. (Interview with K M Peyton)

Peyton well understands the pony obsession. She read pony books: Joanna Cannan, Primrose Cumming, *Moorland Mousie*, and *The Ponies of Bunts*, which she loved so much that she still has two copies. As a child she had an extensive stable of imaginary horses, each with its own page in her notebook: 'I just thought up a new horse or pony every day, imagined how it looked, how it behaved, and wrote it down in my book until I had over 2000. My friend did it too and we discussed our new ones at school every day.' She had no horse of her own until she was an adult, and, because she could not have the real thing, made her fantasies live through her books. In *Sabre, the Horse from the Sea*, the writing has the hypnotic, erotic pulse of fantasy. Set in the Second World War, it is the story of Liza, living with rich and unsympathetic relatives while evacuated, who one day comes across a horse emerging from the sea:

> She stood with bare feet in a pool of water left by the receding tide, and looked at the grey. It did not seem strange to her to find a horse standing half in and half out of the sea, no stranger than it felt to be standing there herself. She only thought that she had never seen anything so beautiful as this animal, with the sea-water running down his legs, and with a piece of seaweed caught up in his tail.
>
> She stretched out her fingers to him. His ears came up and forward, and one hoof took a step towards her. She murmured:
>
> 'Come on you beautiful fellow,' and he walked straight up to her and rubbed his nose on her dress. Liza took off her belt and buckled it round his neck, standing on

tip-toe, and holding her breath. But the grey horse only knuckered deep in his throat, and pushed his muzzle against her hips, searching for her pockets.

Victor Watson, author of *Where Texts and Children Meet* (2000), argues that this novel, along with other similar ones by teenage authors, does not have a wide perspective with characters who change and develop over a period but instead offers 'directness, linguistic and narrative passion, and an ability to communicate the excitement and intensity of adolescence'. Peyton undoubtedly expressed this in her earlier novels, but her later ones also show she kept that ability to portray the passion of adolescence. Not only that, she wrote about what happens after the storms of passion have ended, or change their object. Ruth, the heroine of *Fly-by-Night* (1968), for example, does not maintain her passion for the horse. In *The Beethoven Medal* (1971) she has transferred her obsession from the difficult and untameable pony to the equivalent in teenage boy form: Patrick Pennington.

In 1968, Peyton wrote the first of the Flambards series, set in pre-First-World-War England. This marked a return to the horse, and to writing solo, most of the books prior to it being written with her husband (Mike, the 'M' in K M Peyton), and focusing on his obsession, sailing. K M Peyton says:

> My first real books were all based on sailing as that's what we did all the time. Three of them were runners-up for the Carnegie Medal. Then I had a great yen to go inland and write about my first love, horses, and this resulted in the Flambards series.

Flambards introduces twelve-year-old Christina, an orphan. Like her predecessor Liza (*Sabre, the Horse from the Sea*), and Ruth (*Fly-by-Night*) who was to follow, she is an isolated child. Christina has been shuttled about between relations since her parents died. When she is 21, she will inherit her parents' money and be rich, a fact that makes her suddenly attractive to her Russell relations, who are in desperate need of money to shore up their house, Flambards, and, more importantly, maintain their stables. And so she is sent off to a household where she knows no-one, and where each relative is obsessed in his own way. Her Uncle Russell is a ranting, violent, hunting-mad bully. Her cousin Mark is the favoured, arrogant son, and William (Will), the younger son, is the cuckoo in the nest who is utterly determined to build a machine that can fly. He is condemned by his father and brother as a coward because he lacks the desire and courage to throw himself and his horse over fences. 'There's never been a Russell rode as badly as William,' says Uncle Russell. It is Will with whom Christina forms an almost instant bond.

Christina has had very little to do with horses when she arrives at Flambards, but she is left in no doubt that learning to ride is essential: and not only learning, but being dashing about it. When she has been riding for only a few weeks, Mark puts her on his wild horse, Treasure. The horse bolts, taking one jump successfully but then heading for a vast thorn hedge which, if he tries to jump it, will result in certain disaster for them both. Dick, the groom, stops Treasure. Despite this experience, Christina learns to ride, and comes to appreciate the joy of riding through Dick's kindness and understanding:

Dick stood up in his stirrups and Woodpigeon started to gallop, Sweetbriar beside him, and this time Christina was confident, utterly trusting in her own ability, and in the infallibility of Dick. She looked across at him and laughed. Now it was right to be galloping: a great joy surged through her.

Though Christina is attracted to Dick, it is her cousin Will whom she comes to love, and with whom she elopes. In the succeeding books in the series, romance takes over. Christina crashes through the men in Flambards: after Will is killed in the First World War, she marries in succession Dick and, finally, Mark. With him, in *Flambards Divided* (1981), she comes at last to a sort of peace, though a controversial one. It is a book which divides Flambards fans; some feel that Christina's final settling with Mark, so spectacularly unsympathetic in the first book, is unsatisfactory.

The Flambards novels are not traditional pony books (the Carnegie Medal winner *The Edge of the Cloud*, 1969, has virtually no pony content at all). The horses are there to reveal the characters' motives and obsessions. To Mark and Uncle Russell, horses represent the only way of life they are prepared to countenance; in the pursuit of it, they ignore the estate crumbling round them, and their debts. To Will, horses represent being bullied and belittled. Horses to Christina are freedom, and the means through which she learns about life. Through riding she manages to escape some of the unhappiness of living at Flambards, and later to assert herself. Christina does become that dashing rider to hounds, 'a hunting Russell, for sure', but she does not swallow the Russells' views wholesale. After her mare Sweetbriar is seriously injured (*Flambards*), Christina fights the Russells' decision to send her to the hounds. Together with Dick and Will, she spirits the horse away. The results are disastrous. Will is severely beaten, and Dick is dismissed without a reference. Destitution is the most likely result for him and his family.

Christina has never before considered Dick, or any of the other servants, as human beings with their own lives, and now she is brought up, hard, against reality when she visits Dick and his family, riven with guilt over what she has done:

She had always thought the little village cottages picturesque, but there was nothing picturesque about the interior of this one, with its sagging, damp-stained ceiling and floor of broken flags. There were a rickety table and two hard chairs, no other furniture … Christina could not help her eyes going round nor the dismay showing in her face; yet she knew enough to realize that she was hurting him, by intruding on his poverty.

In the end, the world of the horse is sharply contrasted with the new world of machines: the old world is indeed shattered by the new. The race Mark is desperate to win is ruined when Will's flight goes wrong and his floundering plane terrifies the horses. Christina and Will elope in a Rolls-Royce; Mark tries to catch them on his horse, but fails. Christina takes the middle way: though she loves the excitement and invention of cars, she never loses her love for horses.

In this Christina is unlike Ruth, the heroine of *Fly-by-Night* (1968). This has a more conventional girl-gets-pony plot. Ruth, though pony obsessed, is not even at the periphery of the local equine world. From a family who struggle to make ends meet, the nearest she can get to a pony is skulking at the edge of the field where the local Pony Club rally is taking place. Ruth's wistful, desperate longing was a far better fit with most readers of pony books, whose circumstances meant they would never learn to ride, let alone get a pony. Peyton writes about Ruth's situation with what Marcus Crouch describes as 'unfailing realism and great good-humour':

> She ... walked over to the collecting-ring, shivering with cold and excitement. She half expected to be told to leave by one of the cold adults, but she was ignored. The girls on the ponies looked at her without expression. This suited Ruth very well. She did not want to be noticed. She only wanted to look at the ponies.

Ruth and her family have moved from London to a new house tacked onto the edge of an East Anglian village. Ruth does not like her new school. She longs for a pony; anything to do with a pony makes her virtually quiver with excitement:

K M Peyton: Fly-by Night

> She did not want her mother or Ted to see how excited she felt, and she knew it showed. She walked nonchalantly out of the room. She could feel the hot pounding of her joy in her inside: a great flushing of gorgeous anticipation. The unexpectedness of it unnerved her ... Her father told her she cared too much. 'Nothing matters that much,' he said to her quite often. But wanting a pony did.

Ruth does manage to buy a pony. She uses her National Savings, but the pony she buys, Fly, is anything but ideal. He is an unbroken three year old, 'a character', based on Cracker, the first pony Peyton bought for her daughter, Hilary. Although he eventually became a model pony, with a waiting list of Pony Club mothers wanting him for their children, Cracker's early days with the Peytons were difficult. 'He broke us in, rather than the other way round … Many of our traumas I used when I wrote *Fly-By-Night*.' It is Cracker unregenerate that we first meet as Fly-by-Night:

> He crashed down the ramp, skidded on the concrete, and pulled up, quivering, nostrils wide, held sharply by the rope halter. A quiet one, Ruth remembered, was what she should have had. No animal that she had ever seen, she thought at that moment, looked less quiet than Fly.

Ruth does not have a kind Pony Club or riding school there to help her. Fly is unbroken and difficult to handle. The Hollises' back garden very soon proves inadequate—'she thought

K M Peyton: Fly-by-Night

she had never worried so much in her life as since she had bought Fly'. But Ruth does fulfil the pony book dream. Fly is, eventually, schooled, with the help of the Hollises' foster-child, who turns out to be not the expected small child but Peter McNair, the teenage son of the local horse dealer with whom he has spectacularly fallen out. Ruth manages to provide for Fly's keep, but it is at times a desperate struggle. Ruth's whole progress through the book is summed up by her and Fly's undisciplined and wildly enthusiastic progress through the Hunter Trials. Ruth is not entirely in control of Fly, and they get lost:

> She thrust her cap back, but could still see nothing but a blur of clutching branches through which Fly-by-Night was forcing his way in a series of excited bounds. Whatever had hit her face was agonizing; she realized that she could not see for blood. When she put her hand up it came away all red.

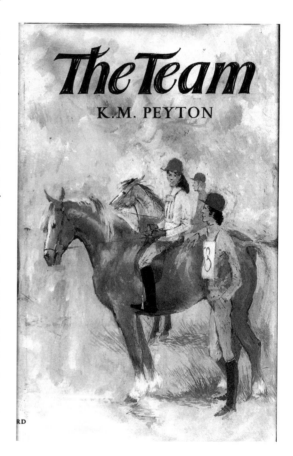

The sequel to *Fly-by-Night*, *The Team*, appeared in 1975. It was a fill-in, written after Ruth's fate with Patrick Pennington had already been decided in 1973's *Pennington's Heir*. *The Team* picks up Ruth's story at the age of fourteen. She has outgrown Fly, and so has no realistic chance of getting on the Pony Club team. If she can manage to find a larger pony, she might. *The Team* opens with a picture of the relaxed relationship between Ruth and Peter McNair, the Hollis family's former foster-child. All this changes when Ruth goes to buy a replacement for Fly at a local horse sale, and finds Peter's beloved Toadhill Flax, the one horse he wanted his father not to sell and whose going precipitated their falling out. Ruth buys Toad and tells Peter, fully expecting him to share in her excitement that she has managed to find herself another pony, and Toad at that. But Peter does not:

> Ruth looked at Peter in the lamplight.
> He looked very odd, she realized, almost shocked. She knew he was a moody character, and that his good humour and banter could subside into long periods of gloom and resentment, but she hadn't expected this reaction from him in this particular circumstance. She had been expecting him to join in a general rejoicing. His insistence that she take the pony to his home seemed to her rather like a taking-over attitude.

K M Peyton: The Team

Peter's father offers to buy Toad back, or exchange him for any pony in his stables, but Ruth—stubborn, and nearly as obsessed with the pony as Peter is—refuses. Ruth goes on, eventually, to ride Toad more or less successfully, and to repair her relationship with Peter. *The Team* maintained Peyton's firm grip on realism: Ruth is unable to take part in a competition because it coincides with the first day of her period, and she is too unwell to ride. The interest of the book lies in far more than the usual what-the-pony-did-next—it is in the relationships between the characters and how they work out.

Peyton is just as good at male characters as female, at adult as at child. The awkward relationship between Jonathan Meredith, a fellow Pony Club team member, and his mother, developed over several books, is equally compelling. Jonathan is never the horse obsessive that Peter and Ruth are. His riding is done in part because Mrs Meredith, the über-Pony Club mother, drives her children on. In *Prove Yourself a Hero* (1977) Jonathan is kidnapped. He and his family react in their different ways to his kidnapping and subsequent release, but it is the portrayal of the Meredith parents, easy to write off as heartless, which is the most interesting. Jessica, Jonathan's sister, describes what she thinks will happen when or if Jonathan is released:

> 'You know, even if he does come back all right, I think everything is going to be awful for a bit.'
> 'How so? Great rejoicings all round, I would have said.'
> 'Well, you know what they're like … I mean, it's not actually losing the money, but being—well—sort of beaten, I suppose.'

'Held to ransom. Having to do what someone else wants, for a change.'

'Yes. I'm sure they won't just forget it. I think it's going to be horrid .... I bet, when they get over being glad to see Jonathan, they'll be cross with him,' Jessica said.

They are. They are even more so in *The Last Ditch* (1984), after Jonathan is tricked into making love to a fellow sixth-former, Iris, and she becomes pregnant. But it is what Mrs Meredith sees as Jonathan's desertion of Iris and the baby that she minds more, after Jonathan and Peter seek refuge from their problems by keeping and training a racehorse, Dogwood, for the Grand National.

Ruth enters adulthood in the same crashing fashion as that in which she met the world of the pony. In *The Beethoven Medal* she transfers her obsession to Patrick Pennington. Although she has a plan to work with horses once she leaves school, this falls utterly by the wayside once she meets Patrick:

> It occurred to her, quite inappropriately, that once these strange feelings had been to do with ponies and winning something very special, the times when she had looked at the sky and been filled with inexplicable longings. It was the only thing she had to compare this present ache with.

After Ruth becomes pregnant very young, she and Patrick have a stormy relationship. Peyton's characters have a lot to contend with: the author does not leave them marooned at the childhood stage. Alison Haymonds argues that in pony books 'the seeds of the adult relationships the girls will have to cope with are sown'. For Ruth, and for Peyton's heroines and heroes who were to follow, learning to live is part of the books, and we see them grow into adulthood.

It is difficult to think of a poor book by Peyton. With her, the pony book reached its finest expression. John Rowe Townsend says 'she knows in her fingers how to handle a boat or a horse ...', and in all her novels there is 'the moment of rejoicing at simply being here, to love and suffer and take what comes'. Her characters really do grow up, and what is most important to them changes as they age: with Ruth it is ponies, then Patrick Pennington; with Christina it is Will, then Flambards. Joy Whitby, writing in *Twentieth-Century Children's Writers*, says that all Peyton's characters are determined to 'achieve whatever is most important at the time'. Ruth's transference from ponies to boys is a transference of that desire to look after, to tame the difficult. Over the course of the Pennington books, Ruth learns that human beings are not as amenable to schooling as a horse. Christina in Flambards, too, comes to accept her place in post-war society; never a fitter-in, she remains a figure set apart. While Peyton's novels are about passion and desire, they are also about accepting the results of that passion.

The 1960s was in many ways the last flowering of the pony book. Paperback publishing widened what was available to the reader, and meant that writers' back catalogues had a life. The stimulation of demand ensured that new titles kept coming to the market. Sadly, much of what was published was derivative, but there were a few, a very few, inventive new authors like Vian Smith and K M Peyton determined to give children the best.

CHAPTER 11
'AND A FAST HORSE GAVE YOU WINGS'
Patricia Leitch and Monica Dickens

The 1970s saw a falling-off in quality, and in numbers, of pony books, with just over half as many being printed in that decade as had been in the 1960s. However, perhaps in response to a generation more likely to watch fast-moving adventures on television than read a book, the pony adventure story, the sub-genre so popular in the 1950s, reappeared in even greater numbers.

There was not a great deal of innovation in the 1970s, but it was in this decade that two major authors in the genre produced their most notable work. In 1963, Monica Dickens had written *Cobbler's Dream*, an uncompromising and at times bleak adult novel about Follyfoot, a home of rest for horses. In the early 1970s, a television series called *Follyfoot* appeared which developed the characters' stories (although it changed some of their names). Monica Dickens then wrote four books—the Follyfoot series—to tie in with the television programmes. The greatest pony series of the 1970s, however, and one which is now being reprinted, owed nothing to television at all. Patricia Leitch's Jinny books combined

Monica Dickens and cast members of Follyfoot

mysticism, a teenage heroine completely in tune with her readers, and a wild Arabian mare. It was an intoxicating mix.

Monica Dickens's pony books were earthier. They do not feature comfortable middle-class children and neat pony adventures; the difficulty of surviving without a steady source of income is a recurring theme, as is the mistreatment of animals. Dickens (1915–92), the great-granddaughter of Charles Dickens, came from a privileged background. After being expelled from St Paul's School for Girls for throwing her school uniform over Hammersmith Bridge, she did not take the conventional route of her class: a social whirl as a debutante followed by marriage. Instead, she went out to earn her living, and, as described in her autobiographical *One Pair of Hands* (1939), became a cook-general. She then worked as a nurse and a journalist and in 1951 married Commander Roy Stratton, a former US Marines Officer, and moved to the United States. Having worked with both the Samaritans (she founded the first American branch in Boston in 1974) and the RSPCA, she had a keen appreciation of the cruelty to which humanity could stoop.

Dickens's first equine novel, *Cobbler's Dream*, intended as an adult novel, and sold in its Puffin paperback printing as one for teenagers, is considerably more graphic than most children's pony series; the incidences of cruelty and neglect described are, in some cases, horrific. The book opens with Cobbler's Dream, a successful showjumping pony, being beaten by his spoiled and vindictive owner, Chrissy. The pony is left blind in one eye; the other will probably also lose its sight, and Chrissy's father decides to have the pony put down and collect the insurance. Paul, his ex-Borstal groom, leaves enough money to buy the pony and spirits him away, both of them ending up at a home of rest for horses, Follyfoot Farm. The farm is home to a collection of worn-out, wounded and awkward beings, both human and equine.

Life at Follyfoot Farm is a struggle—a struggle to find enough money to support the animals, to rescue suffering animals, and to manage the horses—with a cast of disparate and not always sympathetic characters. The Captain, who runs the farm, is generally unsentimental, but in *Cobbler's Dream* he is unable to take the decision to put down the aged pit pony, Charley, even after the vet recommends it:

> 'My doctor,' the vet said, 'envies me because I can release my patients when they're past it and get to be a problem. It's not the patients that's the problem, I tell him. It's the owners.'

In a book which is otherwise bleakly realistic, Charley is found by Tom, the miner who used to look after him, just before the pony dies. It is a moot point whether what then happens is sentimentality, or, as it is portrayed in the book, sensitivity:

> Corinne was not there, fortunately, to cry: 'Oh, he knows him! Look, he's trying to say he's glad in his own funny way. If only he could speak!'
> But the Captain saw, and Dora saw, that there was something in the stable that could not be expressed in words. Charley looked the same—grizzled, sagging, bearded, with

a blurred blue eye and a loose wet jaw. And yet there was an unmistakeable difference, a rallying of the spirit, as if Tom's voice and touch awoke in him as many memories as the sight and feel of him brought surging back to Tom.

The Follyfoot books which sprang from *Cobbler's Dream* were less hard-hitting but still a world away from the conventional pony story. The series ran to four books: *Follyfoot* (1971), *Dora at Follyfoot* (1972), *The Horses of Follyfoot* (1975) and *Stranger at Follyfoot* (1976). Although marketed as a tie-in to the TV series, the books did not simply parrot its storylines. Dickens maintained her own take on her creations, though it confused readers who had come to them from the television series. Suzy, the administrator of a Follyfoot Internet Forum, describes the book series as 'confusing as it wasn't very much like the TV series I watched avidly in the 70s. In the book Steve was called Paul, Dora wasn't the pretty TV Dora but a more horsy, down-to-earth girl, Ron hardly appears at all, the Colonel was called the Captain and Slugger had a wrestling wife called Tiny!' But Dickens's style hooked her readers in despite these differences. Sabrina, the moderator of the Follyfoot Forum, says:

Monica Dickens' writing style worked its magic on me. She was a very engaging writer, using the second person to draw the readers in and make them feel part of the book. In her Follyfoot series it's a crueller world than the TV show, particularly with *Cobbler's Dream*, which is certainly adult/young adult rather than children's fiction. The subsequent books in the series tamed down the violence and cruelty somewhat, but the writing style was the same—engaging, with beautiful bursts of humour, and best of all the books don't treat the readers as children in terms of vocabulary or character development.

The series in book form has some of the normal girl-loves-pony passion, provided by teenage Dora, who works at the farm, and Callie, whose mother marries the Captain, but it also has an eccentric panoply of adult characters who provide a depth of experience rare in the pony book world: the Captain; Callie's family; the stable worker Ron Stryker, essentially lazy and selfish; Slugger Jones, the ex-wrestler who also helps look after the horses. In most pony stories, a pony is rescued from dire circumstances and then goes on to win prizes; that does not happen here. The horses and ponies rescued are often incapable of being ridden. The books have important things to say about what takes place after the pony book dream has passed: what happens to those horses and ponies who have done the gymkhana and show, grown old and are no longer wanted.

Dickens's other pony series, World's End, had its initial premise in that hoary chestnut of children's book plots, the absent adults. The pony book does not tend to enter this world. There are any number of unaccompanied treks, and the occasional journey to escape from an unpleasant situation to a better one, but survival on one's own for any length of time with animals is such an implausible task that it is almost never attempted in fiction. One of the very few exceptions is this series. The first book, *The House at World's End* (1970), opens with the Fielding family—Tom, Em, Carrie and Michael—and their animals living with their Uncle Rudolph and Aunt Valentina. Their father is trying to sail round the world; their mother is in hospital after being severely burned.

The Fieldings are initially agog with excitement when Uncle Rudolph, only too glad to get rid of the children, allows them to live in an old pub he has bought, World's End, and be supported by the teenage Tom, as long as he can find a job. Carrie, whose love of horses means she has a dream world peopled by horses that talk, is delighted by the move. At last she will be able to have a horse, she thinks. And the animals do appear, rescued from cruelty by the children, but life for the family is a constant and at times desperate struggle. Social workers pursue them, and the family being taken into care is only averted by the last-minute appearance of their mother, spirited out of hospital too early by Tom. In only one book of the succeeding three are the Fielding parents present. In *World's End in Winter* (1972) their father is shut away in his study, writing a book about the unsuccessful attempt to sail round the world that took him away in *Summer at World's End* (1971). The parents are off sailing again in the last book of the series, *Spring Comes to World's End* (1973), crewing yachts to try to earn enough money to buy World's End.

This series is peopled by a cast of characters often larger than life: Mr Mismo and his fat, much-boasted-of cob, Princess Margaret Rose, and Carrie's friend Lester, completely unbound by rules. Uncle Rudolph and Aunt Valentina are at times almost cartoonishly awful. Virtually every appearance they make offers a new opportunity to smile at their towny pretensions. There is a sly humour that makes the exaggeration bearable. Aunt Valentina has some finer feelings, though she does an excellent job of suppressing them, in the interests of maintaining her own lifestyle:

'That boy sounds wheezy,' Valentina said. 'Are you sure you're all right here on your own?' Her painted face was twisted with the struggle between feeling she ought to say, 'You must come back with us,' and dreading they might say, 'Yes.'"

The books are not depressing. The children's passion for animals, and their ability to carry on despite dreadful setbacks, are cheering, and underlying it all is Dickens's sly observational humour. Carrie and Michael make money for the horses' keep over winter by selling manure. They smell all the time, and their sister Em will not sit in the same room with them.

The series has considerable charm, appealing as it does to what the critic Nicholas Tucker calls 'a host of pre-adolescent fantasies and prejudices'. He goes on to say that this is 'at a uniformly undemanding and facile level'. Most children, I think, knew perfectly well it was a fantasy: the charm of the books is that they bring the fantasy almost within reach. Alison Flood, writing in *The Guardian* on the books' reissue, says: 'In this case it felt like the loving, but scatty and selfish, Fielding parents' departure on a sailing trip could actually have happened.'

Spring Comes to World's End is the weakest of the four books. In the end, it is adult benevolence that ensures the family can stay at World's End, but that only comes about as a result of a thoroughly unrealistic kidnapping. But the exaggeration, on the whole, works. The overriding impression left by the series is of the charm of the family's life with animals, allied to the precariousness of their financial situation. The elder brother Tom's job at the vet's is not secure; and, when it seems as if all will finally be well, Uncle Rudolph starts to demand rent.

It is the children who are truly the heroes; the children's father is, alas, just the feckless, self-absorbed being his brother Rudolph thinks he is. Mrs Fielding is too kind, or too blinkered, to tell her husband that any plan to write a book with her as the glamorous swim-suited companion will not work; when the two go off manning yachts in an attempt to earn enough money to buy World's End (*Spring Comes to World's End*), on one occasion Mr Fielding leaves his earnings in a jacket pocket, forgetting to tell his wife he has done so, and she gives the jacket away to a beggar. When Uncle Rudolph gives World's End to the Fieldings in gratitude for their rescue of his wife from kidnappers, he makes it over to the children, not their father:

'I've given it away.' Uncle Rudolf paused for an eternity.
'To you. Not to that feckless father of yours. He'd gamble it away, or set fire to it, or let it get dry rot.' (*Spring Comes to World's End*)

Like Dickens's other series, World's End is occasionally subject to unlikely plot devices—why Valentina should be kidnapped is never made clear. The incident does, however, reveal an unexpected softness of feeling in Uncle Rudolph, and of course serves its main purpose by allowing the Fieldings to keep World's End.

Monica Dickens's books are bleaker than most pony books; the goodness of humanity has to struggle against considerably more than normal, and at times it is not enough. Neither of her pony series is set in a comfortable and predictable world. Survival is not certain. The amount that horses cost, and the knowledge needed to take care of them properly, are facts that are hammered home. But both series are far more than protests against animal mistreatment; their spiky and exuberant casts of characters ensure that both, in the end, fall just about on the side of the angels.

Before Patricia Leitch's Jinny series was launched in 1976, she had written a range of solid (and at times outstanding) pony stories. Despite this, she was not well known. Only a few of her books had made it into paperback by the early 1970s, although she had by that time written fifteen titles, four under the name Jane Eliot. This belies just how good her books were: she rarely wrote a poor one. Alison Haymonds considers her as one of the major writers in the genre. *Dream of Fair Horses* (1975) she describes as 'a remarkable work of imagination', and the Jinny series as 'still deservedly popular'.

Patricia Leitch (1933–) was born in Paisley, Scotland. She had a varied career, but her jobs as a riding instructor, librarian and primary school teacher all honed her ability to communicate. Despite two teaching careers, Leitch did not write didactic books. She understood the longings of the ponyless: she had to wait until adulthood before she bought her own first pony, Kirsty, a Fell-Highland cross who 'almost broke her', and who provided the inspiration for many of the Highland ponies who feature in her books. She understood, too, the haunting equines who stalked the imaginations of her readers, and she created one of the most vivid of them all: Shantih, a creature so real that some readers have gone on, years later, to buy their own chestnut Arab mares. Shantih was, Leitch wrote in correspondence with me, 'all dream. In fact, I used to dream about the chestnut Arab mare long before I wrote about her … I still feel, if I could walk out onto the moor and call her she would hear and come galloping over the skyline to me. But then what is imagination for if not to call up the past?'

Shantih

The Jinny series introduced new elements into a genre in which mysticism was a rare visitor, and a wild, tantrumming heroine even more so. There are two intertwining worlds in the books: the everyday one of family life and going to school, and that of the ancient spirits and Celtic gods who inhabit the moors. Leitch's earlier books had hints of what was to come—wild Scottish settings, Highland and Arab ponies, teenage drama, and, occasionally, mysticism—but these early titles were rather more prosaic than the Jinny books. They were influenced, at least in style, by the Pullein-Thompsons and their mother, Joanna Cannan. Angy, the heroine of *Riding Course Summer* (1963), comes out with sentences that could have trotted, unaltered, from a Cannan heroine: 'She said that I was the most careless child that she had ever known and a lot more meaning the same thing.' That is not to say the early books are bad; they are not. Margery Fisher commends *Janet, Young Rider* (1963) for its 'exceptional character interest as well as good technical details'.

From the start, Leitch did not enter wholeheartedly into writing the pony story as a fairy tale. Her first book, *To Save a Pony* (1960), although it nods to several conventional elements of the pony book genre, showed that its author was not going to produce plots that provided pat solutions. The Dallas family relocate to Scotland and start a riding school. They go to a local horse sale to find ponies, and Jane sees a pony she is desperate to save. However, no miraculous means to buy the pony appear, and Jane has to wait until the end of the book before she sees the pony again, when she discovers her condemned to the dreadful pony book fate of pulling a cart. But Jane is writing a pony book, and she is sure that if she can only get the manuscript to a publisher, it will provide her with enough money to buy the pony. (This had worked for other pony book heroines, Josephine Pullein-Thompson's Christabel in *I Had Two Ponies* for one.) Gregory, who runs the riding school and has lived with the family since he was five, challenges Jane.

> 'And where will you get twenty pounds from? No, don't tell me. I can guess. Your book!'
> 'Well, why not?' I demanded.
> 'Jane! Jane! Jane! Will you never grow up? Things like that just don't happen. You've got to face up to it that life is brutal and hard and not a fairy tale with you as the principal fairy godmother.'

Her book is rejected.

Jane does get the money, but only by conquering her fear and doing what she has flatly refused to do before: jump a pony in a show. An author refusing to allow the pony book heroine to be 'the principal fairy godmother' was almost heretical at the time: title after title saw miserable ponies rescued by the strenuous efforts of the heroine. In Leitch's world, which was a more realistic one than most, girls do not necessarily get ponies. The heroine of *Riding Course Summer* doesn't have a pony at the beginning of the book, and she still doesn't by the end.

Patricia Leitch maintained her ability to detach herself from her characters; she could stand back and see the humour in some of the situations in which pony lovers find themselves. The pony book can be a humourless beast (and the Jinny books, for all their strength, cannot be said to be funny), but among her books Patricia Leitch produced several which show a wry and understated humour. She was a fine observer of family dynamics. In *Riding Course Summer* Angy has set up a riding course, but won't be able to take part herself, as she has no pony. She bemoans the fact to her family:

> 'I do wish I had a pony,' I told my family.
> 'I do wish I had a fridge,' said Mummy.

'I do wish I had a new suit,' said Daddy. And if Liz had been in she would have said that she did wish she had a new typewriter.

The later *Pony Surprise* (1974) has one of those identikit pony book titles which leads the reader to assume it is a conventional trot around the usual tropes. The book is much better than that. Ewan and Penny are both pony mad, but have no pony. Their potter friend, Miss Frobisher, who knows virtually nothing about ponies, agrees to look after a friend's Highland, Augustus, for the summer. The children are delighted, and offer to take the burden of pony care from her. Augustus has other ideas. From the moment he appears, it is clear that he's not a pony to be trifled with:

> It was not the first time that Augustus had met children who stared at him with a gymkhana look in their eyes. In his long life Augustus had often had to deal with such children.

Harold, the pony in *Cross Country Pony* (1965), is a similar hard case. Jinty, who rides him, says:

> Cynically Harold regarded me, a gleam in his wicked little eyes. I was absolutely at his mercy. It was merely a question of what he decided to do with me.

Leitch was just as acute at describing the settings of her books. Her powers of description are way beyond those of most authors in the genre, where the setting is completely unimportant compared with the pony and its doings. The wild beauty of Scotland springs off the page in what was an atypical book in her early works, *The Black Loch* (1963). Kay Innes and two of her cousins, Sara and Edgar, are going to stay with their uncle Vincent and his family in Deersmalen, the family home in the Highlands. The exact reason for their going takes time to emerge: the Innes family are guardians of the Water Horse. A giant black horse, it lives in a loch, occasionally emerging to thunder across the glens. It seems to be a lone survival—no others are ever mentioned, and it appears to be extraordinarily long-lived, as the Innes family have protected it for generations. Nevertheless, it is as much a beast as any other that lives in the world, and Kay rides it away from danger when its freedom is threatened. Its existence

Patricia Leitch: The Black Loch

is never explained: it is there to act as a symbol for all those things better left alone and not interfered with by man. The horse's survival is threatened by those who learn of its existence and want to capture and study it rather than let it live free. It, and the Scotland it inhabits, are untamed and beautiful:

> We rose over the last of the encircling hills, and stretching away in a billion sparkling diamonds was an island-fretted sea. Without pausing the Horse sped down towards it.

Leitch's real-life horses are similarly magnificent. She understands the almost mystical reverence the observer can feel for the horse. The part-Arab Falcon in *Rebel Pony* (1973) 'jumped for the joy of it, jumped as a salmon swims or an eagle soars'. And Shantih, the Arabian star of the Jinny books, 'moved round the ring like a bright flame, her pricked ears delicate as flower petals   After the dull ache of the rosinbacks, she was all light and fire.' (*For Love of a Horse*, 1976)

In Leitch's tenth book, *Jacky Jumps to the Top* (revised 1973), the eponymous heroine rides the pony she hopes to buy, Flicka:

> And in those moments nothing existed for Jacky but the willing pony beneath her, the surge and power of the gallop and the freedom of the open land and sky. They had escaped from time. No yesterday. No tomorrow. Only now. The drumming freedom of the now.

It is a temptation to want to possess that beauty, one that Leitch explores in *Dream of Fair Horses* (1975), which preceded the Jinny series. Gill Caridia is one of a family of seven whose father, Laurence, is an author. He writes 'strange novels' which critics love but nobody buys. He has now written a pot-boiler, a detective novel, which has sold very well, and out of the proceeds he has bought back the family home, Hallows Noon. Gill, the only horse lover of the family, discovers a field of horses and a beautiful grey pony at the other side of a lake. Gill is desperate to discover to whom the pony belongs, and to ride her if she can. Eventually she meets the pony's owner, Mr Ramsay, and is asked to ride her. It is a magical experience:

> Perdita changed from a trot, her hoofs pounding the ground. Suddenly she broke out of the circle and flung herself madly away from the rein. She snaked her head, her tangled mane tossing and wild and then she reared up, touched down and reared again proud and defiant. For a second she balanced there. It was as if a tree had sprung from the ground surging in the instant from a seed to a full blossomed tree, blazing and brilliant. As if for a second I could hear the rage of the sun.
>
> I caught my breath and heard Mr Ramsay laughing with a deep gravel sound. A flow, a current, strong as an electric shock passed between the three of us.

Gill loves Perdita with every fibre of her being. To Gill, because she loves her, the pony is hers. And when Mr Ramsay dies, he leaves the pony to Gill, not to his family. But by this time financial disaster has closed in upon the Caridias again. Hallows Noon has had to be sold to pay their debts and they are on the move again, probably to inner-city Birmingham. There will be no fields, no stable, and no money: no way to keep Perdita. Gill thrashes round frantically trying to find a way, but her father points out with a relentless lack of sympathy just how hopeless the case is.

> 'You can't keep her the way she should be kept. Can't afford to feed her. But you don't care, that doesn't matter; as long as you can possess her, you don't care what happens to her.'
>
> 'But I love her.'
>
> 'Love! You call what you want to do to Perdita love? You only want to hold on to her, never let her go. She's bred for the show ring … Do you think she'd be happy shivering in a field while you deliver your papers …'

Gill lets Perdita go. By the end of the book she has met a boy, and plans to live in a commune with him 'to build a new way of living together, or sharing love': a doubly poignant ending, as Gill has reached peace with herself over Perdita, but we suspect she has still more to learn about the nature of life and love. With the Jinny books that followed, Leitch carried on exploring what it means to want to possess another living thing.

Leitch started the Jinny series after her publishers, Collins, asked her to write a three-book series about a girl and her horse. Twelve books eventually followed, tracing the adventures of

Jinny and her Arabian mare, Shantih, the series only ending because Collins was taken over, and the resulting company dropped it. The Jinny books have kept their popularity; they are being republished today. Jinny seems to have a quite extraordinary ability to fasten herself into her readers' lives. Having interviewed the author and published the results online, I get letters from Jinny fans, many talking about what an impact the books had on them as teenagers—they talk of the 'hours of joy and comfort' they had from the series, of how 'her Jinny series was responsible for getting me through teenagerdom'. One reader, Jess Allen, says:

… it is remarkable how influential her books were for me—probably the single most influential source—from her writing to the underlying philosophy and horsemanship, particularly valuing the actual relationship one has with one's horse, as … an individual and not as an object or vehicle for competing.

The series opens, in *For Love of a Horse*, with the Manders family packing up their house in Stopton. Mr Manders has inherited money from his mother, and is taking his family to live in the Highlands of Scotland, where he plans to support the family through a new career as a potter. His daughter Jinny is a talented artist but has no love for school, and will miss little of Stopton save her art teacher, who loads the departing girl up with art materials, determined that she will not give up her painting.

On the way up to their new house, Finmory, the family stop off overnight, and go to see a circus. There Jinny sees Shantih, 'Yasmin the killer horse', ill-treated and wild. When an accident to her travelling wagon decants Shantih onto the moors, Jinny begins an obsessive pursuit of the mare, who eludes the girl until she finds her close to death, nearly frozen in the harshness of the Highland winter. After Jinty nurses Shantih back to health, she buys the mare from the farmer who bought her from the ringmaster after her escape.

Jinny dreams of becoming like the pony book heroines she reads about, but her efforts to ride the recovered Shantih meet with dismal and constant failure:

'Always finish your schooling on a happy note so that both rider and mount feel satisfied with what they have achieved,' Jinny quoted from her book. 'So that's what we'll do. Not that we've achieved much,' she added, knowing that if she tried to take Shantih round the field twice there wouldn't be a happy note. (*A Devil to Ride*, 1976)

Successful show ring appearances are not, as is the case in earlier Leitch stories, the central point of these books. Jinny may have swallowed the pony book dream of competition success, but much of the series is taken up with her coming to terms with Shantih's essential nature, and with learning to share. Alison Haymonds comments that in earlier books, like *Dream of Fair Horses*, Leitch had 'serious things to say about the dangers of trying to possess living beings', and she continues this exploration with Jinny. Jinny's love for Shantih is all-consuming, and possessive. She wants the pony-girl dream in which Shantih is the horse only she can ride. But it is Ken, the eighteen-year-old former offender who lives with the Manders family, who rides the mare effortlessly:

Jinny could just make out the comforting whisper of his voice as he soothed Shantih, gentled her, assured her of the rightness of the world when he was with her. Jinny sighed to herself, feeling her own distress flow out of her into the calm silence of the hills. She let go of her jealousy—jealousy that Ken could ride her horse better than she could. It didn't seem worth bothering about. There was nothing in Ken that said, 'Look at me. See how clever I am.' He only showed you how easy it all was, how simple, if you would only learn to let it be. (*A Devil to Ride*)

Jinny does succeed in schooling Shantih, and manages the mare with tact and sensitivity, but it is the combination of speed and the utter joy of being with her horse that she loves most:

> Over the moors they galloped. Dry-stone walls rose up before them and fell away behind them as Shantih soared over them and galloped on. There was no tomorrow, only this now of space and light. Joy in Shantih, and in this flying freedom sang through Jinny's whole being. She rode entranced, the Arab mare part of her own being. On and on they went. (*The Magic Pony*, 1982)

It may be hard to let someone share your mare when they can ride infinitely better than you; it is much harder when they are worse. In *The Summer Riders* (1977) Bill and Marlene Thorpe, two children Mr Manders knows from his time as a probation officer, are to stay during the summer. Jinny is appalled, having planned a summer full of horses and improving Shantih, and is anything but accommodating to Marlene. The visitor longs to ride Shantih; Jinny is utterly determined not to let her. Eventually Jinny comes to appreciate Marlene and to understand something of what her life is like with a criminal brother she will probably spend her whole life trying to protect. Jinny finally appreciates that other people are as entitled as she to experience the wild joy that Shantih brings:

Jinny knew that it was what she would have wanted to do if she had been Marlene.

If she had had to leave Shantih tomorrow and go back to Stopton, Jinny would have wanted to gallop by herself over the sands of Finmory Bay; to be alone with Shantih, sharing the ecstasy of galloping together—the freedom, the joy. To hoard the moments in her mind so that she would always have them there, to bring them out, to re-live them, during the black times … The part of Jinny that clutched tight and hard on to anything that belonged to her had released its hold, just a little bit.

And in the tenth book of the series, *Jump for the Moon* (1988), Jinny finally manages to let Shantih go. She finds out that the mare was stolen from her breeder, who comes up to see Wildfire, as she was known. Jinny is raging and desperate, but comes to terms with the parting. As she rides the mare into the last round of a show jumping class, she says: 'Fast as the wind … It's the last time. Make it the best.' After the glorious, triumphant gallop round the ring when they have won the class, Jinny hands the mare over:

'She's yours,' said Jinny, looking up at the blazing saffron eyes and the streaked hair of Mrs Raynor. 'I'm glad you found her.' And again Jinny held out Shantih's reins to her.

But Mrs Raynor has come only to see that Jinny is the right person for her mare, and she gives Shantih to her.

Jinny fails frequently, but she is a fighter. She is part of a loving family, but is slowly separating herself from it and learning to find her feet in the adult world, as many of her readers must have been. She is pigheaded and stubbornly pursues her desire for conventional equestrian success, despite knowing what Shantih is like. In *A Devil to Ride* she makes friends with wealthy Clare Burnley purely because Clare is a success at shows and Jinny believes the girl will be able to help her make Shantih a well-schooled, competitive horse. Jinny knows full well that Clare is a selfish bully, but she manages to suppress the knowledge, dazzled by the golden glory of the Burnleys' wealth and their apparent achievement of the successful equine dream she wants:

'D'you think,' Jinny asked her mother, 'you could alter that pair of Petra's cavalry twill trousers for me?'

Arms full of shopping, half in, half out of the car, Mrs Manders turned in astonishment.

'I've been trying to get you to try them on for months!' she exclaimed. 'Whatever made you think of them just now?'

'Dunno,' said Jinny, but she did. Clare had been wearing cavalry twills. (*A Devil to Ride*)

Leitch brilliantly captures Jinny's dazzling by those who seem to have everything she ever wanted: she wants to be like them, dress like them, impress them. Clare is a constant selfish presence in the books, though at the end Jinny realises that they have more in common than she thought: in *Running Wild* (1988) they are both competing in a long-distance ride, which ends in disaster for Clare after she loses her way in the fog. When Jinny finds her, Clare's first concern is her horse. Jinny's is too.

Jinny has more to contend with than just difficult humanity: the supernatural and the mystical force their way into her life, much as she desperately wants them not to. So does literature. Besides including elements of Buddhism, Christianity and Celtic mythology, Leitch must also be the only pony author to quote Kerouac. Jinny is in some ways a younger Gill Caridia: by the end of *Dream of Fair Horses*, Gill is old enough to have a boyfriend and, one suspects, might not long remain a horse devotee. Jinny retains her passion for horses, and in particular for Shantih, throughout the series. Shantih (whose name, ironically, means 'peace') is the wild, difficult thing who can never be really possessed, and the story of the series is Jinny's and Shantih's own interpretations of peace.

Epona, the Celtic Goddess of the Horse, is personified through the Red Horse that stalks Jinny's dreams and the mysterious man known as The Watcher who communicates with her more directly in later books. *Night of the Red Horse* (1978) has archaeologists visiting Finmory to look at the mural of the Red Horse on Jinny's bedroom wall. A statue of Epona had been found nearby many years ago and given to a small collection in Inverburgh, the Wilton Collection. The archaeologists want that statue, and if they can't have it they are keen to take whatever else they can find, particularly as they are convinced there is another statue still buried. Once they have visited, Jinny starts to see the Red Horse: staring, alive, from her mural; in the fire; and in her dreams. The conventional pony book world is here used as a counterpoint to Jinny's utter terror of the Red Horse. *Night of the Red Horse* is a genuinely disturbing book, unlike the placid, fluffy unicorn adventures which were to succeed it as the pony book attempted to combine the mystical with the pony. The Red Horse is ferocious, relentless; night after night it haunts Jinny's dreams. One particularly dreadful night, Jinny cowers by the Aga, reading her favourite pony book, using it as a sponge to soak up her terrors:

No danger. No dreams. Only summer days filled with riding school ponies. They held back the terror of the Red Horse.

Unlike those many, many pony books where the major problem is whether or not a rosette will be won at the gymkhana, Jinny's problem is the Red Horse, and the haunting, screaming nightmare that awaits her when she sleeps:

> The need for sleep was a lead weight inside her head. In a moment of total terror, Jinny knew that she must sleep, and that in her sleep the Red Horse was still waiting for her.

Jinny's fear of the Red Horse is worse than its reality; as the personification of Epona, it leads Jinny to find the missing statue, and eventually, to reunite the two statues in the Wilton Collection. Susanna Forrest, writing about the Jinny books in her equine memoir *If Wishes Were Horses*, said that Jinny 'learns to have an existence that overlays the two worlds like lamination, the older richer Celtic world enhancing the modern and showing her which parts of it are false'.

Patricia Leitch's world was not the conventional, Sunday morning church-going one of earlier pony book heroines, though Jinny and Ken are just as open to Christianity as they are to Epona and her wild horses. The eleventh book in the series, *Horse of Fire* (1986), has Jinny and Shantih taking part in a nativity play put on by the local minister. Jinny is as open-minded about this as she is about mythology: if the series has a message, it is of acceptance of belief, no matter what that might be.

Jinny is a completely recognisable teenager: stubborn, determined on her own way, frequently refusing to listen to wiser counsel, and finding her own way to salvation. It is in the accuracy of her portrayal of a moody, tempestuous teenager, clashing with family, friends and society, that Patricia Leitch succeeded in moving beyond the traditional pony book. Susanna Forrest wrote: 'Leitch's great strength was to make both those worlds vivid and real.'

Marcus Crouch wrote that in the 1960s the pony book was 'almost dead, killed by sheer exhaustion of possibilities and also, perhaps, by affluence—for children who have a pony hardly need the vicarious experiences offered by pony stories …'. He saw K M Peyton as the pony book's saviour: maybe she was, but some writers who followed her, such as Patricia Leitch, also deserve to be remembered.

My Favourite Pony Book: *Dream of Fair Horses* by Patricia Leitch

I discovered this remarkable novel when I was fourteen and I have never forgotten it. It is a story of a girl and a beautiful horse—the quintessential quest story, in the mythology of pony literature—the young heroine who dreams of horses and overcomes obstacles to be united with her pony, and to triumph at the show. So far, so ordinary. What made this book so extraordinary, for me, was the beautiful, lyrical writing; the heroine, Gill Caridia, and her amazing bohemian family; the vivid poetic descriptions of the pony Perdita; and the themes of self-actualisation, connection and freedom that add a moving philosophical thread to the book.

I was utterly enchanted by the end of the first, brief chapter. Gill Caridia is one of seven children. Her father—wild-eyed, black-haired, oddly dressed—is a critically acclaimed, commercially unsuccessful writer of 'strange novels'. The children are all bright, eccentric and unconventional. Gill's passion is horses: 'I lived in a dream world where horses moved ghostlike at my side. I went to new schools, riding an Arab stallion who moved windfleet beneath me.' Every night she prays to ride at the Horse of the Year Show.

At the birth of his seventh child, Gill's impecunious father capitulates by writing a thriller, a commercial success that enables him to buy the gloriously named Hallows Noon: a grand, dilapidated house in the country, by a lake. Here Gill sees the horse of her dreams, the lovely Perdita. Gill's fledgling riding talent is recognised by the pony's elderly owner, Mr Ramsay, and they work together over the year to prepare Perdita for the Horse of the Year show.

Patricia Leitch taps into the passionate, fairy-tale yearning of girls in which horses aren't simply interesting animals but the key to transformation, the path to a larger, more marvellous, magical realm:

> I was no longer a skinny, ugly girl on an old pony that didn't belong to me. I was changed to Velvet on The Pie, Gandalf on Shadowfax, Bellerophon on Pegasus, Tom o' Bedlam astride his horse of air. The magic that had haunted my life for as long as I could remember was still as powerful as ever.

The book is crammed with brilliant scenes: Laurence Caridia visiting Gill's headmaster; Gill's sister Fran's bizarre pop career; the touching references to Gill's relationship with her older brother, the intellectual Ninian, with whom she shares her thoughts about her adventure. The novel quotes Shakespeare, William Blake and Dylan Thomas, while the dog is called Dante. As a teenager I loved the Caridia family; I didn't know anything about Blake or Dylan Thomas at the time, but their words leapt out at me, even as I was relishing the sheer flesh-and-blood, hardworking, mud and sweat, straw and stables, bits and bridles horsiness of the story.

Gill is by no means a perfect heroine. She can be, in her brother's words, a perfect prig, and is, like so many in her family, devoted to her cause to the point of utter selfishness. We know from the very first page that Gill will not ride off into the sunset with Perdita—girl does not get horse—but at the end of the novel she has an almost mystical vision of the world's beauty, a sense of universal connection, and realises that no-one (not even a horse) can be truly owned.

Sarah Singleton
Author of *Century, Heretic, Sacrifice* and *The Amethyst Child*

CHAPTER 12
AND FEET THAT IRON NEVER SHOD
Wild horses

British authors generally restricted themselves to the domestic scene; whether their stories were of winning at the local gymkhana or pony-filled adventures, they were firmly based in Britain. The story about wild horses was one which was mostly American or Australian. Authors like Marguerite Henry, Mary O'Hara and Elyne Mitchell wrote about wild horses, and their books became immensely popular in Britain, all going into several reprints. It is noticeable that while most pony book authors of the classic period are now out of print, all these authors are still available. There is something about the wild horse which has a perennial appeal. Although they do not fall within the strict definition of a pony book, it is worth looking at those books by overseas authors and their British imitators which were, and are, so popular with British children.

Britain has wild ponies, but they are not invested with the same romance as other countries' wild horses. There are plenty of stories about Britain's native ponies running wild on the moors, but generally, with the exception of the ones that appear in the stories of Allen Seaby—whose books, written in the 1920s and 1930s, are more nature study than adventure narrative—they are only wild until they are caught and broken in. The Moorland Mousie of 'Golden Gorse', Allen Chaffee's Wandy and their ilk live the rest of their lives as the servants of man.

Hazel M Peel wrote three books about wild horses in Australia, though most of her literary efforts were expended on her seven-book series about the Leysham stud run by Ann and Jim Henderson, set in England, in which each book deals with the problems arising from working with a new horse, and a different equestrian sport. Peel had travelled to Australia in her youth, and had come across wild horses. Her time there produced probably her best book, *Jago* (1966), which is is spare and unstinting in style. Jago is not, initially, a wild horse; he is a Thoroughbred, being trained to race. There is, however, something of the wild in him, and he is a failure on the track, being far too headstrong to succeed. He is sold off to a rancher, and life goes spectacularly wrong when Warrigan, a stockman who is used to breaking the will of horses swiftly, brutally and successfully, comes up against the full might of an enraged stallion. Jago cripples him, and takes off. The story of the horse's adaptation to the wild is compelling and convincing; Peel does not anthropomorphise him. His lethal hatred of man, and his life in the harsh conditions of the outback, almost ruin him.

Peel's first book, *Fury, Son of the Wilds* (1959), had used the same theme in reverse: in it a wild horse is tamed. Sadly for Jago, Peel brings him and the Hendersons together in *Untamed* (1969), where Ann forms enough of a bond with the stallion to think of using him for breeding. Jago will stay in Australia and have mares shipped out to him, but with the author having created such a symbol of freedom—'Jago, the Supreme. King of the outback'—it leaves the reader with a sense of being let down that this equine wildness is to be used for human gain.

Helen Griffiths had a similarly realistic attitude to the brutalities of life in the wild. She started writing young, with *Horse in the Clouds* (1957), based on her own childhood in Argentina, appearing when she was just sixteen. Griffiths wrote mostly about animals; her wild horses are compelling and memorable. She spares neither animals nor humans; her aim was to 'show animals free from the sentimental light in which they are so often portrayed in fiction'. All Griffiths's horse stories are set in the Spanish-speaking world. They are starkly realistic: horses die, sometimes by the hundred when they are hunted down by the Gauchos for their skins; people die too. There is cruelty, often unthinking but nonetheless brutal. Griffiths's heroes sometimes share in the cruelty, though it is generally through ignorance rather than inclination, and they learn that there is a better way.

Griffiths's most memorable books are set in South America. *The Wild Heart* (1963) is the story of La Bruja, a mare with an amazing turn of speed. As in *Stallion of the Sands* (1968), the equine hero is hunted. A young boy befriends the mare, the first human to be able to do so. In the end he realises that, because of her amazing speed, she will always be vulnerable. In a spare and brutal, but believable, episode, he lames the mare. She will never be the subject of cruel pursuit again, but neither will she be free to run the Pampas.

La Bruja loses her speed. Loss is a consistent theme for Griffiths: of freedom, of loved ones, of innocence. Generally the loss is coped with and a degree of understanding reached, but the process doesn't always make comfortable reading. It does, however, make for stories which explore themes often missed by the average horse or pony story. Griffiths's books ask real questions about the nature of freedom and what it means.

America's mustangs and wild horses are the subject of many stories. The number of books written about boys (generally, though girls get a look-in too) who come across a wild horse out on the range, and resolve to tame it, is legion: just a few examples are Albert G Miller's

Fury (1959), which inspired a television series, and Thomas Hinkle and Glenn Balch, notable authors who produced over thirty books between them. Taming the horse often means that its young rescuer will save it from a worse fate at the hands of those who want it for their own, possibly cruel, purposes: rodeos or racing. The rescuers often rescue something within themselves as they tame the wild horse.

Some of these books were reprinted by British publishers, but most did not achieve wide circulation. The exceptions were the Golden Stallion series by Rutherford Montgomery (published in the 1950s in the UK) and the Flicka one by Mary O'Hara (published in the UK in the 1940s, and in every decade since). Both have ranch settings. The Golden Stallion books feature Charlie Carter and his horse, Golden Boy. Ranch horses in America can lead a semi-wild existence: a stallion is broken in and ridden, but spends much time out on the range living with his mares, and this is what Golden Boy does. He and his ilk achieve wildness on humanity's terms, though Montgomery's books do not shy away from the sometimes cruel realities of ranch life.

The Flicka books of Mary O'Hara take this same scenario, but without quite the attitude of good cheer that inhabits the Carters' Bar L Ranch. Ken is a dreamer who, unlike his brother, returns home from school with poor reports. His father does not find him easy to understand, and is infuriated by him. Nell, Ken's mother, persuades her husband to give him a foal to help him to grow up. Ken chooses Flicka, a filly out of one of the hellion mares sired by the Albino, a rogue wild horse. Flicka is terribly injured trying to escape from captivity, and as Ken nurses her both he and Flicka change.

The Flicka series reflected some of O'Hara's own experiences on a Wyoming ranch, though in real life Flicka died of her barbed-wire wounds, and Mary's husband was a philanderer, not the capable (if pigheaded) Rob of the novels. Ken's parents are fully part of the books too: Nell and Rob McLaughlin are probably two of the most fully realised adults in children's horse books. Their relationship is sensitively and gently written; in *Thunderhead* (1943) it is that, rather than the children, which is central. Their marriage is close to disintegration, as the horse business is close to outright failure.

Marguerite Henry's *Misty* books start with a wild pony for whom the call of the wild is much stronger than the love of any comfort humanity can provide. The Misty books were hugely popular in both America and Britain, first appearing in the latter in the 1960s. They were much more popular in Britain than Henry's other excellent horse stories, the majority of which are historical. *Misty of Chincoteague* (1947) was based on a real-life family, the Beebes, who live on the island of Chincoteague. Each year, wild ponies are swum over from the neighbouring island, Assateague, on what is known as Pony Penning Day, in order for spare ponies to be sold so that the herd numbers can be kept constant. In *Misty of Chincoteague* the Beebe children, Paul and Maureen, are bewitched by the wild mare Phantom, and want to own her. When the mare is lamed and unable to escape, they take her in. Phantom escapes back to the wild once she has recovered, but the Beebes keep her foal, Misty. Henry went on to write three more books in the series, which tell the stories of Misty's descendants: *Sea Star, Orphan of Chincoteague* (1949), *Stormy, Misty's Foal* (1963) and *Misty's Twilight* (1992). Henry has the knack of writing about a community: she makes the people of Chincoteague spring off the page. Her stories are about whole, believable families, not just children.

The books of Mary Elwyn Patchett (1897–1989) take as their theme wild horses co-existing with man. Born on a cattle ranch in Queensland, she lived in England from 1931 but set most of her books in her native Australia. Her Brumby series starts with *The Brumby* (1958) and shows its hero, Joey Muhan, being unable to accept the stockmen's view of the wild brumbies as vicious and unproductive. He is determined to prove them wrong by catching a brumby and breeding horses in a place safe from hunters. He succeeds, and the remaining titles of the seven-book series show the difficulties of trying to work with semi-wild horses.

An author whose horses were resolutely wild was another Australian, Elyne Mitchell. Her Silver Brumby series went through several printings; the first title, *The Silver Brumby* (1958), is still in print today. Written for Mitchell's daughter, as there was so little good native Australian fiction for her to read, the series is set in the Australian Alps. It took the motifs of freedom and beauty, and made them its totems. The horses think and speak, and the style is sometimes overblown (particularly in the later books: Mitchell, having killed off the equine hero Thowra in *Silver Brumby Whirlwind* (1973), wrote a loosely connected set of later books beginning with *Silver Brumby, Silver Dingo* (1993) whose style is even more high-flown). Mitchell's frequent allying of the horses to wild winds and sweeping snowstorms stresses their beauty and the romance of their wild existence, but the horses do not exist solely in a romantic world of freedom: Thowra's mother, Bel Bel, dies, and her bones bleach on the high mountains. Horses are killed in stallion battles, come close to starvation in the snow and are swept away in floods. Although the horses are part of the wilderness, ultimately it is the landscape, and Mitchell's beloved mountains, that are the constants as the horses come and go.

Mitchell's *The Silver Brumby*, with its vision of wild beauty uncontaminated by humanity, is still casting its spell. Where wild things are, there will always be conflict between their needs and humanity's. When the horse book has considered the wild horse, it has ranged from considering the simple want of the child for a companion to tame to the nature of freedom and what achieving it might mean. Romanticism has tended to be more popular than brutal reality, and still is today. The American author Terri Farley has written a lengthy series, The Phantom Stallion (2002–9), whose purpose is to encourage the protection of mustangs rather than the system of management promoted by the authorities. Until there is no longer any land for the wild horse to range over, its lot will still prove potent stuff to the equine writer.

CHAPTER 13
A SHORT HORSE IS SOON CURRIED
Pony annuals and the short story

Once, pony book authors could cut their teeth on the short story. The Pullein-Thompsons produced so many that 30 were gathered together in their *Treasury of Horse and Pony Stories*, 1995. There were short stories in pony magazines and annuals, in girls' magazines like *Judy* and *Bunty*, in equestrian magazines for both children and adults. These provide a fascinating insight into authors' early careers and tantalising hints of directions in which they might have moved—that is, they do if you can find them. Although many annuals have survived the passage of time, their frailer magazine sisters have not been so lucky, so this chapter, after looking at the genesis of the annual in magazines, will concentrate on those short stories the reader stands some chance of tracking down: the ones in annuals.

The pony-annual market had three major players: the *Pony Magazine Annual*, *The Pony Club Annual* and the *Princess Pony Book* (later the *Princess Tina Pony Book*), but preceding them all was *Riding* magazine. From its first issue, in 1936, it featured a short section for the young rider, which included non-fiction articles and a children's letter box. 'Golden Gorse' (Muriel Wace), whose *Moorland Mousie* and its sequel, and *The Young Rider*, were already published by Country Life, contributed short stories in October and November 1936. These are the earliest children's short stories I have found in any equestrian magazine. Two of them, 'Rosalind's Saddle' and 'The Young Pony', are straightforward morality tales. A third one, from December 1936, 'Peter and His Pony see a Ghost', in which what they actually see is a cow with a sack over its head, is a much less didactic and more interesting read. Golden Gorse's next appearance in *Riding* was a ten-part serial starting in April 1937, *The Young Horsebreakers*, illustrated by Anne Bullen. It was a neat example of promotion by Country Life. The story of Jane and Felicity and their attempts to ride two barely broken-in Exmoors, it was published in book form by Country Life in 1937, having already had a partial airing in the magazine.

Although *Riding* acknowledged the existence of its child readers, the majority of its contents was aimed firmly at adults. Children had to wait for a horsy magazine exclusively their own until 1949, when *Pony* was set up by David J Murphy, a journalist. He had served in the Merchant Navy before changing careers to journalism; he worked as a reporter in his birthplace, Liverpool, before moving to London and working as a freelance. During the Second World War he worked for the welfare of servicemen. After the war ended, he founded DJ Murphy (Publishers) Ltd in 1949. David Murphy's two daughters, Jenny and Marion, spent 'every living teenage moment 'eating and breathing' horses and ponies', and it was they who had the idea of *Pony*. David Murphy and Lieutenant-Colonel Charles Evelyn Graham Hope, who became *Pony*'s editor, knew each other through their membership of KEYS, the London branch of the Catholic Writers' Guild, a Fleet Street association for Catholic journalists.

151

In pony stories there are many literary ex-military figures who bail out children with problems; chief among them is probably Josephine Pullein-Thompson's Major Holbrooke, inculcating sense and good horsemanship into the West Barsetshire Pony Club. Colonel Hope (1900–71), *Pony*'s editor, was a real-life example. He served in the Indian Cavalry from 1920 to 1927, and was seconded in 1928 to the Mekran Levy Corps: '… forsaking the horse for the camel—much more comfortable for long distances!' After he retired from the Army he wrote thrillers and contributed pieces to most national papers. In 1938 he became Assistant Editor of *Riding*. During the Second World War he served again in India; he returned to *Riding* when the war ended, leaving in 1949 when he started *Pony* with David Murphy. Besides acting as editor of *Pony* until his death in 1971, he wrote several books on riding for children. It is rather poignant that having lost his own children, twin sons Michael and John, in infancy he devoted such a large period of his life to entertaining and educating other people's children.

Early *Pony* magazines are now very difficult to find, but those editions I have from the 1950s contained serials with several short monthly episodes by authors like Judith M Berrisford, who contributed one called *Silver Star*. It was three years before D J Murphy produced short stories in a more permanent form. The earliest annual connected to the magazine was *Percy's Pony Annual 1953*, published by D J Murphy Ltd in 1952 and edited by Colonel Hope. That annual asked readers to get their contributions in early for the 1954 edition, but my investigations with D J Murphy have not turned up any evidence of a 1954 *Percy's Pony Annual*. It's difficult to see why this was: the content was generally charming. The annual perhaps caused some confusion with its title: only an habitual reader of *Pony* would have known the Percy of the title was a wild horse. Percy, with his friends Allsorts, Joseph, Zebra and Griselda Grey, provided a sort of comic foil for Colonel Hope's editorial in *Pony* magazine, commenting on office life:

> So please place your orders [for the Pony Diary 1952] as early as you can; it will also be doing a good turn to our small staff by avoiding a rush at Christmas time. Percy and Allsorts are back again now but they are not much help on those occasions—NrrrrsssSSH! Wuff! WUFF!—(Oh, dear! I did not know they were listening!) Yes, I know, you are perfectly willing to do anything, Percy, but you can't do *everything*—and one thing you cannot do, nor you, Allsorts, is to address envelopes or tie up parcels.

There was a long gap before another *Pony* annual appeared. Colonel Hope edited other annuals during the 1950s: *Horse and Pony Annual Illustrated* (1954–56) and *Horses and Ponies Pictorial* (1957–60). Both of these need a fair amount of dedication to get through: surveys of the previous year's equestrian scene, they are unrelieved by any fiction, or even by any illustrations, as all photographs are contained in the middle sections. Though interesting historically, they are not a riveting read.

After the demise of *Horses and Ponies Pictorial*, Colonel Hope tried another annual based on *Pony*. The title *Percy's Pony Annual* was dropped altogether, and the new annual, which appeared in 1961, was given the prosaic but accurate title *Pony Magazine Annual 1962*, leaving readers in absolutely no confusion about what they were getting. Once *Pony Magazine Annual* started, it hit a successful formula at once, sold out, and then carried on an unbroken run of yearly publication until 1983. The format was similar to *Percy's Pony Annual*: a mix of stories, articles both serious and not, photographs of equine events and personalities and the Equestrian Who's Who, a biographical survey of famous people in the horse world.

Every annual featured stories: at least three in each edition, with occasionally as many as five. There was a regular comic strip, 'Pat and Pickles', which ran until 1974. The vast majority of writers who contributed stories were not previously published authors (that is to say, they had published no full-length pony book). Those published authors who *did* write for the annual included Kathleen Mackenzie, Susan Chitty, Christine Leslie and Delphine Ratcliff. The Pullein-Thompsons are conspicuous by their absence, though Josephine at least was a regular in a rival publication, *The Pony Club Annual*. Only one story by any of the sisters appears in the period 1962–77: Josephine's 'Bound to Fail' (*Pony Magazine Annual 1975*).

Carol Vaughan was a prolific writer of short stories as well as an author of full-length novels. In book form she produced only the three-book Matilda series, *The Dancing Horse* (1966) and *King of the Castle* (1968), but she contributed more stories to *Pony Magazine Annual* than any other author, 24 in all. She catered for the exotic: six of her stories have a Western or American setting, one is set in Spain, and none of the others is a conventional pony story. One features an Appaloosa imported from Canada saving a cow from a train; another, 'Elegant Eddy'*,* sees a piebald donkey making his mark on a hapless family. Girls, ponies and gymkhanas were areas Vaughan left to others.

The most significant short story author by far in both *Pony* and the *Pony Magazine Annual* was Caroline Akrill, who started writing for the magazine in the 1970s. She was brought in by Michael Williams, who took over as editor after Colonel Hope's death in 1971. She initially contributed non-fiction articles: 'I wrote regularly for Michael Williams, mainly about shows and my own ponies, and he was incredibly supportive (always rapping my knuckles about punctuation, spelling and being rude about people).' In 1973 her first venture into fiction, a serial story about the showing world called *My Top Class Season*, was published in *Pony*. Caroline, the heroine, is sent by her mother to spend the summer with an aunt and cousins she has never met. She is quite happy pottering along on her pony, but her Harrison cousins exist in an entirely different part of the horsy world. They are professionals, participants in the endless round of equine beauty contests that is the showing world. In class after class, ponies are ridden round a judge at various paces, hopefully blinding the judge with both their beauty and their exquisite obedience. Successful show ponies are worth a lot of money, and if you own a pony stud, as Caroline's aunt does, you travel to show after show to prove your ponies' worth. The show pony stud in this series is populated by characters both eccentric and opinionated. Caroline is swept along in the wake of her cousins—Simon, with his long hair and velvet trousers; Becky and her evil (but beautiful) pony, Benjamin; Sarah, always trying to conciliate—and Aunt Sybil, a cigar-smoking law unto herself. The serial was enormously popular. Stuart Hollings, well known now in the showing world as a producer of show ponies, and a regular columnist in *Horse and Hound*, but then a schoolboy, would read out episodes to the other children on the school bus. As a child, I, too, read the story as it came out, entranced.

After the serial's success in *Pony*, Michael Williams sent Akrill off to find a publisher for it. Hodder liked *My Top Class Season*, but commissioned her to write two different novels about the same characters: *I'd Rather not Gallop* (1975), in which the Harrisons decide that the best way of showing their small hunter is for Caroline to learn to ride side saddle, and its sequel, *If I Could Ride* (1976). The latter ends rather tantalisingly with Simon and Caroline almost but not quite

It was a tiny grey pony with huge dark eyes....

An Elaine Roberts illustration for Caroline Akrill's 'The Lamentable Leading Rein'

getting together. *My Top Class Season* finally entered the series when it formed the basis for *Caroline Canters Home*, published in 1977 as a prequel to the other two novels. There the

An Elaine Roberts illustration for Caroline Akrill's 'An International Incident'

series ended; Akrill had been asked to write her Eventers series, and there were no more full-length showing stories. Those fans still reading *Pony Magazine Annual* were provided with a few more Harrison family adventures: 'The Lamentable Leading Rein' (1975), 'An International Incident' (1976) and 'The Celebration' (1979).

My Top Class Season was a very rare example of an equine serial crossing over into novel form. It's probably fair to say that the short stories in *Pony Magazine* generally did not reach Akrill's heights, and were less memorable than those in *The Pony Club Annual*. *Pony* always stressed the importance of contributions by its readers, and many of the stories in the annual were by them. Short stories, because they *are* short, can often lack the characters and plot lines necessary to lodge themselves in the reader's consciousness, and, with the glorious exception of Akrill, this is often true of what appeared in *Pony*.

The stories in *The Pony Club Annual* tended to be of higher quality. They were aimed at an older readership than *Pony Magazine Annual*, as the Pony Club's membership went up to the age of 17 (and 21 as an Associate). *The Pony Club Annual* was first published in 1950, as part of the Pony Club's mission to instruct and inform. In the preface to the first volume the Pony Club Chairman, Guy Cubitt, says: '… the written word can help us to understand what it is we want to achieve in practice, what skills we must strive to master, what mistakes we must seek to avoid.' Cubitt hoped readers would find the annual 'interesting, informative and enjoyable'. As it survived in pretty much the same format until the 1980s, it would appear they did. Authors were allowed much more space: stories in *The Pony Club Annual* were around 4,000 words, whereas *Pony Magazine Annual* stories were only about 2,000 words. The increase in length allowed authors to explore with more depth their characters' reactions and thoughts. Stories were often by established authors and were illustrated by the best equine artists. The early annuals, edited by Alan Delgado, are beautiful pieces of work. The first alone contains original illustrations by Michael Lyne, Joan Wanklyn, Cecil G Trew, Sheila Rose, Peter Biegel, Maurice Tulloch and Marcia Lane Foster. The content was a mixture. Readers were expected to take an intelligent interest in all aspects of the horse—historical, cultural, artistic and practical—as well as amuse themselves by reading stories. Alan Delgado wanted you to *learn*. The first edition was a sell-out success.

The Pony Club Annual (and *The Pony Club Book*—it swapped between the two titles) continued in its original format until 1963. There was no annual in 1964; in 1965 a new editor took over: Genevieve Murphy, the then equestrian correspondent of the *Observer*. The new format she introduced was more obviously aimed at children. Virtually gone were the articles of general horsy interest, replaced by more on the stars of the Pony Club, and more puzzles and competitions. Regular authors were soon established, with the short-story favourites Carol Vaughan, Josephine Pullein-Thompson and Primrose Cumming appearing in virtually every annual—only one in this period appeared without a story by one of them. The content became much closer in style to that of *Pony Magazine Annual*; however, *The Pony Club Annual* tended to attract (or commission) weightier authors: as well as the Pullein-Thompson sisters and Primrose Cumming, Pamela Whitlock, Monica Edwards, Pamela MacGregor-Morris, Joan Phipson and Mary Elwyn Patchett all contributed.

One unusual constant in *The Pony Club Annual* was the Captain Hall series: it ran for thirteen years, from 1951 to 1963, with a new episode in every annual. The author was Major C Davenport, part of the Pony Club organisation committee. The characters were Joan, Betty and Captain Hall, of the fictional Downshire Hunt Branch of the Pony Club, and the series described the club's ups and downs.

'*Betty was holding the offending Tony by his headrope*'.

A Stanley Lloyd illustration for a Captain Hall Story—
Pony Club Annual 2

Pamela Whitlock was the only author featured in the first *Pony Club Annual* (1950), contributing 'The Catsmeat Pony'. It's a good story with an unusual twist: the pony which Marty and her brother Ron fear will be sold for catsmeat unless they can save it from the round-up on Dartmoor turns out to be a farmer's much-loved pony, looked for specially at each round-up, and not one needing the saving power of pony-mad children at all. Whitlock wrote two other stories which appeared in later annuals. 'The Great Desire' (*The Pony Club Annual 5*, 1954) is about Elizabeth, a vet's daughter, who sees her chance to buy a foal at the local sale. It's another Dartmoor story, and is a fine piece of work. In most stories of this kind, the only salient feature that emerges about the heroine is her desire for a pony, but Whitlock manages to convey Elizabeth's whole character—her slight sense of isolation from the world, her fear when faced with going into a house in which there lies a dead person—and the interplay between her and her family is wonderfully done. 'Rare Bridget' (*The Pony Club Book 12*, 1961) is another subtle piece: Jane dreams of racing, and is very put out to have to ride slow old Biddy. Then Jane takes an unscheduled detour during a ride, and finds out Biddy's history. A lesson is learned.

Besides writing stories, Whitlock was keen to use Pony Club members' horsy interests to further their interest in literature. In *The Pony Club Annual 2* (1951) she contributed an article called 'Readers and Riders'. In it she argues that once a horsy child has discovered a horse in a book, the author becomes a friend; the two share an interest, and that shared interest will perhaps lead the child on to discover more of the author's work.

> The things you like best you are alert for, and they hit you in the eye. So it will be when you read. Your first books will be 'pony' books, *Moorland Mousie*, *A Pony for Jean*, *My Friend Flicka*, dozens, till the number of book gymkhanas you have attended, the number of miles through chapters you have cantered, are more than any one person could fit into a lifetime. [But] you will be surprised to find, as you bore your way into them, that from books about all sorts of people and places, by all sorts of authors, written at all sorts of times—because you are tuned to notice them—horses will pop out at you …
>
> While you are listening for hoofbeats, eyes cocked for manes in tales, you will find yourself seeing and hearing in the books through which you jog your way, much that you did not bargain for, much more, perhaps, than you set out to find.

The Pony Club Annual kept up the standard of its short stories. Monica Edwards, despite her wish not to be typecast as a pony book author, wrote two stories for it: 'Sure Magic' (*6*, 1955) and 'The Great Horse' (*11*, 1960). Both stories display Edwards's ear for dialogue and her acute characterisation, and both are departures from the family-based stories she is best known for.

'Sure Magic' isn't quite Monica-Edwards-does-fantasy, but the story does pose the question of whether there really are more things in heaven and earth than this world dreams of. Eleven-year-old Paul is desperate for a horse of his own, but has decided to give up saving for one, as it is going so slowly. His friend Roy is a farmer's son, and Paul spends much of his time at the farm with the farmer's mare, Calluna. She is due to foal, but escapes during a blizzard. Eventually, she and a foal are found alive and restored to the farm; however, Calluna will not settle. Paul is told by an elderly friend that if he goes to where a foal has been born, and wishes, his wish will come true. He does, and finds Calluna's second foal, and thus—by luck, coincidence or magic—it is saved, and becomes Paul's.

Edwards's second story, 'The Great Horse', is historical, set during the English Civil War. Fifteen-year-old Robin has trained the great horse Barbarossa, who is supreme at working in the woods hauling felled trees. His family's landlord, Sir Robert Dudley, has his eye on the horse. Dudley is a supporter of Cromwell, and wants Barbarossa for a war horse; Robin and his family love the horse and support the King. The relationship between Robin and Barbarossa is very much at the centre of this story, whose theme is how people's minds can be changed. Dudley is intent on taking the horse, but once he comes to understand (in a particularly painful way) just how strong and well trained Barbarossa is, he also comes to appreciate the horse's true worth to Robin and his family. Edwards as a writer of full-length historical stories would have been very well worth reading.

Primrose Cumming became a stalwart of *The Pony Club Annual* during Genevieve Murphy's editorship, when she contributed eight stories, all well worth reading. 'The

Jeremy sawed at the black's mouth and turned him towards the fence.

A Charlotte Hough illustration for Pony Club Annual 4

Fermoy Affair' (*The Pony Club Annual* 1975), in which Tansy and Duncan move house, is particularly good. Tansy and Duncan are excited, as they will at last have proper stables; but the stables are haunted. Fortunately, their ponies like Fermoy, the ghost pony, but life is complicated when he comes to the Pony Club rally and causes chaos by standing in the way of jumps. Although the riders don't know he's there, their ponies do. In 'A Matter of Background' (*The Pony Club Annual* 1968), Cumming showed her understanding of the teenage mind. Veronica and Harriet suffer the mortification of totally unhorsy parents but, despite their deficiencies, the parents turn out to have their good points.

The existence of *The Pony Club Annual* meant that a fine equine writer was not totally lost to readers after Cumming published her last book, *Penny and Pegasus*, in 1969. Although she felt she was out of touch with modern youth, her continued presence as a short story writer would argue that modern youth felt in touch with her, as they did with the Pullein-Thompsons, who were frequent contributors to *The Pony Club Annual*. Christine's story 'The Vicious Circle' (*The Pony Club Book 10*, 1959) is a typical Christine production, with a heroine who zooms from depression to elation while sorting out her problems. Diana's contribution to *The*

A Geoffrey Whittam illustration for Pony Club Book 10

Pony Club Book 7 (1956) is 'Looking After Jenny', in which the looked-after becomes the looker-after. Most of Josephine's stories involve daring rescues or morality tales. In the latter category there is a charming story of a girl who learns that, although she is frantically jealous of her sister's inclusion in the Prince Philip Cup team, there are plenty of other ways one can do well with horses ('The Failure', *The Pony Club Annual* 1966). One story which reflects changes in society is 'The Scavenger Hunt' (*The Pony Club Annual*, 1972), which shows that life goes on despite divorce.

All are thoroughly readable stories. *The Pony Club Annual*, at its best, contributed stories of lasting worth to the pony story canon. The pair written by Monica Edwards can hold their heads up anywhere, and Pamela Whitlock's short stories are superior to her juvenile novels written with Katharine Hull. *The Pony Club Annual*'s editors were wise enough to give their authors sufficient space, and a wide enough brief, to allow them to flourish.

A minor player in the pony annual arena was the *Princess* (later to become the *Princess Tina*) *Pony Book*, which was an offshoot of the *Princess* comic published by Fleetway. These annuals differed physically from their rivals: their early editions were landscape in format, and printed in colour, something it took the others decades to catch up with. The target audience differed too: the *Princess Pony Book*s were aimed at the pony fans who did not have ponies. They provided plenty to amuse (including a pattern for making felt ponies which kept me and my friends amused for months), but the balance was firmly on the side of those who were never going to experience ponies in real life. The first annual had fifteen stories, a picture story, a game, two poems, and a few picture features on general pony knowledge. The tone was educative: readers were there to *learn* as well as be entertained.

Many of the stories in the *Princess Pony Books* were from pillars of literature: Charles Dickens (Mr Pickwick as a horseman), as well as selections from R L Stevenson, Lewis Carroll and Mark Twain, featured in the first annual; 'Young Lochinvar' by Sir Walter Scott was one of the poems. Some contemporary authors contributed: Cecily Danby wrote three stories for the first annual, in 1962, the other contributors being Anne Collins, Frances Olcott and Michael Bennett. After 1967, when the annual became the *Princess Tina Pony Book*, stories were no longer credited. They were variable in quality; *Princess* was notable more for leading its readers to some of English literature's major authors than for any original contributions to equine literature.

All the annuals discussed had stopped regular publication by the 1980s, although *The Pony Club Book* appeared briefly in the 1990s. Sales of pony books were slipping; libraries tended not to stock them as they were considered elitist. Sales of pony annuals similarly declined, and it was no longer economic to publish them. However, with the renaissance of the pony book in the first decade of the twenty-first century, both the *Pony Magazine Annual* and *The Pony Club Annual* have reappeared, now in full and glorious colour. *The Pony Club Annual* is a drastic reinvention; it is a photographic record of the Pony Club year, with the occasional non-fiction article thrown in to leaven it, but no stories whatsoever. The *Pony Magazine Annual, s*till published by DJ Murphy, is very different in tone from the old annuals, though, if the ever-present exclamation marks and the teen slang are peeled off, the old mix is still there underneath. In the full colour *Pony: the Annual 2010*, readers are urged to start book clubs, do crafts and, above all, think of their ponies first. The short stories also survive, though in some ways they are a peculiar mix: those contributed by adults are mostly cartoon or photo stories amounting to under a hundred words. With the exception of one story from the editor, Janet Rising, the traditional short stories are provided by the teenage winners of *Pony*'s short story competition.

Although the move from writing a short story to producing a full-length novel was very rare for the writer of the pony story, the two major annuals, *Pony Magazine Annual* and *The Pony Club Annual*, did make valuable contributions to the canon of pony literature. They saw the genesis of at least one major writer's career, with Caroline Akrill launched on the pony book stage by her Showing series. Major authors within the genre—like Primrose Cumming, who had stopped writing books—kept their hands in by contributing short stories. The annuals provided opportunities for contributors who might not write a full-length pony book, like Naomi Mitchison, but who were happy to contribute short stories. Other authors, like Carol Vaughan, based most of their career on the production of the short story, writing relatively few books. The stories provided tantalising glimpses into what might have been: what superior works Pamela Whitlock might have produced, for example, had she written full-length pony books in her prime. The short story gave authors an opportunity to try different elements of the genre. Although these stories are not always easy to source, they are well worth finding.

CHAPTER 14
GILDING THE LILY
Pony book illustrators

The average British child today would find it hard to believe that it was once normal for books to be illustrated past the learning-to-read stage. Illustrations, at least if they are good, find their way into the imagination and live there, welded to the words they illustrate. This is particularly true for pony book illustration from the 1920s to 1960s: the golden age. Horses are not easy to draw, but publishers had the equine sporting artist to turn to. Most had started their careers in illustration, and were happy to ornament pony books. Lionel Edwards, the 'Grand Old Man' of sporting artists, illustrated over thirty children's books, and some of his fellow artists—Cecil Aldin, Gilbert Holiday, Michael Lyne, Thomas Ivester Lloyd and Peter Biegel—contributed some notable examples.

Gilbert Holiday (1879–1937) was one of the earliest equine artists to portray horses in action as they actually were, rather than in the 'two legs stretched fore and aft' style that was usual in the Victorian period. Lionel Edwards says: 'Holiday, by clever manipulation of dust or mud and the consequent blurring of outlines, was able to give a tremendous sense of speed.' Mastering this technique was particularly useful for Moyra Charlton's *The Midnight Steeplechase* (1932), one of the two pony books Holiday illustrated.

Holiday's near contemporary Cecil Aldin (1870–1935) also illustrated just two pony books, but was influential far beyond that achievement. During the First World War, too old for active service, he ran a remount depot in Purley. These depots looked after horses recuperating after being wounded during service, and bought and trained new horses and mules for the Army. Responsible for around three hundred horses, Aldin found there were very few men available to care for them, so,

"HE HEARD FOX-TROT THUNDERING UP"

Moyra Charlton: The Midnight Steeplechase
(illustration by Gilbert Holiday)

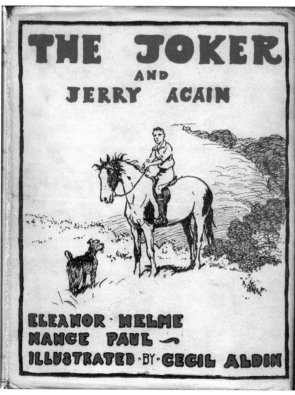

despite the War Office's dim view of his project, he started to employ women and girls to do so—almost unheard of at the time. The Purley remount depot became the first to have an all-female staff: a major development in the move of women into all areas of equestrian life. The pony book girl, 'heroine of her own story', could not have been the independent carer of horses she was without Aldin and his ilk.

Not only that, Aldin was instrumental in developing that absolute mainstay of the pony book, the gymkhana and show centred on children. Aldin's grandchildren complained to him that very few classes in shows were open to children, so he organised a show at Cloutsham Meadow on Exmoor in 1926, on his own, without the aid of a committee. The show, with fourteen classes open only to children, was a roaring success, and Aldin was asked to organise another at Dunster. This he did, and it featured a Handy Hunter course designed by the show expert Captain 'Chips' Russell Wood. (Then as now the worried parent was in evidence: parents complained that the course was dangerous, not realising the vicious barbed wire on it was actually string which had been knotted and painted.) Aldin gave the pony book heroine and hero something to aim at: the Handy Hunter class. I'm sure Jill and her friends, as they organised their shows, had no idea that just a couple of decades earlier the child-centred show was unknown.

The only pony books Aldin illustrated were the two Jerry ones by Eleanor Helme and Nance Paul (*Jerry, the Story of an Exmoor Pony*, 1930; *The Joker and Jerry Again*, 1932): a very small proportion of the hundred or so titles he either wrote or illustrated. These two are both set on Exmoor, and were done towards the end of Aldin's life, when his output had decreased because of his arthritis. Both titles show his expertise at depicting horses, ponies and people. Aldin died in 1935, before the main flourishing of the pony book, but he left two gems in the Jerry books.

Lionel Edwards (1878–1966), a member of the London Sketch Club and a pupil of W Frank Calderon, benefited from the explosion in popularity of the pony book, illustrating over thirty. The son of a Chester doctor, Edwards described his education as being of 'a halting and irregular character' owing to his family's straitened circumstances, and probably too to his own attention being elsewhere. The head of the London crammer to which he was sent in an attempt to fit him for the army reported he was 'more interested in artistic than in military matters'. Fortunately, Edwards's mother (his father died when Edwards was seven) rose above the Victorian convention that artists were low, and allowed him to study art.

Like his near contemporaries Cecil Aldin and Gilbert Holiday, Edwards served as a remount officer during the First World War. He was immersed in horse for the duration of the war, saying: 'I'm afraid I did not take the same interest in the men that I did in the horses!' His people, like his horses, have a tendency towards the lean and aristocratically bred, which perhaps did not serve him as well as it ought when he began to illustrate pony books. His first in the genre was one of the classics: *Moorland Mousie* by 'Golden Gorse' (1929). Edwards illustrated another Exmoor some twenty years later, when he contributed the colour dustjacket for Pamela MacGregor-Morris's *Exmoor Ben* (1950). When I look at it, I see the charm of the picture: the alertness of the pony, just about to move, and the beauty of the background. However, to an Exmoor pony specialist, that pony is not an Exmoor; it's altogether too finely boned. Edwards did nevertheless corner the market in illustrating Exmoors; in the period we are considering, Edwards illustrated six of the eleven books which have Exmoors as their heroes.

Most of the pony books Edwards illustrated were done for the publishers Eyre and Spottiswoode, who tended towards a minimalist approach with their dustjackets. The majority consist of a black-and-white drawing dramatised a little by the application of colour, though when this is beige, as with Eleanor Helme's *Suitable Owners* (1948) and *Shanks's Pony* (1946), it's not much of a dramatisation. This style of dustjacket does have the unfortunate effect of deadening even the liveliest drawing, and it's especially sad to compare these titles with full-colour contemporary examples also illustrated by Edwards. The illustrations for Moyra Charlton's *Tally Ho* (1930) and Kipling's 'The Maltese Cat' (1898) are Edwards at his best: they are things of beauty.

Michael Lyne (1912–89) was trained (albeit briefly) at the Cheltenham School of Art. Like Stubbs before him, he learned equine anatomy through dissection. He published five books himself, though the manuscript and illustrations of one, *Hunting Here and There*, were lost in the Blitz. Lyne worked on relatively few pony books, and had a genius for illustrating ones that would later become very difficult to find; among them are the 1958 UK edition of the American Don Stanford's *The Horsemasters*, and Pamela MacGregor-Morris's *Blue Rosette* (1950).

Peter Biegel (1913–86) painted in a similar style to both Lionel Edwards and Michael Lyne, and was Edwards's only pupil. Having written to the artist while he was at school, Biegel had a chance meeting with him on a train, on his way to a medical board after he had been invalided out of the Army in 1944: he offered his fellow passenger some sandwiches, only to discover who he was. Having studied earlier with Lucy Kemp-Welch, Biegel was now accepted as a pupil by Edwards, and stayed on even after his study had ended, becoming almost a member of the family.

Biegel's style is very similar to Edwards's, although he was not as prolific, but his humans, although lively, aren't as successful. Most of his book illustration was done for Shirley Faulkner-Horne's work, and fell into that period where many publishers used black and white illustrations with added title and border colour on their dustjackets. Faulkner-Horne's *Mexican Saddle* (1946) was given a shocking-pink background, a rare dash of bright colour in a genre distinguished by muted tones. Publishers also used a torn-from-the-sketchbook approach to add some visual excitement to their dustjackets: Faulkner-Horne's *Parachute Silk* (1944) and, perhaps the oddest, *Crab the Roan* (1953) by Kathleen Herald (K M Peyton) were two of Biegel's titles to receive this treatment. His most successful illustrations are generally the ones where he is uninhibited by the presence of a human being, those for Veronica Westlake's *The Ten-Pound Pony* (1953) being particularly so. Biegel's work for the Collins 1949 reprint of John Thorburn's *Hildebrand*, though lacking the mania of the illustrations by 'The Wag' for the original printing (1930), does capture the horse's essential quality. Here, you feel, is a horse you really do not want to mess with.

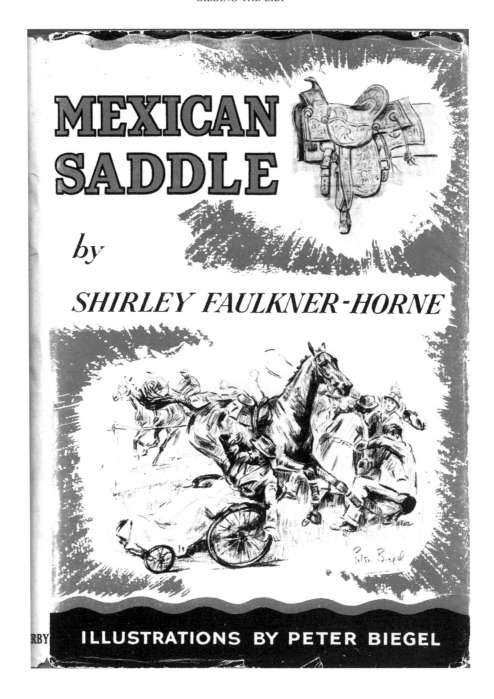

Not all illustrators were sporting artists. Anne Bullen (1914–63), who illustrated some of the earliest examples in the genre with Joanna Cannan's Jean books, was educated at the Académie Julian School in Paris and Chelsea School of Art. She and her husband founded the Catherston Stud, and bred a very successful series of show ponies which were often ridden by some of their six children, three of whom (Jennie, Michael and Jane) went on to ride for Britain in the Olympics. Bullen was particularly successful at capturing the dream feeling

His smooth, soft muzzle came round to meet her.

Monica Edwards: The Summer of the Great Secret *(illustration by Anne Bullen)*

of pony books: if you were a ponyless girl, Bullen's ponies, unimaginably, blissfully breedy, were the ponies who cantered through your sleep. They look too noble to kick craftily while giving the impression they're thinking of something else, or nip their owner on the bottom when she was using the hoof pick. Bullen's ponies have their owner's best interests at heart. I ran a poll on my website on pony book fans' favourite dustjacket, and a Bullen won it: her cover illustration for Diana Pullein-Thompson's *A Pony to School* (1950) trounced even Lionel Edwards.

However lovely Bullen's ponies may be, her people didn't always meet with quite such acclaim. Monica Edwards, whose first four books (*Wish for a Pony*, 1947; *No Mistaking Corker*, 1947; *The Summer of the Great Secret*, 1948; *The Midnight Horse*, 1949) were illustrated by Bullen, thought her children 'too ill and bony looking'. Edwards's daughter, Shelley, was used as the model for Tamzin, heroine of *Wish for a Pony*, and stayed with the artist's family for a week to be drawn; perhaps Bullen had not caught Shelley well enough for a fond mother. Of the four Bullen dustjackets, only *The Summer of the Great Secret* has people as a major part of the composition.

"*Diccon you're* not *to pull the kitten's tail.*"
Monica Edwards: The Summer of the Great Secret *(illustration by Anne Bullen)*

As the pony book moved on to the 1950s, publishers began to use illustrators who were known for general book illustration, not just for horses. Geoffrey Whittam (1915–?98) illustrated a wide range of children's fiction. After a war in which he was awarded the Distinguished Service Cross (DSC), he studied at the Central School of Arts, and was launched as an illustrator by a commission from the *Radio Times*. He is an iconic figure in pony book illustration, principally because he was responsible for the illustrations for Judith M Berrisford's lengthy Jackie series. He also famously illustrated many of Monica Edwards's stories, avidly read by many pony book aficionados. Whittam was her favourite illustrator, and often visited her and her family at Punch Bowl Farm.

Whittam has never been my choice of illustrator; he is at his best when drawing children and landscape, when he is very good indeed, but his horses and ponies are very often awkward, with oddly foreshortened necks and inaccurate legs. They are amazingly distinctive: a Whittam pony will always have a thick thatch of mane (imagine

Judith M Berrisford: Jackie's Showjumping Surprise *(illustration by Geoffrey Whittam)*

trying to groom that without recourse to the dandy brush), be on the stocky side and have an immensely wide forehead.

Geoffrey Whittam was not the only author to be indelibly associated with particular authors. Caney (Clifford Caney) illustrated all of Ruby Ferguson's Jill books. Although his illustrations were lost from some of the titles when Knight published them in paperback, they were not universally cut, and so generations of pony book fans up until the late 1980s were still able to see at least some of his illustrations. Caney does a marvellous job of putting over the characters of Jill and her friends as well as the ponies. His style is unique. He is particularly good at capturing those moments in the stories where something dramatic happens—though not everyone likes my particular favourite, *Jill and the Perfect Pony* (1959), where Jill has just been dumped onto the ground by Plum (see p74): one comment on this picture on my forum called it 'overly sexualised', which I must admit had not occurred to me until then.

Stanley Lloyd (dates unknown) is indelibly associated with Primrose Cumming. He was part of a family who both wrote and illustrated pony books: his brother was Thomas Ivester Lloyd (1873–1942), the illustrator of several, particularly those of his son, John Ivester Lloyd. The latter's daughter, Delphine Ratcliff, herself wrote two pony books as well as contributing articles to equine magazines. Stanley Lloyd illustrated three books for Primrose Cumming: *The Wednesday Pony* (1939), *The Chestnut Filly* (1940) and *Silver Snaffles* (1937). Stanley Lloyd produced recognisable people and ponies, though his ponies' bulgy foreheads and large eyes aren't to everyone's taste. His illustrations for *Silver Snaffles* do succeed in portraying a world of kind but lively ponies, ticking all wish-fulfilment boxes. His portrayal of Jenny sitting on Tattles's manger is a particular delight, showing a child in silent communion with a pony.

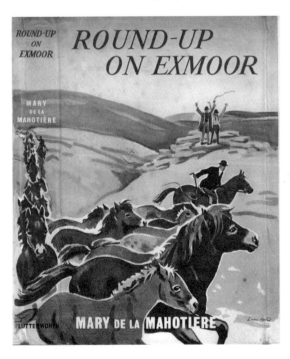

There are illustrators whom one would wish to have done more: Marcia Lane Foster (dates unknown) was one of the very few to regard the spine as an integral part of the dustjacket design. She was a prolific illustrator, working on many of Pamela Brown and Viola Bayley's titles, but she illustrated only four pony books: Christine Pullein-Thompson's *We Hunted Hounds* (London, 1949); Kitty Barne's *Rosina and Son* (1956); Mary de la Mahotière's *Round-Up on Exmoor* (1961); and Gillian Baxter's *The Team from Low Moor* (1965). Her dustjacket for *Round-Up on Exmoor* is particularly good, with the herd of Exmoor ponies streaming down the spine before careering off across the front panel.

Jenny thought Tattles was the wisest creature she knew

Primrose Cumming: Silver Snaffles *(illustration by Stanley Lloyd)*

Sheila Rose (b1929) carved out a niche in pony book illustration during the 1950s and 1960s when she illustrated over fity such titles, which made her one of the most prolific illustrators of the period. She was born in Bishop's Stortford, and was educated at Hitchin Grammar School and Harrogate College. She started riding her own ponies, and drawing them, when she was four, and, according to her entry in *Who's Who* in the *Pony Magazine Annual* 1968, 'competed at all shows in Hertfordshire between 1940 and 1945'. Allowing for the fact that it was wartime, when there were fewer shows than normal, that record still shows formidable determination, especially as she also found time to hunt with the Puckeridge and South Herts.

Rose is another of those very rare creatures who can draw both animals and people. She illustrated her first book in 1948 and had done over eighty by 1968, as well as either writing or illustrating various articles. I have always been very fond of her drawings, and especially like her depiction of Olga in Christine Pullein-Thompson's *The Horse Sale* (1960). She is particularly good, I think, at portraying horses and ponies jumping. Her illustrations always have considerable vim, and a marvellous sense of movement.

Although Rose produced some of the most iconic illustrations for the Pullein-Thompsons' early books, she didn't meet with universal approval among her authors. When I met Josephine, I asked her if she liked Rose's illustrations for her stories. It soon became clear that no illustrator had matched up to Josephine's internal pictures of her creations: none, she thought, ever read the books properly, and none got the illustrations completely right. The worst offender in this respect was Charlotte Hough (1924–2008), who illustrated *Prince among Ponies* (1952). Adonis, the princely pony of the title, is marvellously handsome, and finely bred. The entire story centres around his beauty, which isn't matched by his behaviour until Patrick and Sara meet him and manage to ride him. In the first illustrations, Adonis appeared as a stocky cob-type pony; they were duly returned to be done again.

Hough's pony book illustration was only a small part of her output. Neither she nor her husband was trained for anything when they married, so Hough took her sketches around publishers until she managed to find work as an illustrator of children's books. Her style is sketchy and usually rather perky in feel. There's always plenty of life, but I wonder if she was less than happy using colour: her two dustjackets for Christine Pullein-Thompson (*Goodbye to Hounds*, 1952, and *I Carried the Horn*, 1951) have minimal colour, and what there is seems applied without confidence. Hough's pony book illustration spanned just three years, ending with Anna Sewell's *Black Beauty* for Puffin in 1954. Her drawings are lively, and often fun, but they never seem to have engendered the same affection that other equine illustrators have.

Although she provided very little in the way of internal illustrations—one notable exception is Diana Pullein-Thompson's *Janet Must Ride* (1953)—Mary Gernat (1926–98) is another author whose name is indelibly linked with the pony book. She worked for Collins, and was responsible for producing covers for their paperback imprint, Armada. These printings were the bulk of many people's pony book experience during the 1960s and 1970s, and Gernat provides an instant pull back to that time.

Gernat was born in Ewell, in Surrey, and trained at the Central School of Arts and Crafts and at Regent Street Polytechnic. She had five children, who were pressed into service as models. Although she did not ride herself, she portrayed her equine models with sympathy, and her drawings are full of energy and life. The range of titles Gernat provided covers for was wide: from the St Clare's, Malory Towers and Mystery series of Enid Blyton (whom she met, and found strange) through countryside authors like Monica Edwards to Malcolm Saville's adventures. It's probably fair to say that Gernat is better known as a cover artist than as an illustrator, although she did also illustrate many children's books. She has a very distinctive, sketchy style, which is well suited to situations full of action. I am particularly fond of her cover for the 1960s Armada printing of *I Carried the Horn* (1964), which I think wonderfully captures the awful tension of the moment: the desperate struggle to snip a wire while holding a horse.

Victor Ambrus (1935–) was born László Gyözö Ambrus in Hungary. He studied art for three years at the Hungarian Academy of Fine Art, but left Hungary for Britain in 1956, after the Hungarian uprising. Once in London, he continued studying at the Royal College of Art, illustrating his first book in his last year at the college. He became a freelance illustrator, and has worked on over a hundred books. He won the Kate Greenaway Medal for children's book illustration in 1965 (for *The Three Poor Tailors*) and in 1975 (for *Horses in Battle* and *Mishka*). He was notable for his illustrations for K M Peyton's Flambards series (*Flambards*, 1967; *The Edge of the Cloud*, 1969; *Flambards in Summer*, 1969), horsy dreams for a generation bewitched by the 1970s television series. He was the Australian Elyne Mitchell's illustrator from 1971 to 1981. Ambrus's impressionistic style is well suited to tales of wild horses: he illustrated no conventional girl-gets-pony books, but seems to have been the illustrator of choice whenever a publisher had a book involving wild horses which needed illustrations. He did Mary Elwyn Patchett's *Brumby Foal* (1965), Gerald Raftery's *Snow Cloud, Stallion* (1967) and several titles for Helen Griffiths, whose output was almost all about the wild horse. The nearest Ambrus came to illustrating a conventional pony book was with Mary Treadgold's first two books about a crumbling house, the Heron: *The Heron Ride* (1962) and *Return to the Heron* (1963). I love his impressionistic backgrounds, but think he's generally best at the horse in motion. His standing horses for Helen Griffiths's *The Wild Horse of Santander* (1966) seem rather awkward, in complete contrast to the dramatic struggle of *Stallion of the Sands* (1968) for the same author, where the swirl of the sea matches the movement of the horse.

The artists I have discussed so far generally produced good illustrations. There were plenty of poor, and inaccurate, examples. One of the primary demands of any illustration is that it should reflect the story accurately, though if readers are caught up enough in the twin enchantment of the story and the illustrations they may not necessarily spot any inaccuracies. I did not notice for decades that Peter Biegel showed Gipsy, in Veronica Westlake's *The Ten-Pound Pony*, with a saddle. The children don't have a saddle, want one desperately and spend considerable time thinking about it. Occasionally the error is so blatant it is almost impossible to miss. Diana Pullein-Thompson's skewbald Clown became grey on a 1970s Armada edition of *A Pony to School*.

A change to a well-loved fictional pony's colour can generate decades of argument. Is Black Boy, the equine hero and companion of Jill in Ruby Ferguson's Jill series, black or piebald? (See my discussion on pp81–82.) If an illustration did reflect the story accurately, it then still had to attempt the twin challenges of portraying two notoriously difficult subjects: the human being and the horse. Being able to do both was so rare that the untrained artist Charlotte Hough received her first commissions because she could draw horses *and* people. Even Lionel Edwards, that master of portraying the horse, fell down when it came to people: the sporting art expert Stella Walker says: 'Never gifted at facial likenesses Edwards would cunningly present human personality by stance and poise.' Otherwise capable artists could prove hopelessly inadequate when it came to portraying horses. The Children's Book Club edition of Monica Dickens's *Cobbler's Dream* (1963), which has a good landscape, ruins it with a pair of stiff and awkward horses.

The Children's Book Club seems to have had a genius for reissuing pony books which had perfectly acceptable original covers in new dustjackets that were anything but. It has been responsible for some of the direst efforts in pony book illustration history. Monica Edwards's Chalice, Lindsay's colt in *The Wanderer* (1953), is transformed from Joan Wanklyn's beautiful picture to a poor deformed creature whose legs do not bend as a horse's do. Even this terrible effort faces strong competition from my own 'favourite', Gillian Baxter's *Horses in the Glen* (1967), another book which started off life with a decent dustjacket (see overleaf). Elisabeth Grant's lovely original painting has been replaced by an effort which is stuffed so full of error it's almost painful, and in addition was copied directly from Mathilde Windisch-Graetz's *The Spanish Riding School* (1958). Particularly haunting are the tiny weeny stirrups. What fairy person would be able to get her feet into those?

First edition (left) and Children's Book Club (right) dustjacket illustrations

The horse is not easy to draw. Pony book characters found it equally hard. Tamzin Grey, Monica Edwards's heroine in *Wish for a Pony* (1947) cannot get hind legs right:

> 'Mummy, the legs just WON'T come right. They never will.'
> 'Not chalk in here, PLEASE, Tamzin …'
> 'Oh, all right, Mummy, I forgot. But I wanted to show you. I've been trying to get the hocks right for ages, but they just won't.'

First edition (left) and Children's Book Club (right) dustjacket illustrations

Fortunately, Mrs Grey, having taught riding herself, and presumably drawn horses, is able to help Tamzin with the construction of hocks.

Alas for Tamzin and those who followed her, there are now very few pony book illustrations. Some American titles still have specially commissioned cover art, but the modern British pony book makes do with photographs. There are many equine artists still working; the Society of Equestrian Artists is not short of members, and good sporting art is still being produced. It's sad that twenty-first-century children will not have their own Caney or Lionel Edwards. These artists, and many more whom I have not been able to include in this survey, produced images which still canter through their readers' minds, even when they are grown up and quite possibly no longer ponyless.

CHAPTER 15
WHAT HAPPENED NEXT
The 1980s and onwards

By the 1980s, most of the major pony book writers had stopped writing, or were no longer at the top of their powers or were producing books for the younger reader. The number of old titles being republished in paperback obscured the fact that the number of new pony titles published had plummeted: only half as many were printed in the 1980s as in the 1960s.

The pony book did survive, but it was limping along in the final decades of the twentieth century, affected by the winds of change that were blowing through children's literature as a whole. In earlier decades this had featured children from middle-class backgrounds, but in the 1960s authors like Leila Berg started to write books which moved away from the comfortable middle-class world of *Janet and John*, and showed one where houses had no internal water and children played on dumps.

All children need to read about their own worlds, and a change was long overdue. However, as critical opinion swung behind the new movement, a corresponding one arose against the perceived elitism of some children's books. Pony stories, with a world only fully accessible to the moneyed, were among the most obvious targets. Cadogan and Craig memorably described the pony book heroine as a 'dumb thoroughbred'. To other critics, those who spent their childhoods obsessing about ponies did so to cope with their nascent sexual desires. Bruno Bettelheim wrote that '... by controlling this powerful animal, she can come to feel that she is controlling the male, or the sexually animalistic, within herself. Imagine what it would do to a girl's enjoyment of riding, or her self-respect, if she were made conscious of this desire which she is acting out in riding. She would be devastated ...' Surprised, certainly.

And yet the strong-minded, independent rider was still out there, if in smaller numbers than before. She was actively looking for romance, in defiance of Bettelheim's characterisation of her as an innocent abroad. Samantha Alexander's heroine Alex Johnson combined her riding adventures with a romance with the eventing star Ash Burgess in the eight-book Riders series (1996–97). Caroline Akrill's fine Eventers series (*Eventer's Dream*, 1981; *A Hoof in the Door*, 1982; *Ticket to Ride*, 1983) brought unforgettable characters to the pony book world.

Akrill was an important figure in that world in the 1980s and 1990s. Her *Flying Changes* (1985) gave critics all the anguish they could desire. Its hero, Oliver, is a dressage rider whose perfectionism and ruthlessness drive him to destruction. The publishers, Arlington, were aghast when Akrill delivered the book. In an interview with me the author said: 'It was far, far darker when it was delivered to Arlington Books. They were simply horrified by it because it was not at all what they were expecting ... They took out all the darker bits.' Whatever the publishers thought, Oliver's teenage readers loved him. Decades before the tortured vampiric hero of *Twilight*, Oliver haunted his readers' imaginations. One wrote: 'I look for him

CAROLINE AKRILL
Flying Changes

everywhere, everywhere I go, every show, every dressage event, I look for him. I just know he's there somewhere.'

Akrill became a publisher, working for the equestrian house J A Allen. They were known for publishing non-fiction, but Akrill introduced a children's fiction line, the Junior Equestrian Fiction series, a well-written set of books aimed at the teenage reader. Despite covering difficult topics like rape (Susan Millard's *Against the Odds*, 1995), suicide (Akrill's own *Flying Changes*, reprinted in 1989) and illiteracy (Diana Pullein-Thompson's *This Pony is Dangerous*, 1990), these were not stocked by libraries, which now saw them as elitist fiction. What they and the pony book world acquired instead was series.

Americans have never had the same difficulty with pony books as the British. Their writers have continued to churn them out, and their libraries to stock them, keen to encourage horse-crazy girls to read. In the 1990s, Bantam Books published the American Saddle Club series in the UK. Bonnie Bryant's creation was the story of three girls who keep their horses at a livery stable, and have endless equine-themed adventures with them. Bryant only wrote the first few stories herself; most titles in the series, which eventually numbered over a hundred books, were farmed out to other authors. Joanna Campbell's equally lengthy Thoroughbreds series (90 titles including spin-offs, 1991–2005) was another nineties import, and was again taken on by other authors after the first few titles. These series are the soap operas of the pony world: on and on they go, sucking in readers. All readers always want to know what happens next, and both these series told them in exhaustive detail. The academic Jenny Kendrick suggests, persuasively, that just as toys such as My Little Pony leave little to the child's imagination, so does series fiction—what is there to do imaginatively with it other than 'get another'?

The Saddle Club was the start of a near total take-over of the pony book world by series fiction. The early years of the twenty-first century saw a return to the numbers of titles published of the 1950s, but with a major difference. Just three names—Linda Chapman, Lauren Brooke and Jenny Oldfield—appeared on almost 50 per cent of the total of titles published. The series was king, and any author who could produce a lengthy series was a publisher's dream. Most of these authors' series are notable for their exotic settings: no longer are they tales of girls and ponies and gymkhanas. Many of Oldfield's books are set on American ranches (Half Moon Ranch, 24 titles including specials, 1999–2002); Brooke's series are also set in the USA, her Chestnut Hill one (2006–10) having twelve books. Her Heartland series had an interesting beginning: the early titles were written by the British author Linda Chapman under her own name, with the original intention of setting the series in Cheshire, but when the first publisher interested in the series was American the setting was changed to Virginia; Chapman later adopted the pseudonym 'Lauren Brooke' under which the majority of the books (25 titles, including specials, 2000–08) appeared. Amy, the teenage heroine and mistress of time management, runs Heartland, a horse-healing business, as well as coping with school, a relationship and, later, veterinary studies. The series is an interesting example of the pony book continuing to reflect changes in equestrian fashion. The 'join-up' techniques expounded by Monty Roberts and his followers have taken the equestrian world by storm, and they are right there in pony books too. The Olympic eventing medallist Pippa Funnell is (with a ghostwriter) writing a pony book series, Tilly. Tilly has a gift for communicating with horses, and she has had a long series of endearing adventures.

There began to be a shift in the reader age at which pony books were aimed. Younger readers, previously at the shallow end of the pony book pool, now had their own series; a particularly charming example is Peter Clover's *Sheltie* (24 books, 1996–2001), in which a young girl and her Shetland pony live a life of occasional comfortable adventures. Sheltie is a rare example of a straightforward pony series: most books aimed at the younger reader combined ponies with fantasy. The pony book has often nodded towards what was going on in the children's book genre as a whole: adventure in the 1950s, realism in the 1970s, and, from the 1990s, fantasy. In 1997, J K Rowling's *Harry Potter and the Philosopher's Stone* was published: it and its sequels were such overwhelming successes that pony author after pony author leapt, with sometimes miserable results, into the world of fantasy. Elizabeth Lindsay's Magic Pony series (twelve books, 1997–2006), the story of a miniature magical pony, was the first but by no means the last. Linda Chapman wrote several series on unicorns. The prolific Jenny Oldfield wrote the My Magical Pony series (fifteen books, 2005–2007); Sue Bentley wrote the violet-eyed Magic Ponies series (eight books, 2009). Even Babette Cole, scourge of nits and snot, wrote a four-book series based on unicorns, Fetlocks Hall (2010–11). Unfortunately most of these magical ponies seem to inhabit a world of inhuman goodness, and pontificate at their readers: '… Friendship is important. Is it not worth fighting for?' says Comet in Bentley's series. The addiction to vampires seen in young adult (YA) fiction seems to have passed the pony book by, but there are now titles which inhabit a more interesting and gothic territory. The American Maggie Stiefvater's brilliant *Scorpio Races* (2011) reworks the myth of the water horse to terrifying effect.

Scorpio Races is a rare example in a field which in parts is sadly infantilised. Most pony books have long ago left behind the realistic covers of the 1950s and 1960s. A substantial proportion of those aimed at the younger reader are badged with pink and sparkles, and winsome straplines: 'Could you', asks the front covers of Bentley's Magic Ponies series, 'be a little pony's special friend?' The princess of pink, Katie Price, who first hit fame as the glamour model Jordan, has written (with a ghostwriter) the Perfect Ponies series (twelve books, 2007–10), emblazoned in pink and silver, about a group of four friends and their adventures at a riding school. In a world which places so much emphasis now on how girls look, it's sad to see the riding instructor continually praised because she 'was living proof that you could be glam and still be a brilliant horsewoman'. This is fair enough, but it is a pity if it is made an issue for the books' target audience, children of around eight.

The pinkification of covers obscures even decent stories: Diana Kimpton's sparky Pony Mad Princess series (twelve books, 2004–07) is very much better than its covers would have you believe. Susanna Forrest, in her equine memoir *If Wishes were Horses* (2012), discusses the pinkification of the horse world. 'Horses used to be an alternative to pink and princesses and playing mother; now horses are pink princesses with Lullabye Nurseries™ and sparkly handbags,' she writes. The twinkly cover appears to be a British phenomenon. The American Pulitzer Prize-winning author Jane Smiley has written a three-book Young Adult horse series (*Nobody's Horse*, 2010; *Secret Horse*, 2011; *Mystery Horse*, 2012) whose original American editions have straight-down-the line photographic covers. In the UK, Faber has given them the sparkle factor. Whatever the covers are like, behind them are fine horse stories.

And there are still good pony stories being produced, still jolly pony girls living lives centred around ponies. Janet Rising's Pia, juggling her divorced parents' idiocies with a wry eye in the Pony Whisperer series (six books, 2009–11), is perhaps the best of them, with Victoria Eveleigh's Exmoor stories (three books, 2002–05, republished and retitled 2012) offering rare examples of good, straight-down-the-line pony stories. Older teenagers are well served by Sheena Wilkinson's stories of bolshie Declan, set in Northern Ireland: *Taking Flight* (2011) and *Grounded* (2012). K M Peyton has carried on writing excellent titles: her

Blind Beauty (1999) is deservedly popular. Meg Rosoff's *The Bride's Farewell* (2009) and Linda Newbery's *The Damage Done* (2001) have added fine titles to the genre.

The pony book is not dead; or at least, stories of girls and horses are not dead. Alison Haymonds writes that 'while adolescent girls continue to have a passion for ponies, the pony book will survive'. Despite critical disapproval, the pony book has not only survived but also adapted, if not always with staggering literary success. It will be interesting to see what impact self-publishing and the ebook have on the pony story, now it is freed from the constraints of publishers' demands. Even if they will never, ever have ponies of their own, children still want to read about the pony. He or she is still a companion in adventure; and there are still girls riding, striking forth and living life on their own terms, demanding books which reflect their passions.

My Favourite Pony Book: *Flying Changes* by Caroline Akrill

I've never been one for happy endings. My favourite film is *Vertigo*: murder, melancholia, manipulative behaviour—yummy!

Caroline Akrill's *Flying Changes* tells the story of the talented and self-absorbed dressage star Oliver through the eyes of his sister, Kathryn. Perfectionist Oliver is thoroughly unlikeable—but he is no exaggeration. You can find less talented Olivers everywhere in horsy circles, the novelty of their sex setting them on pedestals upon which they grow and fester. *Flying Changes* tells of power shifts, of a life untested by disappointment and ill-equipped to deal with tragedy, of changing relationships and destroyed expectations, of love and adoration and disastrous obsession.

From the first page you know this is going to be no cosy, happy-ending pony tale. With any book I want to be dragged through hedges of emotion, to gasp, to laugh, to cry. I want my mind to whirl with possibilities, and still be surprised by the author drawing me into their literary maze, turning me back from my own dead ends of ideas, relentlessly sweeping me along their chosen path. The plot must linger in my mind after I've turned the last page—and *Flying Changes* does not disappoint. Would I have liked it as a child? Probably not. Would I even have understood it? Doubtful. But as a grown-up I liked it, and I still do.

Flying Changes tells of what happens when the characters in pony books grow up. It's for anyone wanting something beyond Pony Club camp and first rosettes, something more sinister than the clichés of spoilt brats and rich parents. It's the pony book for grown-ups not yet ready to leave the genre behind. And that's me.

Janet Rising
Editor of *Pony* magazine

BIBLIOGRAPHY

The entries are in many cases partial; only those titles which involve horses are mentioned, and generally only the ones published before the 1970s cutoff applied to most of the book. I've only included books published after 1970 if they are covered in the text. For full bibliographies on all the authors featured, go to my website, www.janebadgerbooks.co.uk , which has details of reprints, synopses, and much more.

Caroline Akrill
I'd Rather not Gallop, Hodder & Stoughton, 1975, illus Elisabeth Grant
If I Could Ride, Hodder & Stoughton, 1976, illus Elisabeth Grant
Caroline Canters Home, Hodder & Stoughton, 1977
Eventer's Dream, Arlington, 1981
A Hoof in the Door, Arlington, 1982
Ticket to Ride, Arlington, 1983
Flying Changes, Arlington, 1985

Anon
The Memoirs of Dick, the Little Poney (Supposed to be written by himself; ...)
  (J Walker, 1800)

M E Atkinson
Steeple Folly, Bodley Head, 1950
Hunter's Moon, Bodley Head, 1952, illus Charlotte Hough
The Barnstormers, Bodley Head, 1953, illus Charlotte Hough
Riders and Raids, Bodley Head, 1955, illus Sheila Rose
Horseshoes and Handlebars, Bodley Head, 1958, illus Sheila Rose

Enid Bagnold
National Velvet, Heinemann, 1935, illus Laurian Jones

Gillian Baxter
Horses and Heather, Frederick Warne, 1956, illus Sheila Rose
Jump to the Stars, Evans, 1957, illus Anne Gordon
Tan and Tarmac, Evans, 1958, illus Anne Gordon
The Difficult Summer Evans, 1959, illus Anne Gordon
Ribbons and Rings, Evans, 1960, illus Anne Gordon
The Stables at Hampton, Evans, 1961, illus Anne Gordon
Horses in the Glen, Evans, 1962, illus Elizabeth Grant
The Perfect Horse, Evans, 1963, illus Ivan Lappe
The Team from Low Moor, Evans, 1965, illus Marcia Lane Foster
Sweet Rock, E J Arnold & Son Ltd, 1966

Special Delivery, Methuen, 1967
Pantomime Ponies, Methuen, 1969, illus Elisabeth Grant
Save the Ponies, Methuen, 1971, illus Elisabeth Grant
Ponies by the Sea, Methuen, 1974, illus Elisabeth Grant
Ponies in Harness, Methuen, 1977, illus Elisabeth Grant
Ponies to the Rescue, Methuen, 1983

Judith M Berrisford
Timber, the Story of a Horse, University of London Press, 1950, illus Caney
Sue's Circus Horse, University of London Press, 1951, illus Leslie Atkinson
Red Rocket, Mystery Horse, University of London Press, 1952, illus Leslie Atkinson
The Ponies Next Door, University of London Press, London, 1954, illus Geoffrey Whittam
Ponies all Summer, University of London Press, 1956, illus Geoffrey Whittam
Pony Forest Adventure, University of London, 1957, illus Geoffrey Whittam
Jackie Won a Pony, Hodder & Stoughton, 1958, illus Geoffrey Whittam
Ten Ponies and Jackie, Brockhampton Press, 1959, illus Geoffrey Rose
A Pony in the Family, Brockhampton, 1959, illus Anne Gordon
Trouble at Ponyways, University of London Press, 1960, illus Elisabeth Grant
Jackie's Pony Patrol, Brockhampton, 1961, illus Geoffrey Whittam
Nobody's Pony, University of London Press, 1962, illus John Ward RA
A Colt in the Family, Brockhampton, 1962, illus Anne Gordon
Five Foals and Philippa, Burke, 1963, illus Barbara Crocker
Jackie and the Pony Trekkers, Hodder & Stoughton, 1963, illus Geoffrey Whittam
Sue's TV Pony, Hutchinson, 1964, illus Sheila Rose
A Showjumper in the Family, Brockhampton Press, 1964
Jackie's Pony Camp Summer, Brockhampton, 1968, illus Geoffrey Whittam
Jackie and the Pony Boys, Brockhampton Press, 1970
Jackie's Show Jumping Surprise, Brockhampton Press, 1973, illus Geoffrey Whittam
Jackie and the Misfit Pony, Hodder & Stoughton, 1975, illus Geoffrey Whittam
Jackie on Pony Island, Hodder & Stoughton, 1977, illus Geoffrey Whittam
Jackie and the Moonlight Pony, Hodder & Stoughton, 1977, illus Geoffrey Whittam
Jackie and the Pony Thieves, Hodder & Stoughton, 1978, illus Geoffrey Whittam
Jackie and the Phantom Ponies, Hodder & Stoughton, 1979, illus Geoffrey Whittam
Jackie and the Pony Rivals, Hodder & Stoughton, 1981, illus Geoffrey Whittam
Jackie and the Missing Showjumper, Hodder & Stoughton, 1982, illus Geoffrey Whittam
Change Ponies, Jackie!, Hodder & Stoughton, 1983, illus Geoffrey Whittam
Jackie's Steeplechase Adventure, Hodder & Stoughton, 1984, illus D E Walduck

Hilda Boden
Pony Trek, A & C Black, 1947, illus Mary Shillabeer
One More Pony, A & C Black, 1952, illus Mary Shillabeer
Treasure Trove, Lutterworth, 1955
Pony Boy, Lutterworth, 1958

Pony Girl, Lutterworth, 1959
Little Grey Pony, Lutterworth, 1960
Joanna's Special Pony, Burke, 1960, illus Lilias Buchanan
Joanna Rides the Hills, Burke, 1961, illus Lilias Buchanan

Joanna Cannan
A Pony for Jean, John Lane, 1936, illus Anne Bullen
We Met our Cousins, Collins, 1937, illus Anne Bullen
Another Pony for Jean, Collins, 1938, illus Anne Bullen
London Pride, Collins, 1939, illus Anne Bullen
More Ponies for Jean, Collins, 1943, illus Anne Bullen
They Bought Her a Pony, Collins, 1944, illus Rosemary Robertson
Hamish, the Story of a Shetland Pony, Puffin Picture Books 1944, illus Anne Bullen
I Wrote a Pony Book, Collins, 1950, illus Sheila Rose
Gaze at the Moon, Collins, 1957, illus Sheila Rose

Sheila Chapman
A Pony and his Partner, Burke, 1959, illus Geoffrey Whittam
The Mystery Pony, Burke, 1960
Pony from Fire, Burke, 1960, illus Geoffrey Whittam
Ride for Freedom, Burke, 1961, illus Sheila Rose

Moyra Charlton
Tally Ho, Putnam, 1930, illus Lionel Edwards
The Midnight Steeplechase, Methuen, 1932, illus Gilbert Holiday
Three White Stockings, Putnam, 1933, illus Gilbert Holiday
The Echoing Horn, Putnam, 1939, illus Lionel Edwards

Marion Coakes
Sue-Elaine Draws a Horse, Marion Coakes and Gillian Hirst, Pelham, 1971

Primrose Cumming
Doney—a Borderland Tale of Ponies and Young People, Country Life, 1934,
    illus Allen W Seaby
Spider Dog, Country Life, 1936, illus Barbara Turner
Silver Snaffles, Blackie, 1937
The Silver Eagle Riding School, A & C Black, 1938, iillus Cecil Trew
The Wednesday Pony, Blackie, 1939, illus Stanley Lloyd
Ben: The Story of A Cart-Horse, Dent, 1939, illus Harold Burdekin
Rachel of Romney, Country Life, 1939, illus Nina Scott Langley
The Chestnut Filly, Blackie, 1940, illus Stanley Lloyd
Silver Eagle Carries On, A & C Black, 1940, illus Cecil G Trew
Owls Castle Farm, A & C Black, 1942, illus Veronica Baker

The Great Horses, Dent, 1946, illus Lionel Edwards
Trouble at Trimbles, Country Life, 1949, illus Geoffrey Whittam
Four Rode Home, Dent, 1951, illus Maurice Tulloch
Rivals to Silver Eagle, A & C Black, 1954, illus Eve Gosset
No Place for Ponies, Dent, 1954, illus Maurice Tulloch
The Deep-Sea Horse, Dent, 1956, illus Mary Shillabeer
Flying Horseman, Dent, 1959, illus Sheila Rose
The Mystery Trek, Dent, 1964, illus Sheila Rose
Foal of the Fjords, Dent, 1966, illus Wendy Marchant
Penny and Pegasus, Dent, 1969, illus Mary Gernat

Monica Dickens
Cobbler's Dream, Michael Joseph, 1963
The House at World's End, Heinemann 1970, illus Peter Charles
Summer at World's End, Heinemann, 1971, illus Peter Charles
Follyfoot, Heinemann, 1971
Dora at Follyfoot, Heinemann, 1972
World's End in Winter, Heinemann, 1972
Spring Comes to World's End, Heinemann, 1973
Horses of Follyfoot, Heinemann, 1975
Stranger at Follyfoot, Heinemann, 1976

Monica Edwards
Wish for a Pony, Collins, 1947, illus Anne Bullen
No Mistaking Corker, Collins, 1947, illus Anne Bullen
The Summer of the Great Secret, Collins, 1948, illus Anne Bullen
The Midnight Horse, Collins, 1949, illus Anne Bullen
Black Hunting Whip, Collins, 1950, illus Geoffrey Whittam
The White Riders, Collins, 1950, illus Geoffrey Whittam
Punchbowl Midnight, Collins, 1951, illus Charles Tunnicliffe
Cargo of Horses, Collins, 1951, illus Geoffrey Whittam
The Spirit of Punchbowl Farm, Collins, 1952, illus Joan Wanklyn
Hidden in a Dream, Collins, 1952, illus Geoffrey Whittam
The Wanderer, Collins, 1953, illus Joan Wanklyn
Storm Ahead, Collins, 1953, illus Geoffrey Whittam
Punchbowl Harvest, Collins, 1954, illus Joan Wanklyn
No Entry, Collins, 1954, illus Geoffrey Whittam
Joan Goes Farming, Collins, 1954
The Nightbird, Collins, 1955, illus Geoffrey Whittam
Frenchman's Secret, Collins, 1956, illus Geoffrey Whittam
Rennie Goes Riding, Collins, 1956, illus Sheila Rose
Hidden in a Dream, Collins, 1952, illus Geoffrey Whittam
Strangers to the Marsh, Collins, 1957, illus Geoffrey Whittam

Operation Seabird, Collins, 1957, illus Geoffrey Whittam
The Cownappers, Collins, 1958, illus Geoffrey Whittam
Killer Dog, Collins, 1959, illus Sheila Rose
No Going Back, Collins, 1960, illus Geoffrey Whittam
The Outsider, Collins, 1961, illus Geoffrey Whittam
The Hoodwinkers, Collins, 1962, illus Geoffrey Whittam
Dolphin Summer, Collins, 1963, illus Geoffrey Whittam
Fire in the Punchbowl, Collins, 1965, illus Geoffrey Whittam
The Wild One, Collins, 1967, illus Geoffrey Whittam
Under the Rose, Collins, 1968, illus Richard Kennedy
A Wind is Blowing, Collins, 1969

Shirley Faulkner-Horne
Bred in the Bone: A Tale for Children, H. F. & G. Witherby, 1938, illus Peter Biegel
Pat and her Polo Pony, The Power of a Charm, Country Life, 1939, illus Peter Biegel
Riding with the Kindles, H. F. & G. Witherby, 1941, illus Peter Biegel
Parachute Silk: A Story for Young Riders, H. F. & G. Witherby, 1944,
    illus Peter Biegel and 'Haz'
Mexican Saddle, H. F. & G. Witherby, 1946, illus Peter Biegel
Green Trail, H. F. & G. Witherby, 1947, illus Peter Biegel
White Poles, H. F. & G. Witherby, 1954, illus Peter Biegel
Look Before You Leap, H. F. & G. Witherby, 1955, illus Peter Biegel.

Ruby Ferguson
Jill's Gymkhana, Hodder & Stoughton, 1949, illus Caney
    (US edition *A Horse of her Own*, 1950)
A Stable for Jill, Hodder & Stoughton, 1951, illus Caney
Jill has Two Ponies, Hodder & Stoughton, 1952, illus Caney
Jill Enjoys her Ponies (reissued as *Jill and the Runaway*), Hodder & Stoughton 1954,
    illus Caney
Jill's Riding Club, Hodder & Stoughton, 1956, illus Caney
Rosettes for Jill, Hodder & Stoughton, 1957, illus Caney
Jill and the Perfect Pony, Hodder & Stoughton, 1959, illus Caney
Pony Jobs for Jill (reissued as *Challenges for Jill*), Hodder & Stoughton, 1960, illus Caney
Jill's Pony Trek, Hodder & Stoughton, 1962, illus Caney
Challenges for Jill (reissue of *Pony Jobs for Jill*), Hodder, 1993
Jill and the Runaway (reissue of *Jill Enjoys her Ponies*), Hodder, 1993

Mary Gervaise
A Pony of your Own, Lutterworth, 1950, illus E Herbert Whydale
Ponies and Holidays, Lutterworth, 1950, illus E Herbert Whydale
Ponies in Clover, Lutterworth, 1952, illus E Herbert Whydale
Ponies and Mysteries, Lutterworth, 1953, illus Bowe

Pony from the Farm, Lutterworth, 1954, illus Bowe
Fireworks at Farthingale, Nelson, 1954, illus Robert Hodgson
The Farthingale Fete, Nelson, 1955, illus A H Watson
The Pony Clue, Lutterworth, 1955, illus Bowe
The Farthingale Feud, Nelson, 1957, illus A H Watson
Pony Island, Lutterworth, 1957, illus John Raynes
The Vanishing Pony, Lutterworth, 1958, illus John Raynes
A Pony for Belinda, Lutterworth Press, 1959, illus John Raynes
Belinda Rides to School, Lutterworth Press, 1960
Belinda's other Pony, Lutterworth Press, 1961, illus John Raynes
The Farthingale Find, Nelson, 1961, illus A H Watson
Belinda Wins her Spurs, Lutterworth Press, 1962, illus John Raynes
Puzzle of Ponies, Lutterworth, 1964, illus John Raynes
The Secret of Pony Pass, Lutterworth, 1965, illus John Raynes

'Golden Gorse' [Muriel Wace]
Moorland Mousie, Country Life, 1929, illus Lionel Edwards
Older Mousie, Country Life, 1932, Lionel Edwards
Janet and Felicity, The Young Horsebreakers, Country Life, 1937, illus Anne Bullen
Mary in the Country, Country Life, 1955, illus E H Shepard

Helen Griffiths
Horse in the Clouds, Hutchinson, 1957, illus Edmund Osmond
Moonlight, Hutchinson, 1959, illus Edmund Osmond
The Wild Heart, Hutchinson, 1963, illus Victor Ambrus
The Wild Horse of Santander, Hutchinson, 1966, illus Victor Ambrus
Stallion of the Sands, Hutchinson, 1970, illus Victor Ambrus
Federico, Hutchinson, 1971, illus Shirley Hughes

Catherine Harris
We Started a Riding Club, Blackie, 1954, illus Maurice Tulloch
They Rescued a Pony, Blackie, 1956, illus Geoffrey Whittam
The Ponies of Cuckoo Mill Farm, Blackie, 1958, illus Geoffrey Whittam
Riding for Ransom, Blackie, 1960, illus Joan Thompson
If Wishes were Horses, Blackie, 1961, illus Constance Marshall
To Horse and Away, Blackie, 1962, illus Lilian Buchanan
The Heronsbrook Gymkhana, Blackie, 1964, illus Geraldine Spence

Eleanor Helme
Mayfly the Grey Pony, Eyre & Spottiswoode, 1935, illus Lionel Edwards
Runaway Mike, Peter Lovat, 1936, illus T Ivester Lloyd
Shanks's Pony, Eyre & Spottiswoode, 1946, illus Lionel Edwards
Suitable Owners, Eyre & Spottiswoodem, 1948, illus Lionel Edwards

White Winter, Eyre & Spottiswoode, 1949, illus Lionel Edwards
Dear Busybody, Eyre & Spottiswoode, 1950, illus Lionel Edwards

Eleanor Helme and Nance Paul
Jerry, Eyre & Spottiswoode, 1930, illus Cecil Aldin
The Joker and Jerry Again, Eyre & Spottiswoode, 1932, illus Cecil Aldin

Marguerite Henry
Misty of Chincoteague, Rand McNally, 1947, illus Wesley Dennis
Sea Star, Orphan of Chincoteague, Rand McNally, 1949, illus Wesley Dennis
Stormy, Misty's Foal, Rand McNally, 1963, illus Wesley Dennis

Lorna Hill
Marjorie & Co, Art & Educational, 1948, illus Gilbert Dunlop
Stolen Holiday, Art & Educational, 1948, illus Gilbert Dunlop
Border Peel, Art & Educational, 1950 (artist unknown)
They Called her Patience, Burke, 1951, illus Gilbert Dunlop
It Was All Through Patience, Burke, 1952, illus Gilbert Dunlop
Castle in Northumbria, Burke, 1953, illus Gilbert Dunlop
So Guy Came Too, Burke, 1954, illus Joanna Curzon
The Five Shilling Holiday, Burke, 1955, illus Joanna Curzon
No Medals for Guy, Nelson, 1962, illus Gilbert Dunlop
Northern Lights, 1st ed Brockleside Press, 1999; 2nd ed Girls Gone By, 2009; both illus the author

Katharine Hull and Pamela Whitlock
The Far-Distant Oxus, Jonathan Cape, 1937, illus Pamela Whitlock
Escape to Persia, Jonathan Cape, 1938, illus Pamela Whitlock
Oxus in Summer, Jonathan Cape, 1939, illus Pamela Whitlock

Rudyard Kipling
'The Maltese Cat', illus Lionel Edwards, in *The Day's Work*, Macmillan, 1898

Patricia Leitch
To Save a Pony, Hutchinson, 1960, illus Sheila Rose
A Pony of our Own, Blackie & Son 1960, illus Constance Marshall
The Black Loch, Collins, 1963, illus Janet Duchesne
Riding Course Summer, Collins, 1963
A Rosette for Royal, Blackie 1963, illus Anne Linton
Janet, Young Rider, Constable, 1963
Highland Pony Trek, Collins, 1964
Cross-Country Pony, Blackie 1965
First Pony, Spitfire, 1967 (as Jane Eliot); extended version, Collins, 1973

Jacky Jumps to the Top, Spitfire, 1967 (as Jane Eliot); extended version, Collins, 1973
Pony Club Camp, Spitfire, 1967 (as Jane Eliot)
Afraid to Ride, Spitfire, 1967 (as Jane Eliot); extended version, Collins, 1974
Rebel Pony, Collins Pony Library, 1973
Pony Surprise, Collins Pony Library, 1974
Dream of Fair Horses, Collins, 1975
For Love of a Horse, Armada, 1976
A Devil to Ride, Armada, 1976
The Summer Riders, Armada, 1977
Night of the Red Horse, Armada, 1978
Gallop to the Hills, Armada, 1979
Horse in a Million, Armada, 1980
The Magic Pony, Armada, 1982
Ride like the Wind, Armada, 1983
Chestnut Gold, Armada, 1984
Jump for the Moon, Armada, 1985
Horse of Fire, Armada, 1986
Running Wild, Armada, 1988

Patience McElwee
Match Pair, Hodder & Stoughton, 1956
Dark Horse, Hodder & Stoughton, 1958
The Merrythoughts, Hodder & Stoughton, 1960

Pamela Macgregor-Morris
Topper, Noel Carrington, 1947, illus Lionel Edwards
High Honours, H. F. & G. Witherby, 1948, illus Lionel Edwards
Lucky Purchase, Gryphon, 1949, illus Lionel Edwards
Exmoor Ben, Gryphon 1950, illus Lionel Edwards
Blue Rosette, H. F. & G. Witherby, 1950, illus Michael Lyne
Not such a bad Summer, Latimer House, 1950
The Amateur Horsedealers, 1951, Gryphon Books, illus Lionel Edwards
Clear Round, Collins, 1962

Kathleen Mackenzie
The Four Pentires and Jimmy, W G Harrap, 1947, illus Violet Morgan
We Four and Sandy, Evans, 1947, illus Violet Morgan
A Green Fox, Evans, 1949, illus Violet Morgan
The Badgers of Quinion, Evans, 1950, illus Violet Morgan
Vicky and the Pentires, Evans, 1951, illus Violet Morgan
Red Conker, Evans, 1952, illus Violet Morgan
Minda, Evans, 1953, illus Maurice Tulloch
Jumping Jan, Evans, 1955, illus Violet Morgan

Three of a Kind, Evans, 1956, illus Violet Morgan
Chalk and Cheese, Evans, 1957, illus Violet Morgan
Nancy and the Carrs, Evans, 1958, illus Violet Morgan
Prize Pony, Evans, 1959, illus Violet Morgan
Nigel Rides Away, Evans, 1960, illus Violet Morgan
The Cave in the Cliff, Evans, 1961, illus Violet Morgan
Pony and Trap, Evans, 1962, illus Violet Morgan
The Pageant, Evans, 1964, illus Violet Morgan

Elyne Mitchell
The Silver Brumby, Hutchinson, 1958, illus Ralph Thompson
Silver Brumby's Daughter, Hutchinson, 1960, illus Grace Huxtable
Silver Brumbies of the South, Hutchinson, 1965, illus Annette Macarthur-Onslow
Silver Brumby Kingdom, Hutchinson, 1966, illus Annette Macarthur-Onslow
Moon Filly, Hutchinson, 1968, illus Robert Hales
Silver Brumby Whirlwind, Hutchinson, 1973, illus Victor Ambrus
Son of the Whirlwind, Hutchinson, 1976, illus Victor Ambrus

G Rutherford Montgomery
The Capture of the Golden Stallion, Little, Brown & Co, 1951, illus George Giguere
The Golden Stallion's Revenge, Little, Brown & Co, 1953, illus George Giguere
The Golden Stallion to the Rescue, Little, Brown & Co, 1954, illus George Giguere
The Golden Stallion's Victory, Little, Brown & Co, 1956, illus George Giguere
The Golden Stallion and the Wolf Dog, Little, Brown & Co, 1958, illus Percy Leason
The Golden Stallion's Adventure at Redstone, Little, Brown & Co, 1959, illus George Giguere
The Golden Stallion and the Mysterious Feud, Little, Brown & Co, 1967, illus Albert Michini

C Northcote Parkinson
Ponies Plot, John Murray, 1965, illus Violet Morgan

Mary O'Hara
My Friend Flicka, J B Lippincott, 1941
Thunderhead, J B Lippincott, 1943
Green Grass of Wyoming, J B Lippincott, 1946

Marjorie Mary Oliver
Riding Days in Hook's Hollow, Country Life, 1944, illus Stanley Lloyd
Horseman's Island, Country Life, 1950, illus Stanley Lloyd
Land of Ponies, Country Life, 1951, illus Charlotte Hough
A'Riding We Will Go, Lutterworth, 1951, illus Stanley Lloyd
Menace on the Moor, Nelson, 1960, illus Drake Brookshaw

Mystery at Merridown Mill, Nelson, 1962, illus Robert Hodgson
The Riddle of the Tired Pony, Nelson, 1964, illus Drake Brookshaw

Marjorie Mary Oliver and Eva Ducat
The Ponies of Bunts, Country Life, 1933
Sea Ponies—The Story of a Children's Riding Holiday, Country Life, 1935
Ponies and Caravans, Country Life, 1941

Mary Elwyn Patchett
Ajax the Warrior, Lutterworth, 1953, illus Eric Tansley
Tam the Untamed, Lutterworth, 1954, illus Joan Kiddell-Monroe
The Brumby, Lutterworth, 1958, illus Juliet McLeod
Come Home, Brumby, Lutterworth, 1961, illus Stuart Tresilian
Circus Brumby, Lutterworth, 1962, illus Stuart Tresilian
Stranger in the Herd, Lutterworth, 1964, illus Stuart Tresilian
Brumby Foal, Lutterworth, 1965, illus Victor Ambrus
Summer on Wild Horse Island, Brockhampton Press, Leicester, 1965, illus Roger Payne
Quarter Horse Boy, Harrap, 1970, illus Roger Payne
The Long Ride, Lutterworth, 1970, illus Michael Charlton
Rebel Brumby, Lutterworth, Guildford, 1972, illus Roger Payne

Hazel M Peel
Fury, Son of the Wilds, Harrap, 1959, illus Joan Kiddell-Monroe
Pilot the Hunter, Harrap, 1962, illus Keith Money
Pilot the Chaser, Harrap, 1964, illus Keith Money
Easter the Showjumper, Harrap, 1965, illus Michael Lyne
Jago, Harrap, 1966, illus Sheila Rose
Night Storm the Flat Racer, Harrap, 1966, illus Clyde Pearson
Dido and Rogue, Harrap, 1967, illus Phyllida Legg
Gay Darius, Harrap, 1968, illus Robert Hodgson
Untamed, Harrap, 1969, illus Mortelmans

K M Peyton
Sabre, the Horse from the Sea (as Kathleen Herald), A & C Black, 1948,
    illus Lionel Edwards
The Mandrake, a Pony (as Kathleen Herald), A & C Black, 1949, illus Lionel Edwards
Crab the Roan (as Kathleen Herald), A & C Black, 1953, illus Peter Biegel
Flambards, OUP, 1968, illus Victor Ambrus
Fly-by-Night, OUP, 1968, illus the author
The Edge of the Cloud, OUP, 1969, illus Victor Ambrus
Flambards in Summer, OUP, 1969, illus Victor Ambrus
Pennington's Seventeenth Summer, OUP, 1970, illus the author
The Beethoven Medal, 1971, OUP, 1971, illus the author

A Pattern of Roses, OUP, 1972
Pennington's Heir, OUP, 1973, illus the author
The Team, OUP, 1975, illus the author
The Right-Hand Man, OUP, 1977, illus Victor Ambrus
Prove Yourself a Hero, OUP, 1977, illus the author
A Midsummer Night's Death, OUP, 1978
Marion's Angels, OUP, 1979, illus Robert Mickelwright
Flambards Divided, OUP, 1981
The Last Ditch, OUP, 1984 (US edition *Free Rein*)

Christine Pullein-Thompson
It Began with Picotee (with Josephine and Diana Pullein-Thompson), A & C Black, 1946, illus Rosemary Robertson
We Rode to the Sea, Collins, 1948, illus Mil Brown
We Hunted Hounds, Collins, 1949, illus Marcia Lane Foster
I Carried the Horn, Collins, 1951, illus Charlotte Hough
Goodbye to Hounds, Collins, 1952, illus Charlotte Hough
Riders from Afar, Collins, 1954, illus Charlotte Hough
Phantom Horse, Collins, 1955, illus Sheila Rose
A Day to Go Hunting, Collins, 1956, illus Sheila Rose
The First Rosette, Burke, 1956, illus Sheila Rose
The Impossible Horse (as Christine Keir), Evans, 1957, illus Maurice Tulloch
Stolen Ponies, Collins, 1957, illus Sheila Rose
The Second Mount, Burke, 1957, illus Sheila Rose
Three to Ride, Burke, 1958, illus Sheila Rose
The Lost Pony, Burke, 1959, illus Sheila Rose
For Want of a Saddle, Burke, 1960, illus Anne Bullen
The Horse Sale, Collins, 1960, illus Sheila Rose
Ride by Night, Collins, 1960, illus Sheila Rose
The Empty Field, Burke, 1961, illus Anne Bullen
The Open Gate, Burke, 1962, illus Barbara Crocker
Bandits in the Hills, Hamish Hamilton, 1962, illus Janet Duchesne
The Doping Affair (reissued as *The Pony Dopers*), Burke, 1963, illus Enid Ash
Little Black Pony, Hamish Hamilton, 1967, illus Lynette Hemmant
Riders on the March, Armada, 1970
Phantom Horse Comes Home, Armada, 1970
Phantom Horse Goes to Ireland, Armada, 1972
They Rode to Victory, Armada, 1972
I Rode a Winner, Armada, 1973
The Pony Dopers (reissue of *The Doping Affair*), Burke, 1987, illus Enid Ash

Diana Pullein-Thompson
It Began with Picotee (with Josephine and Christine Pullein-Thompson), A & C Black, 1946, illus Rosemary Robertson

I Wanted a Pony, Collins, 1946, illus Anne Bullen
Three Ponies and Shannan, Collins, 1947, illus Anne Bullen
The Pennyfields, Collins, 1949
A Pony to School, Collins, 1950, Anne Bullen
A Pony for Sale, Collins, 1951, illus Sheila Rose
Janet Must Ride, Collins, 1953, illus Mary Gernat
Horses at Home/Friends Must Part [two-in-one], Collins, 1954, illus Sheila Rose
Riding with the Lyntons, Collins, 1956, illus Sheila Rose
The Boy and the Donkey, Collins, 1958, illus Shirley Hughes
The Hermit's Horse, Armada 1974

Josephine Pullein-Thompson
It Began with Picotee (with Christine and Diana Pullein-Thompson), A & C Black, 1946, illus Rosemary Robertson
Six Ponies, Collins, 1946, illus Anne Bullen
I Had Two Ponies, Collins, 1947, illus Anne Bullen
Plenty of Ponies, Collins, 1949, illus Anne Bullen
Pony Club Team, Collins, 1950, illus Sheila Rose
The Radney Riding Club, Collins, 1951, illus Sheila Rose
Prince among Ponies, Collins, 1952, illus Charlotte Hough
One Day Event, Collins, 1954, illus Sheila Rose
Show Jumping Secret, Collins, 1955, illus Sheila Rose
Patrick's Pony, Brockhampton, 1956, illus Geoffrey Whittam
Pony Club Camp, Collins, 1957, illus Sheila Rose
The Trick Jumpers, Collins, 1958, illus Sheila Rose
All Change, Ernest Benn, 1961, illus Sheila Rose
Race Horse Holiday, Armada, 1971

Anna Sewell
Black Beauty, Jarrolds, 1877

Vian Smith
Question Mark, Constable Young Books, 1961
Martin Rides the Moor, Constable Young Books, 1964
Green Heart, Doubleday & Company, 1964
The Horses of Petrock, Constable Young Books, 1965
King Sam, Constable Young Books, 1966, illus Peter Forster
Come Down the Mountain, Constable Young Books, 1967
The Lord Mayor's Show, Constable Young Books, 1968
Moon in the River, Longmans Young Books, 1969, illus Anthony Colbert
Minstrel Boy, Peter Davies 1970

Pat Smythe
Jacqueline Rides for a Fall, Cassell, 1957, illus J E McConnell
Three Jays Against The Clock, Cassell, 1958, illus J E McConnell
Three Jays on Holiday, Cassell, 1958, illus J E McConnell
Three Jays go to Town, Cassell, 1959, illus J E McConnell
Three Jays Over the Border, Cassell, 1960, illus J E McConnell
Three Jays go to Rome, Cassell, 1960, illus J E McConnell
Three Jays Lend a Hand, Cassell, 1961, illus Keith Money
A Swiss Adventure, Cassell, 1970
A Spanish Adventure, Cassell, 1971
A Cotswold Adventure, Cassell, 1973

Glenda Spooner
Royal Crusader, Latimer House, 1948, illus Michael Lyne
The Earth Sings, Latimer House, 1950
The Perfect Pest, Jonathan Cape, 1951, illus Charlotte Hough
Minority's Colt, Cassell, 1952
The Silk Purse, Cassell 1963, illus Anne Bullen

John Thorburn
Hildebrand, Country Life, 1930, illus 'The Wag'; reprinted Collins, 1949, illus Peter Biegel

Mary Treadgold
We Couldn't Leave Dinah, Jonathan Cape, 1941, illus Stuart Tresilian
No Ponies, Jonathan Cape, 1946, illus Ruth Jervis
The Heron Ride, Jonathan Cape, 1962, illus Victor Ambrus
Return to the Heron, Jonathan Cape, 1963, illus Victor Ambrus
The Rum Day of the Vanishing Pony, Brockhampton, 1970
Journey from the Heron, Jonathan Cape, 1981

Veronica Westlake
The Ten-Pound Pony, Blackie, 1953, illus Peter Biegel
The Intruders, Routledge & Kegan Paul, 1954, illus Sheila Rose
The Unwilling Adventurers, Blackie & Son, 1955, illus Robert Hodgson
The Mug's Game, Routledge & Kegan Paul, 1956, illus Sheila Rose

Williams, Dorian
Wendy Wins a Pony, Burke, 1961, illus Mary Gernat
Wendy Wins her Spurs, Burke, 1962, illus Sheila Rose
Wendy at Wembley, Burke, 1963, illus Juliette Palmer
Pancho, the Story of a Horse, Dent, 1967, illus Owen Ward
Kingdom for a Horse, Dent, 1967, illus Val Biro

ACKNOWLEDGEMENTS

Thank you to my husband, Jonathan, and Sue Howes, Kate Hills, Sharon Booth and Catherine Hawley, who nobly read everything I threw at them and came back with endless helpful suggestions.

Thank you too to my family, particularly my children: Miranda, who patiently fed herself and got on with life while her mother's attention was elsewhere, and Fred, who attempted to pin his mother down to working on the book at the same time as she attempted to pin him down to revising for his A-levels, both attempts meeting with only partial success.

To the ever-wonderful Tig Thomas, editor supreme, who must have wondered (as did I) if I would ever get my act together and finish the book. Tig is definitely in the beyond-rubies camp.

To all the wonderful contributors: Susanna Forrest, Stacey Gregg, Linda Newbery, Janet Rising and Sarah Singleton.

To all the authors and their families who answered my endless questions, which were occasionally separated by months: Caroline Akrill, Gillian Baxter, Linda Chapman, Sheila Chapman, Patricia Leitch, Linda Newbery, Hazel M Peel, K M Peyton, Diana and Josephine Pullein-Thompson, Janet Rising and Meg Rosoff; Alison Haymonds, Sarah Ferguson, John Wright and Peter Howson of the Methodist Church for information on Ruby Ferguson; Birte Scheel, John Rees and the Jill Facebook group; the Follyfoot Forum and its wonderful administrators, the Jinny and Shantih Facebook group; Anne Bullen's family: Jennie Loriston-Clarke, Jane Holderness-Roddam and Sarah Vey; Kate Austin of DJ Murphy; the Pony Club; Roderick Macleod and Kay Whalley for information on Moyra Charlton; Vanessa Robertson for help with Ruby Ferguson and K M Peyton; Carol Hewson for information on Stanley Lloyd; Deborah Moggach for help with her mother, Charlotte Hough; Mary Lewis for information on Kathleen Mackenzie; Jim Mackenzie for information on Lorna Hill; Roger How for help with his mother, Mary Gernat; David Addis for help with Katharine Hull and Pamela Whitlock; Harriet Hall for help with Patience McElwee; and the members of my Facebook page, Jane Badger Books, and forum, horsebooks.proboards.com, for being a brilliant source of information, humour and encouragement.

To Dawn Harrison, Sarah Beasley and Hannah Fleetwood for lending me books I didn't have.

To Clarissa and Ann for publishing the book, Laura Hicks for copy-editing, Sarah Woodall for typesetting and Ken Websdale for cover design and for taking the front cover photograph.

To anyone who has helped me and whom I have managed to miss off this list: I am grateful, and sorry.

And lastly, to that noble creature the horse, particularly the piebald who bit me firmly, several times, when I was two. He failed to dim my enthusiasm.

Illustrations

The author and publishers would like to express their thanks to the many artists who gave permission to reproduce their material in this book and are glad to acknowledge their contribution. Every effort has been made to trace the holders of copyright illustrations used in this book. The publishers and author would be glad to hear from any copyright holders they have failed to trace.

Illustrations by
- Anne Bullen, by kind permission of the Bullen family
- Caney, by kind permission of Fidra Books
- Gilbert Dunlop, by kind permission of Girls Gone By Publishers
- Mary Gernat, by kind permission of Roger How
- Charlotte Hough, by kind permission of Deborah Moggach
- Elaine How, by kind permission of the artist
- Stanley Lloyd, by kind permission of Sue Vincent and family
- Susan Millard, for *Against the Odds*, by kind permission of the artist and J A Allen
- Violet Morgan, by kind permission of Nicki Braithwaite
- Geoffrey Whittam, by kind permission of Girls Gone By Publishers

Credits

page 11 © Charlotte Hough
page 12 by kind permission of Bridget Major
page 15 (top and bottom) The Wag
page 16 Gilbert Holiday
page 18 unknown
page 19 Cecil Aldin
pages 23 and 24 © Anne Bullen
pages 27 and 29 (top and bottom) © Stanley Lloyd
page 31 © IPC Media
page 33 © Veronica Baker
page 40 © Rosemary Robertson
page 41 unknown (Armada edition)
page 42 © Anne Bullen
page 44 © Geoffrey Whittam
page 46 © Anne Bullen
page 48 © Charlotte Hough
page 52 © Mary Gernat
page 55 © Anne Bullen
page 56 unknown (Armada edition)
page 57 © Mary Gernat
pages 61 and 62 © Anne Bullen
pages 63, 64, 65 (top) and 66 © Geoffrey Whittam
page 65 (bottom) © Mary Gernat
pages 70–75, 77, 79, 81–82 © Caney
page 85 unknown (Armada edition)
page 86 © E Herbert Whydale
pages 88–91 © Geoffrey Whittam
pages 92 and 94 (top) © J E McConnell
page 94 (bottom left and bottom right) © Mary Gernat
page 97 © Anne Bullen
page 100 © Mary Gernat
page 104 © Geoffrey Whittam
page 106 © Gilbert Dunlop
page 108 © Violet Morgan
page 110 © Peter Biegel
page 112 © Caney
page 115 © Mary Gernat
page 119 © Violet Morgan

pages 124–7 © K M Peyton
page 129 © ITV, Rex Features
page 131 © Yorkshire Television
page 134 unknown
page 136 © Geoffrey Whittam
page 137 © Janet Duchesne
page 140 unknown (Armada edition)
page 142 unknown (Armada edition)
page 147 unknown (Armada edition)
page 149 © Peter Archer
page 154 (top and bottom) © Elaine Roberts
page 156 © Stanley Lloyd
page 158 (top) © Charlotte Hough
page 158 (bottom) © Geoffrey Whittam
pages 161 and 162 (top) Gilbert Holiday
page 162 (bottom) Cecil Aldin
page 164 © Michael Lyne
page 165 © Peter Biegel
page 166 (all) and page 167 (top) © Anne Bullen
page 167 (bottom) © Geoffrey Whittam
page 168 © Marcia Lane Foster
page 169 © Stanley Lloyd
page 170 (top) © Sheila Rose
page 170 (bottom) © Charlotte Hough
page 171 © Mary Gernat
page 173 (left) © Joan Wanklyn
page 173 (right) © Children's Book Club
page 174 (left) © Elisabeth Grant
page 174 (right) © Children's Book Club
page 176 © Elaine How
page 177 © Susan Millard
page 200 © Joan Wanklyn
Back cover (top left) © Caney
Back cover (bottom left) unknown (Armada edition)
Back cover (top right) © Gordon Crabb
Back cover (bottom right) unknown (Children's Press edition)

INDEX OF AUTHORS

Main entries are in **bold type**

A

Akrill, Caroline **153–5**, 160, **175–7, 181**
Alexander, Samantha 175
Anon [*The Memoirs of Dick, the Little Poney ...*] 9
Atkinson, M E **103**, 116

B

Bagnold, Enid **20–22**, 23
Balch, Glenn 148
Ball, Richard 12
Barne, Kitty 168
Baxter, Gillian 101, 102, 110, **114–16**, 117, 168, 173, 174
Bennett, Michael 159
Bentley, Sue 179
Berrisford, Judith M 26, 70, 84, **87–91**, 95, 117, 152, 167
Boden, Hilda **103–4**
Brooke, Lauren *see* Chapman, Linda
Bryant, Bonnie 58, 155, 178

C

Campbell, Joanna 178
Cannan, Joanna **22–26**, 34, 38, 40, 41, 47, 70, 121, 134–5, 157, 165
Carey, Catherine 117
Carroll, Lewis 159
Chaffee, Allen 146
Chapman, Linda ('Lauren Brooke') **178**, 179
Chapman, Sheila **109**

C (continued)

Charlton, Moyra **15–17**, 20, 31, 161, 163
Chitty, Susan 101, 153
Clover, Peter 178
Coakes, Marion **101**, 102, 114
Cole, Babette 179
Collins, Anne 159
Cumming, Primrose 14, **27–30**, 32, 33–34, 103, 117, 118, 121, 155, **157–8**, 160, 168, 169

D

Danby, Cecily 159
Davenport, C 156
De la Mahotière, Mary 168
Dickens, Charles 159
Dickens, Monica **129, 130–3**, 172
Ducat, Eva 17, 121

E

Edwards, Monica 8, 9, **60–69**, 103, 117, 155, **157**, 159, 166–7, 171, 173–4
Eliot, Jane *see* Leitch, Patricia
Enriquez, C M 12
Eveleigh, Victoria 179

F

Farley, Terri 150
Farley, Walter 8, 103
Faulkner-Horne, Shirley **32–33**, 164, 165
Ferguson, Ruby 8, 26, 43, 44, **70–83**, 114, 162, 168, 172
Forest, Antonia 103
Forrest, Susanna 59, 143, 179
Funnell, Pippa 178
Furminger, Justine 114

G

Gervaise, Mary 26, 70, **84–87**, 95, 117
'Golden Gorse' [Muriel Wace] **12–14**, 121, 146, 151, 157, 163
Gregg, Stacey 83

Grey, Peter 117
Griffiths, Helen **146–7**, 172

H

Hance, J E 22
Harris, Catherine **104–6**
Havers, Elinore 117
Helme, Eleanor **18–20**, 163
Henry, Marguerite 103, 146, **148–9**
Herald, Kathleen *see* Peyton, K M
Hill, Lorna **106–7**
Hinkle, Thomas 148
Hirst, Gillian *see* Baxter, Gillian
Hope, Charles Evelyn Graham **151–3**
Hull, Katharine 22, 159

K

Keir, Christine *see* Pullein-Thompson, Christine
Kimpton, Diana 179
Kipling, Rudyard 11, 163
Knowles, Cecilia 12

L

Leitch, Patricia 22, 70, 84, 114, **129–30, 134–45**
Leslie, Christine 153
Lindsay, Elizabeth 179
Lloyd, John Ivester 168
Lyne, Michael 31, 155, 161, 163–4

M

McElwee, Patience 110, **112–14**, 116
Macgregor-Morris, Pamela **98–99**, 102, 155, 163, 164
Mackenzie, Kathleen **107–9**, 153
Millard, Susan 175, 177
Miller, Albert G 147–8
Mitchell, Elyne 8, 146, **149–50**, 172
Mitchison, Naomi 160
Montgomery, G Rutherford 103, **148**
Moray Williams, Ursula 12

N

Newbery, Linda 9, 69, 180
Northcote Parkinson, C **117–18**

O

O'Hara, Mary 8, 103, 117, 146, **148**, 157
Olcott, Frances 159
Oldfield, Jenny 178, 179
Oliver, Marjorie Mary **17–18**, 20, 31, 121

P

Patchett, Mary Elwyn **149**, 155, 172
Paul, Nance 18–19, 163
Peel, Hazel M **146–7**
Penney, Joan 12
Peyton, K M 117, **120–8**, 143, 164, 172, 179–80
Phipson, Joan 155
Price, Katie 101, 179
Pullein-Thompson sisters 8, 24, 26, **38–59**, 103, 117, 134, 151, 153, 155, 158, 170
   Christine 38, 39, **51–58**, 158, 168, 170, 171
   Diana 7, 38, 39, **41–46**, 51, 158–9, 166, 171, 172, 177
   Josephine 31–32, 38, 39, 43, 44, **46–51**, 54, 99, 107, 134, 152, 153. 155, 170

R

Raftery, Gerald 172
Ransome, Arthur 103
Ratcliff, Delphine 153, 168
Rising, Janet 160, 179, 181
Rosoff, Meg 9, 180

S

Seaby, Allen 12, 146,
Scott, Walter 159
Seredy, Kate 22
Sewell, Anna **10–11**, 171
Singleton, Sarah 145
Smiley, Jane 179
Smith, Vian 9, 117, **118–20**, 128
Smythe, Pat 26, 84, **92–95**, 96, 101, 102
Spender, Brenda E 22
Spooner, Glenda **96–98**, 99, 102
Stanford, Don 164
Stevenson, R L 159
Stiefvater, Maggie 179

T

Thorburn, John **14–15**, 118, 164
Treadgold, Mary 32, **34–37**, 117, 172
Trease, Geoffrey 103
Twain, Mark 159

V

Vaughan, Carol **153**, 160

W

Wace, Muriel *see* 'Golden Gorse'
Westlake, Veronica **110–12**, 116, 164, 172
Whitlock, Pamela 22, 155, **156–7**, 159, 160
Wilkinson, Sheena 179
Williams, Dorian **100–1**, 102
Wynne, May 12

Girls Gone By Publishers

Girls Gone By Publishers republish some of the most popular children's fiction from the 20th century, concentrating on those titles which are most sought after and difficult to find on the second-hand market. Our aim is to make them available at affordable prices, and to make ownership possible not only for existing collectors but also for new collectors so that the books continue to survive. We also publish some new titles which fit into this genre.

Authors on the GGBP fiction list include Margaret Biggs, Elinor Brent-Dyer, Dorita Fairlie Bruce, Patricia Caldwell, Gwendoline Courtney, Winifred Darch, Monica Edwards, Josephine Elder, Lorna Hill, Clare Mallory, Dorothea Moore, Violet Needham, Elsie Jeanette Oxenham, Malcolm Saville and Evelyn Smith.

We also have a growing range of non-fiction titles, either more general works about the genre or books about particular authors. Our non-fiction subjects include Girl Guiding, Monica Edwards and her books, Elsie Oxenham's books, and Geoffrey Trease. These books are in a larger format than our fiction titles, and some of them are lavishly illustrated in colour as well as black and white.

For details of availability and when to order see our website—www.ggbp.co.uk—or write for a catalogue to GGBP, 4 Rock Terrace, Coleford, Radstock, BA3 5NF, UK.

Some of our books are available as eBooks. These are only available from our website, www.ggbp.co.uk .